Sex, Crime, and the Law

Sex, Crime, and the Law

Donal E. J. MacNamara
and
Edward Sagarin

THE FREE PRESS
A Division of Macmillan Publishing Co., Inc.
NEW YORK
Collier Macmillan Publishers
LONDON

The Free Press
A Division of Macmillan Publishing Co., Inc.
866 Third Avenue, New York, N.Y. 10022

Collier Macmillan Canada, Ltd.

First Free Press Paperback Edition, 1978

Library of Congress Catalog Card Number: 77-5231

Printed in the United States of America

printing number

1 2 3 4 5 6 7 8 9 10

Library of Congress Cataloging in Publication Data

MacNamara, Donal E   J
    Sex, crime, and the law.

    Bibliography: p.
    Includes index.
    1. Sex crimes--United States. I. Sagarin, Edward
          joint author. II. Title.
KF9325.M3   345'.73'0253   77-5231
ISBN 0-02-919680-9
ISBN 0-02-919690-6 pbk.

To Gladys Topkis
A superb editor is
an author's best friend

Contents

Preface

Events, movements, organizations, and changes in sociosexual attitudes over the past few decades have brought the relationships among sex, crime, and the law into newly sharpened focus. Foremost among these dynamic factors has been the sharp rise in violent crime, more specifically the astonishing increase in forcible rape, which has elicited widespread anger, fear, frustration, and indignation. At the same time, the new feminism has been waging an aggressively effective campaign to protect the complainants in rape cases from the humiliations they have all too often experienced during police and prosecutorial investigations of their allegations and the embarrassing probes into their previous sex lives by defense counsel during cross-examination in court. As a result more rape victims are reporting attacks; police have set up special sex-crimes units staffed by women detectives; more vigorous prosecutions and less leniency are the rule; both court procedures and in some states the amount and type of evidence necessary for conviction have been changed; and some improvement in public attitudes toward rape victims has been noted.

Paralleling these developments, a strong movement toward eliminating legal sanctions against consensual sexual activity engaged in by adults in privacy (adultery, fornication, homosexuality, and non-coital sex play), reducing penalties for public-nuisance type sex activity (exhibitionism, voyeurism, nonassaultive fetishism), a much more tolerant attitude toward what was once denounced as obscene and pornographic, and recodifications of the penal laws for certain offenses to prevent their misuse have been evident not only in the United States but in most European countries as well. These changes, generally subsumed under the concept of decriminalization, antedate in some respects the so-called moral revolution that has markedly relaxed the puritanical American reaction to the open cohabitation of unmarried persons and to public manifestations of homosexuality.

Laws change slowly, unevenly, in one jurisdiction or geographic area sooner than in another; sometimes the changes are made by legislative enactment, at other times by judicial interpretation, and perhaps even more frequently by policy changes at the police or prosecutorial level. Neither laws, nor courts, nor enforcement policies are always in pace with the attitudes, beliefs, and more important the sexual practices of a society, particularly when the society is heterogeneous, its mores in conflict and in flux, with little agreement as to sociosexual standards. Such a society will find itself confronted with difficult problems due to this disjunction of laws and attitudes, enforcement and conduct.

Legal changes, on the one hand, and what has been perhaps exaggeratedly described as the "sexual revolution," on the other, are given greater clarity and meaning by the proliferating body of significant research into the dynamics of human sexual behavior, and specifically into sexual criminality, published in the past thirty years. Before the landmark work of Alfred C. Kinsey and his colleagues was published in 1948, sex research was sporadic, seldom scientific, frequently confined to reports on a handful of bizarre case histories, and even more frequently imbued with an all too evident moral indignation that brought into question the objectivity of the data and interpretations. Now, however, a body of solid research is available: on rape, on child molestation, on prostitution (male and female), on homosexuality, and on pornography. Not all of this material is impeccable (scientific research rarely is); ideology is not absent (though the author bias is now more likely to be permissive than punitive); but cumulatively it provides a strong input toward an understanding of the triad around which this study is organized: sex, crime, and the law.

There is available today not only this strong body of useful research but also an even larger bibliography of thoughtful and informative volumes on all aspects of sex-related criminality. A mere listing of recently published books on rape would be as extensive as many of them are impressive; probably the number of titles dealing with homosexuality exceeds those concerned with rape; and there are literally dozens of works on prostitution and pornography and a somewhat smaller but still significant listing devoted to child molestation, exhibitionism, incest, and some of the lesser paraphilia. Nevertheless, it is difficult to find significant studies since Morris Ploscowe's *Sex and the Law* (1951) and Isabel Drummond's *The Sex Paradox* (1953) that have reviewed the entire problem, taken note of changes in the law and in the mores, summarized the voluminous new literature, and placed the problems of sexuality and crime in a combined legal, sociological, and psychological frame of reference.

There comes a time in social science (and within this rubric we would include law, criminal jurisprudence, corrections, and therapy) when it appears useful to summarize the distant and recent past, to attempt to capture the direction in which social currents are flowing, to note both the consensus and the dissensus in society, to the end that further research, the legislative determination of social policy, and perhaps even more important the socialization of the young and the resocialization of some of their elders may be based on empirically derived evidence rather than on myth and prejudice, superstition and tradition. It is upon such a foundation that we believe social and creative thinking, leading to a sexually more mature and tolerant society, can be solidly based. It is this yawning gap in the literature on sex, crime, and the law that we seek to bridge in this modest volume. If parts of what we report are overtaken by fast-moving events, judicial or legislative, before our work can reach the hands of scholars, students, and those seriously concerned with the sociosexual mores, this is the more reason, rather than less, for bringing such a book into being at this time.

DEJ MacN and ES

NYC   June 1977

1 | Sex, Crime, and the Law

Sexual behavior that violates the prevailing norms in a society has been a matter for social control, and in modern societies for legal control through criminal sanctions, in all countries of the world. There is a widespread belief that the United States, with its Puritan tradition, has been more repressive and more regulatory with regard to sex than most other nations, but this view is generally not supported by comparisons of penal codes, prosecutions, and sentences actually meted out to transgressors. The Communist nations, some but not all countries with a strong Catholic Church influence, and the Islamic world generally have sex laws and punitive sanctions as repressive and severe as ours.

The social and legal control of sexual behavior is based, on the one hand, on the need felt in many societies for the channeling of sex drives into forms of conduct leading to procreation, stable family units, and care and socialization of the child (with unquestioned knowledge of paternity in order to ensure proper passing on of property); and, on the other, on the assumption that the libido, or sexual drive, is a force that has antisocial potential. This assumption is expressed succinctly by Kingsley Davis.

> The development and maintenance of a stable competitive order with respect to sex is extremely difficult, because sexual desire itself is inherently variable. Erotic relations are subject to constant danger—a change of whim, a loss of interest, a third party, a misunderstanding. Competition for the same sexual object may inflame passion and stir conflicts; failure may injure one's self-esteem. The intertwining of sex and society is a fertile ground for joy, happiness, paranoia, homicide, and suicide.[1]

1

Not all social thinkers agree with Davis. Some, particularly John Gagnon and William Simon,[2] argue that human sexuality is "socially scripted," that without social intervention there would be neither the instability nor the anarchy that Davis has described. Nevertheless, in modern societies in which legal controls have been extended over many other aspects of social life, there is general agreement that such controls and the punitive sanctions that support them are needed in order to discourage certain forms of sexual behavior.

Sigmund Freud, most notably in *Civilization and Its Discontents,* contended that civilization itself is made possible by the "renunciation of instinctual gratifications," including particularly the demand for sexual gratification. "The existence of civilization," Freud wrote, "presupposes the nongratification of powerful instinctual urgencies."[3] For those who have not been socialized to make such renunciation, there is the law, as well as religion, to guide, channel, deter, threaten, and punish—thereby to encourage and assist in resisting the drives toward disapproved sex behavior.

The Scope of Law and Typologies of Sex Crime

Sexual conduct can take a variety of forms differentiated by the degree of consent, the number of partners, their ages, previous relations, responsibilities, and gender, the physical nature of the contact between partners' bodies, and the use of animals, inanimate objects or oneself to obtain gratification. Some types of sexual behavior meet social approval and in fact are encouraged. A modern society with written penal codes must decide which acts, from among the multitude that do not meet the standards of an accepted code of sexual conduct, should be discouraged without the use of law and which are to be defined as criminal and prosecuted as such. Not every society is a conglomerate of persons with strong agreement on such matters, nor are sexual mores and folkways fixed over long periods of time. There are opposing emphases not only in different countries but also within the same society among various segments of the population, and opposing views are set forth by philosophers, scholars, and social commentators. While concurrence is occasionally found within this array of differing views—as, for example, on the need to illegalize and punish sex obtained by violence and without the consent of the partner—disagreement is more frequent.

In the United States, any examination of sex crimes involves the problem of the multitude of jurisdictions (fifty states, a federal code that covers both interstate and District of Columbia activities, a military code, and others), which differ in nomenclature, definition, interpretation, inclusion or exclusion of various types of behavior, sentencing, laxity or severity of prosecution, and police-arrest policies, for example. Add to this list the differences among neighborhoods, cities, and counties within a single state and the putative differential prosecution and sentencing linked to the social class and race of offender and victim, and one can readily see that a single, overall survey of sex crime is far from simple. For example, in all states except Nevada prostitution is illegal; still, prostitution in Nevada is legal only in certain counties and only in brothels. Age of consent differs as one travels across state borders—a complex matter because merely crossing the state line with a consenting partner of the other sex for the purpose of engaging in sexual relations constitutes a federal offense (a violation of the Mann Act) unless the partner is one's spouse. Adult consensual homosexual relations in private are illegal, as of this writing, in thirty-six of the fifty states, but several states are considering new permissive penal codes. Even in the states in which such acts are legal, however, there are diverse definitions and interpretations of what constitutes adulthood, consent, and privacy, and there are numerous laws, under such headings as public disorder, public indecency, lewd and lascivious conduct, and solicitation for immoral purposes, that can be invoked in the absence of a law against homosexuality per se.

To focus on these differences, important and often tragic as their results are, would give a false picture of sex and American law if one were not at the same time to take note of the direction in which the laws and courts are going. There is a new sexual morality, or an old morality that has become self-assertive and is no longer pretending to be what it is not. There are trends toward uniformity in interpretations of law, traceable in large measure to the decisions of the Supreme Court of the United States (the movement that came to be known as the nationalization of the Bill of Rights).* Furthermore, there is a powerful progressive force in

---

* The first ten amendments to the Constitution were interpreted in the early years of the nineteenth century as being applicable only to federal law. Thus, historically the individual's rights to be free from unreasonable search and seizure, not to have excessive bail imposed, and not to be subject to cruel and

judicial circles, led by the American Law Institute, for hammering out a model penal code and urging its adoption by the various states, with such minor modifications as may reflect local needs.* Geographic mobility, industrialization, and ease of communication seem to be fostering the homogenization of American society, not along age and other lines, but across state and regional ones. The result is a movement, slow but of unmistakable direction, toward uniformity of definitions and punishments in the penal codes and similarities in police practices. Moreover, the trend toward national homogenization does not proceed in a unilinear manner; for example, it was set back when the Supreme Court declared that it was not unconstitutional for a state to legislate against sodomy—i.e., so-called unnatural acts or crimes against nature, including homosexual activity.

ON DEFINING SEX, CRIME, AND SEX CRIME

Crime is here defined in the legal and common-sense meaning of the word: an act that violates the penal code of a governmental jurisdiction and that is punishable by the criminal courts of that government. This definition embraces, in addition to sexual assaults and the molestation of children, such obsolete and unenforced laws as involve seduction, fornication, and adultery, for example, although they are closer to what are sometimes called infractions, violations, or offenses than to crimes. These are "minor crimes," for the most part ignored, no longer reflecting (if ever they did) the moral judgment of the people but deserving of attention if only because they have been, and in some cases still are, part of the penal laws governing sexual conduct. Those sex crimes that arouse the greatest indignation and public concern involve force and violence,

---

unusual punishment, for instance, were not applicable to state prosecutions for violations of state laws. In a series of decisions starting in the 1930s, the Court ruled piecemeal that some of the amendments and sections thereof protected those accused in state prosecutions, as a result of the due process clause of the fourteenth amendment.

The early case that denied Bill of Rights protection to persons in matters involving state rather than federal law was *Barron v. Baltimore*, 32 U.S. (7 Pet.) 243 (1833). An entire series of cases starting about a century later reversed the impact of *Barron;* among the most important were two appeals that reached the Supreme Court in the *Scottsboro* case: *Powell v. Alabama*, 287 U.S. 45 (1932), and *Norris v. Alabama*, 294 U.S. 587 (1935).

* The proposals of the Model Penal Code of the American Law Institute as they apply to sex crime are described and discussed in several of the chapters that follow.

actual or threatened; exploitation of children and others; an important and gross affront to the moral beliefs and standards prevalent in a society (as incest); the possible presence of psychological disturbance (exhibitionism, voyeurism, sadomasochism, bestiality, fetishism, necrophilia); and the pursuit of sex in a manner that has come to be defined as a social problem (e.g., prostitution and homosexuality). Nonsexual acts related to sexuality are often criminalized and considered by many to be sex crimes (abortion, sale of contraceptives, dissemination of birth control advice, production of erotic entertainment, sale or even possession of pornography, nudism, and the advertising of aphrodisiacs, among others).

A further difficulty in defining sex crime is determining whether a given illegal act should logically be classified as sexual. Whatever analytic or therapeutic purposes are served by conceptualizing arson as a sex crime because of the arsonist's unconscious motivations or murder as a sex crime motivated by sexual jealousies and passions, the criminologist would not find such a classification system useful. In the penal codes, conduct is defined or categorized not according to its motivation but only according to its overt forms. Thus, sex crimes would be limited to violations of the law in which the behavior is designed to obtain immediate and conscious sexual gratification, release, or pleasure or to profit from another's obtaining such gratification.

As Max Weber pointed out, to describe something as legal does not imply that it is good or bad, necessary or expendable.[4] There are many illegal sexual acts that, by what has come to be common consent, are not treated as crimes but that, for various reasons, have not been removed from the penal codes. At the other end of the spectrum, there are acts that are widely, if not universally, condemned but that many contend are not the rightful business of the law and should be considered matters of private morality and dealt with by education or propaganda from public health, social, educational, or religious sources. Between these extremes there are a few acts that it is agreed ought to be condemned, discouraged, and punished (as forcible rape); others that can be seen as essentially harmless (although they may or may not be such) except to the person or persons involved, as teenage consensual sex, homosexual relations, and masturbation; and some that overwhelming evidence suggests are manifestations of psychological disturbance whether or not they are in and of themselves antisocial (as transvestism and exhibitionism).

At one time or another, and in one society or another, almost every type of interpersonal sexual activity except adult heterosexual acts between socially recognized mates, directed toward procreation and performed in the so-called "missionary position," has been condemned as immoral and has been punishable as a crime. Indeed, some procreative heterosexual acts were condemned if they were not conducted between legally recognized mates who would be capable and willing to care for the child that could issue from such a union. But it can also be said that almost all types of sexual activity—with important exceptions that will be brought out shortly—have been accepted, even encouraged, by one group or another. Thus, Clellan Ford and Frank Beach,[5] in their cross-cultural study of the varieties of sexual norms and behavioral patterns,* pointed to societies in which masturbation, premarital fornication, adult-child sexuality, oral-genital relations, and other types of conduct have been condoned, and others in which condemnation has been strong.† While their study focused primarily on primitive, nonindustrial, or unsophisticated societies, the punishment meted out to transgressors can be considered the analogue of criminal prosecution in the modern world. Nevertheless, though acknowledging the varieties of approval and disapproval cited by Ford and Beach and many other anthropologists, one should not overlook the significance of cross-cultural similarities. There is universal or near universal condemnation of the rape of women of one's own society; the incest taboo has had some very specialized types of exceptions that do not upon investigation invalidate the claim that it is universal (there have been major trends toward decriminalization of incest); and all societies have favored adult heterosexual relations while not necessarily criminalizing all other forms of sexuality.

Unknown and Unreported Sex Crimes

Several factors make a study of sex crime particularly hazardous and the results of research often speculative. Like most forms of

---

* Their study was cross-specific as well, but only the cross-cultural is relevant here.

† Masturbation alone among these acts has not been a crime in modern societies although it has been severely punished by agents of social control as well as by family authorities. However, Alfred Kinsey and his colleagues pointed out that it has been criminal to encourage masturbation, "encourage" meaning teaching, counseling, or advising; they also demonstrated a class distinction in the social acceptability of the practice, with acceptability and frequency positively correlated with social class. See Alfred C. Kinsey, Wardell B. Pomeroy, and Clyde E. Martin, *Sexual Behavior in the Human Male* (Philadelphia: Saunders, 1948), chaps. 10, 14.

criminal behavior, sex crimes generally are committed in privacy and in secrecy; hence, the researcher, the police, or the compiler of statistics may not know that the act has been committed. This is particularly applicable although not limited to what Edwin Schur refers to as "crimes without victims" in a 1965 book by that title.[6] The acts are crimes in that they are against the law; they are victimless in the sense that they are committed with the willing consent of the parties, and there are no complaining witnesses. Examples include a wide range, as adult homosexuality in private and (where the act is illegal) adultery and noncoital heterosexual activities. The lack of a complaining witness extends even further. One or both of the parties may be under the age of consent, in the adolescent or prepubertal years, but while technically the male has committed statutory rape, solicitation, public indecency, carnal abuse, or impairment of the morals of a child, his partner has been entirely willing and, unless apprehended *in flagrante delicto,* is unlikely to make a complaint.

The "dark figure" of unknown crime extends deeply into the area of sexuality. A very young child may not complain out of fear, lack of understanding, or for some other reason; if she (or sometimes he) does complain, adults may choose to disbelieve the child or may prefer, perhaps because the offender is a member of the family or a close friend, to downplay the incident and handle it without making an official complaint. Furthermore, some professionals have contended that reporting the incident may prove more traumatic for the child than suppressing it (a debated and debatable position) and may convince the parents accordingly. In cases of voyeurism, to take another example, or of transvestism, where this is a criminal offense, only the performer of the act may know of the commission, which certainly would generally be true of the rare (or believed to be rare) instances of necrophilia.

A number of additional, related problems confront the student of sex crimes. First, the percentage of instances of a given crime that has come to the attention of authorities and has found its way into the statistics cannot be determined with reassuring accuracy. Plea bargaining, on the one hand, or indictment and conviction for a lesser offense, on the other, may effectively obfuscate the official statistics—a charge of forcible rape becomes simple assault; exhibitionism, disorderly conduct. Thus, official statistics on the prevalence of various offenses and the nature of offenders and victims are less than reliable, which is not to assert that no accurate information exists: criminologists and other social scientists have developed techniques of estimating prevalence and frequency and for gathering data about most sex crimes. Second, penal codes do not classify sex crimes in a manner that is helpful to the criminologist. A typical example. is taken from the statutes of the state of Nebraska:

> Crimes Against Nature. Whoever has carnal copulation with a beast, or in any opening of the body except sexual parts with another human being, shall be guilty of sodomy and shall be imprisoned in the Nebraska Penal and Correctional Complex not more than twenty years.[7]

Such a law covers oral-genital heterosexual relations (including those between husband and wife), all or almost all forms of homosexuality, and bestiality, categories that are entirely different from a social and psychodynamic viewpoint but that would be linked with one another statistically if all arrests and indictments under this law were recorded and reported as a single figure. Obviously, an investigator who uses only such legal distinctions would be led astray. Finally, psychological classifications are of little help in analyzing the acts and in discovering the relationships between law and conduct although they are no doubt valuable for preventive and therapeutic purposes.

TYPOLOGIES AND CATEGORIES

A useful method of classification would have to take into account major social factors involved in the sexual activity and the legal categories encompassing such acts when these factors are present. In what might be considered a descending order of significance for society, we suggest that sex crimes could be analyzed as follows:

1. The presence of force or the threat or fear of force.
2. Obtaining sex by exploitation of the status or authority differences between victim and offender, as when the victim is considerably younger than the offender, is mentally impaired, or is in a patient-therapist, inmate-custodian, and in some instances student-teacher relationship with the offender.
3. The public visibility of what otherwise might be a private matter, in a manner grossly offensive to a considerable portion of the population, whether intentional, as in sexual ex-

hibitions, or impulsive as in copulation or fellatio committed in public parks, theaters, restrooms, or in other places where persons are likely to be unwilling witnesses.
4. The blood relationship of the partners and, to a lesser extent, adoptive or affinal relationships.
5. Exploitation of sex as an occupation, in a manner contrary to the prevailing social norms.
6. Sex between persons of the same gender.
7. Relationships in violation of trust.
8. Nuisance behavior, usually considered no threat to society but rather important from the viewpoint of psychopathology; for example, exhibitionism, voyeurism, fetishism, and transvestism.
9. Sexual activity which although consensual may result in severe injury or death.
10. Sexual relations between human beings and animals.

This typology is not all-inclusive, and it has some overlapping elements. In addition, the relative social importance of the items for criminal law is a value judgment, on which there will be disagreement. Probably only the first category, involving rape, attempt to rape, and sexual assault, encounters strong and universal hostility. In the second category, people distinguish between the child and the teenager although both may be victims. We would place public solicitation in the third category (in fact, England has legalized prostitution so long as it does not involve open solicitation on public streets); thus, we suggest that there is less concern for sex as occupation when it is concealed than when it is flaunted.

Translating the ten categories into specific offenses:

1. Rape, attempted rape, sexual assault, including forcible sodomy.
2. Carnal abuse of children, child molestation, impairing the morals of a minor, contributing to a child's delinquency, and statutory rape.
3. Public solicitation for sexual purposes, with or without demand for financial remuneration; public indecency; lewd and lascivious behavior.
4. Incest between consenting adults.
5. Prostitution, pimping, operation of a brothel, and other such activities; marginal behavior in some occupations (as taxicab driving) to recruit customers for prostitutes.

6. Adult consensual homosexuality, as well as homosexual acts between consenting minors.
7. Sexual favors obtained through misrepresentation and those that are violations of the marital or quasi-marital trust (e.g., seduction under promise of marriage, faking a marriage ceremony, bigamy).
8. Transvestism, exhibitionism, voyeurism, frotteurism, fetishism, and other such acts when they do not interfere strongly with the ongoing society and do not involve invasion of privacy or the rights of nonparticipating persons who become a victimized public.
9. Sadomasochism.
10. Bestiality.

Without abandoning this system, we suggest further that sex criminality as a social problem might be better understood if these acts were assigned to four groups according to the degree to which the conduct itself can be tolerated in a permissive society, with or without resort to criminal law and punitive sanctions. From this vantage point, and drawing upon our own values, with which there will be disagreement, we suggest the following typology as guide for both analysis and social policy.

1. Conduct beyond the level of tolerance and requiring legal prohibition, both for the protection of potential victims and for the purpose of expressing through codified law the moral outrage of the members of society.
2. Conduct that by agreement of large numbers of people is best seen as psychopathological but that nevertheless requires legal prohibition in order to protect members of the society from being victimized and to facilitate treatment of the offender.
3. Conduct that dominant forces in the society, but by no means in numbers approaching a value consensus, believe should be discouraged through means other than criminal sanctions.
4. Conduct that is best seen as a proper area for private decision by the individuals personally involved.

The first of these categories would include any kind of sexual behavior that regardless of the motive or pathology of the offender justified criminal sanctions and punishment in order to protect potential victims and deter potential offenders. These are the main and, in the opinion of some, the only sex acts that should be legally prohibited in a modern society. Many legal and social thinkers limit this category to conduct in which one party has not given consent or is incapable of giving that consent because of age, mental condition, custodial relationship, or some other reason. Yet even here unanimity seems limited only to forcible rape. There are a few people (a few, but not many) who would not extend legal prohibitions to relationships in which one party is a child, a viewpoint that will be discussed in Chapter 3. While forcible rape and other acts in the first category may be committed by deeply disturbed people, it is agreed that they are nonetheless proper areas for legal action, the nature and extent of disturbance guiding the authorities with regard to postconviction treatment of the offender and guiding the police and public with regard to prevention, deterrence, and apprehension.

The second group consists of those types of sexual behavior that are manifestations of psychological disorders but do not appear to pose any serious public menace (exhibitionism, voyeurism, and other such conduct). The problem here is to decide whether legal toleration is in the interests of the public and the offender. The arrest and prosecution of a patently disturbed individual hardly seems appealing to the American people in the last quarter of the twentieth century; however, unless an exhibitionistic or voyeuristic act is against the law, one cannot make a legal move to apprehend, stop, and offer treatment to the transgressor. Although there is a strong feeling that the social response to such a transgressor should be therapeutic, one is always faced with the outcry against (and the ineffectiveness of) enforced therapy.

The third category consists of acts that by common but far from unanimous consent seem better to discourage than encourage but that have come to be regarded, to use the phrase of Gilbert Geis, as "not the law's business."[8] It is felt that prevention might better be handled through education and socialization by the family or by social mechanisms outside the criminal justice system. Examples are almost always controversial for some will argue that certain activities should not be discouraged at all; others agree with Patrick Devlin that matters of morality should be encoded in the law;[9] and a third group, represented by H. L. A. Hart,[10] would neither defend the conduct nor make it criminal. For the moment, one might list as examples prostitution (male and female), adult consensual homosexual and incestuous relationships, and adultery.

For the fourth group, including oral-genital and other extracoital relationships, fornication, miscegenation, and the like there appears to be little argument in most modern societies that criminal laws are unnecessary and improper; that there is nothing inherently evil or antisocial about the acts; and that such conduct is of concern only to the participants.

Somewhere in this classification one has to find a place for gross acts that are annoying and disturbing yet are not manifestations of pathology. In fact, the perpetrators might well pass every psychological test of normality. Examples would be uninvited and unwelcome touching, rubbing, pinching, or what is known in the vernacular as "goosing." These acts might well be included in the legal definition of a misdemeanor, such as simple assault, or an offense, such as disorderly conduct.

Again, there will be disputes over whether a particular form of activity rightfully belongs in one category or another. But a classification of this type should enable one to determine the rationality and the effectiveness of the criminal law, the alternate modes (if any) for channeling behavior into socially acceptable directions, the potential for social harm that rests with various forms of conduct, and the relative value of modifying undesirable sexual conduct by imprisonment, therapy, compassion, radical nonintervention, and benign neglect.

Certainly this list is not all-inclusive and perhaps could not be. For example, having otherwise legal sexual relations while one knowingly has an infectious venereal disease is not criminal in the sense that in most jurisdictions one cannot find a specific paragraph of a penal code so defining it. Nevertheless, such an act might well involve greater danger to the community than many other sexual acts that commonly result in arrest, trial, and imprisonment.*

SOME CONCOMITANT PROBLEMS

There are a number of related issues sometimes linked to studies of sex crime. One involves the question of explicit sexual material,

---

* However, it is entirely possible that deliberate and willful disregard for the health of another might make one liable for prosecution under a law prohibiting, for example, assault, disorderly conduct, or public endangerment. In a civil suit in the United States, in the 1970s, a woman was awarded heavy damages from a former lover from whom she had contracted a venereal disease. In the Soviet Union (Russian Criminal Code, art. 115), the infection of a person with a venereal disease by someone aware of having such a disease is a violation of the criminal code, punishable by a prison sentence of up to three years. See Harold J. Berman, ed., *Soviet Criminal Law and Procedure* (Cambridge: Harvard University Press, 1966), pp. 194–195.

obscene exhibitions, and hard-core pornography not so much as forms of communication that are often illegal or that border on the margins of legality but rather in terms of their effect on the commission of such acts as rape. Pornography is often studied for its putative and disputed impairment of morals and its effect, if any, on what is called the moral fiber of society. Our interest is not in morality in this general sense but rather in the relationship between pornography, either directly or through its moral impact, on sex criminality.

A second problem is abortion, which cannot be deemed a form of sexual behavior and hence when illegal (as it remains in many parts of the world) cannot be considered a sex crime. Abortion has, however, been regarded as a criminal event of a sex-linked nature.

Also of interest, although diminishing in importance in the United States, is the illegality of the sale of contraceptives, especially to minors; but note that sale of contraceptives, even to married couples, was illegal in Ireland as late as 1977.

There is also the question of the offender as victim, with special reference to such stigmatized persons as prostitutes and homosexuals. Some theoretical approaches turn the tables, regarding the sexual deviant as the victim of a hostile society. But even more directly, some persons, in the pursuit of their sexually deviant ways of life, become highly susceptible to victimization.

The question of victimization leads, further, to the issue of concomitant crime. Consideration of this problem has mostly involved victim-offender relationships: situations in which the customers of prostitutes are robbed or rolled or homosexuals are assaulted, blackmailed, or subjected to extortion by men who are or pretend to be police officers. But concomitant crime goes beyond these examples. There is probably considerable drug addiction today associated with prostitution in the United States. A major example of two crimes associated with each other is felony rape, a term used by Menachem Amir to denote a rape, apparently unplanned, that takes place during the commission of another crime,[11] as a burglary in which the intruder is interrupted by a woman or discovers a sleeping female whom he rapes. Concomitant crime exists with prostitution in an entirely different sense; that is, the prostitution is planned but in the course of solicitation or sexual activity such crimes as robbery, larceny, or blackmail are carried out by the prostitute's accomplice.

A study of sex crime involves not only special categories of people but categories of places as well. It should cover sex in prison, in juvenile detention centers, in institutions for the mentally ill or retarded, and in other settings that provide custodial care to inmates. In addition, we are deeply concerned with the stigma visited upon complainants or victims of a sex crime and, at the other end of the spectrum, with the rights of the accused, the special onus that they carry, and the problems of judicial defense not usually present in other types of prosecution. The issue is complex, for the defendant in a sex case has difficulties not shared with other defendants, as has the victim or complaining witness.

Another aspect of sex criminality involves the public images of the persons who commit the acts, whether these images are founded in reality or fantasy. Are there such people as "sex fiends," and are their modes of conduct in any way related to what people think of them? Is there a stereotype, and is there a kernel of truth in the stereotype? What can be done about offenders: are they aided by rehabilitation and treatment efforts; and are their rights invaded by demanding that they undergo behavior modification, neurosurgery, or even castration under pain of indefinite incarceration for refusal to submit?

The Sexual Content of Nonsexual Crimes

The theme that there is a repressed or unconscious sexual motivation behind apparently nonsexual acts was elaborated most thoroughly by Sigmund Freud, is central to his entire work, and has been generally accepted not only by psychoanalysts but by laymen, men of letters, and scholars in a variety of specialized areas of study. In the early 1970s it was challenged by a new group of thinkers, most persuasively by John Gagnon and William Simon in their work *Sexual Conduct*.[12] They maintain that the very reverse of the Freudian concept is a truer model of how humans behave; namely, that far from sexual gratification being a motive for nonsexual acts (whether legal or illegal, it would make no difference), other goals (power, dominance, money, revenge) lead people to engage in sexual acts. For purposes of categorization and analysis, the thesis of Gagnon and Simon, whatever its merits may be, is not particularly relevant; rape and child molestation, for example, are sex crimes and are best handled as such regardless of motives, values, or goals. The Freudian view, on the other hand, in which the sexual element has been isolated in "ordinary" criminal acts, has led to some interesting efforts, but in the end one winds up in a *cul de sac*.

For statistical purposes, one counts a given number of acts that contravene a certain law; there is no way, nor would it be socially useful, to distinguish between acts that violate the code for reasons of greed and those that are similar in all respects except that the motive is sexual gratification that has been deflected or perverted in a peculiar direction. An act can be considered a sex crime, in our view, only if the immediate goal is apparently sexual gratification or if that type of gratification is shown to be present and indispensable for the commission of the crime in the overwhelming number of known instances. To cite an example, it has been said by several scholars that there is a sexual motive in some cases of arson,[13] but whatever value the data of the *Uniform Crime Reports* have for us would be destroyed if a distinction were made that depended on the presence or absence of a repressed libido in setting fires. To call arson a sex crime, at least in the present state of knowledge, would be very much like referring to the common cold as a venereal disease because it is sometimes transmitted during sexual encounter. The issue is further complicated by the plea of psychological disturbance that may be made by a defendant in order to mitigate his responsibility and diminish expected punishment when guilt has been indisputably established. Nevertheless, if there is a repressed and unknown sexual factor in many ordinary crimes, therapeutic procedures would be impaired by failure to recognize such motivation.

HOMICIDES AND BIZARRE CRIMES

The search for sexual motivation is likely to be most fruitful in bizarre crimes, on the one hand, and in "senseless" crimes, on the other. By the former is meant acts that have characteristics not usually encountered as part of the syndrome surrounding an event, such as homicide followed by the removal and theft of soiled underclothing, as occurred in the *Heirens* case in Chicago. We are using the term "senseless" very much in the manner of Albert Cohen in his discussion of delinquent boys:[14] namely, the act is not rationally oriented toward achieving a goal (unless it be a psychological goal unknown to the perpetrator). It is true that the concept of the senseless crime has been overused and overstated. Acts of terrorism have been called senseless by opponents of the terrorists, but they do make sense—in fact, a great deal of sense—to those who commit them. A bank robbery is not senseless, nor is arson to collect insurance. But there is a peculiar and irrational nature to the act of a man who attacks Michelangelo's *Pietà*, screaming at the marble virgin as he attempts to kill her. Larceny only of women's underwear, and the subsequent use of the stolen garments as pillowcases and bedroom decorations, cannot be explained easily except as a neurotic compulsion that does not make sense. Certainly, violence far beyond that necessary to overcome resistance or the use of violence greater than that required to commit murder would be both bizarre and senseless. (The use of these words is intended not to diminish the enormity of the crimes but to focus on the additional dimension, the psychopathological.)

On a conscious level, sex may play a significant part in many murders. In *Patterns in Criminal Homicide*,[15] Marvin Wolfgang found that a majority of all murders were committed by relatives, "friends," and close associates of the deceased such as fiancés and would-be suitors.* Motivations here may be money, sexual jealousy, or some conscious or unconscious sexual goal. Infidelity has been used as the motive, and sometimes the justification or rationalization for the murder of a spouse and/or lover (this is known as the "unwritten law" defense); seduction was at one time brought forward as the excuse for the murder of a daughter or, more often, her alleged seducer. In two nationally renowned cases, those of Joan Little and Inez Garcia, the defendants confessed to murder but claimed they acted to prevent rape (the *Little* case) or to avenge it (*Garcia*). Psychoanalysts have often found considerable evidence of sexuality in parricides, including latent or repressed homosexuality, repressed incestuous desires, and unresolved oedipal conflicts.

CLASSIFICATION BY MOTIVATION

Some behavioral scientists have argued that crimes ought to be classified on the basis of motivation rather than behavior. "The legal classification of crime," claims Benjamin Karpman, here

---

* The ratio of murders by strangers to all other murders may be increasing and may have changed considerably since Wolfgang's work because there has been an increase in murders committed during the course of robberies without a corresponding rise in killings by relatives and associates.

mentioning parenthetically crimes against property, against persons, and against morals, "has no basis in reality. What appears to be a predatory crime may have a motivation not entirely predatory; a crime seeming to be assault on a person may turn out to be sexual." [16] Karpman makes his position more explicit in the following passage.

> "Sex crimes" include crimes which are sex substitutes. A sex-substituting criminal may have a dream state of relaxation following a crime which is a substitute for masturbation. As there is guilt, it is not remembered. Sane persons cannot recall truly their willful wrongdoings; the option is either suicide or poor memory recall, with distortion. This is not a true amnesia but lack of attention—"I don't care to remember." The greatest thrill, so great that there is a compulsion to repeat, is that which comes to the non-duty killer who gets his victim's blood on his hands. Often there is orgasm, a super-orgasm. Actions are semi-automatic, semi-purposeful; the purpose is to make possible a repetition of the thrill. Such persons are not truly amnesic.[17]

On the other hand, Karpman, true to a consistent framework, would exclude from the area of sex crimes those illegal acts in which the motivation is not sexual although the behavior is. "Bigamy, white slavery, and violation of the Mann Act universally included with sex crimes do not usually belong there." White slavery, Karpman points out, "is essentially a predatory crime, the individual white slaver deriving no personal sexual satisfaction from the procedure." [18] The same type of logical distinction would lead to the exclusion from the sex crime category of pimping and possibly, by extension, prostitution. However, bigamy can be sexually motivated, as can violation of the Mann Act.

Of all apparently nonsexual crimes, arson appears to be the one for which a perverted libido is most often offered as cause or explanation. However, most instances of arson are probably motivated by the desire to obtain insurance money, to get revenge, to commit murder (for other than sexual reasons), or to destroy evidence of another crime. The Freudian could argue that even in such instances the specific form in which the other goals were sought (that is, via fire) indicated unconscious and possibly sexual motivation. Putting aside this argument, there remains a residue, probably a minority, of cases in which the arsonist is a chronic offender; he continues in adulthood to be the child who played with matches; his act is apparently "senseless"; he has no profit in mind;

and he runs after the fire engines and watches the flames with a sexual ecstasy that he himself cannot comprehend. There is not only the "thrill" arsonist but the "hero" fire fighter who sets fires, sends in an alarm, participates in alerting, even saving, residents, and helps fight the fire, all to gain hitherto denied recognition that may be linked to deeply repressed sexual drives.

Donal MacNamara describes acts of larceny whose bizarre character resides in the nature of the objects stolen or mutilated, giving rise to a suspicion, frequently sustained, that the thefts are fetishistic acts.[19] Not all fetishists steal: they may assault (as cutting off locks of hair from an unsuspecting victim), destroy, purchase, window-shop, stare, fantasize. Certainly only a small part of the enormous theft that goes on in America and most other parts of the world is fetishistic or can be accounted for by sexual motivation. But a few such instances do occur, and the search for the sex angle not only may help to solve the crime but also may be of great value in rehabilitating the offender. This is not an unmitigated social good: the emphasis on motive may serve to lessen the punishment suffered by the educated and the middle- and upper-class offender as opposed to the poor offender who had more rational goals.

On rare occasions, the sexual character of an "ordinary crime" is conscious and apparent, although one must be careful that this is not a ruse deliberately perpetrated by an offender who is seeking to deceive the court. Take, for example, the well-publicized bank robbery committed by a man who demanded money in order to finance a transsexual operation for his male lover so that they could become legally wedded.° In many instances, psychoanalysts have suggested that the gun is a symbolic phallus, that shooting is symbolic ejaculation, and that in this sense there is a sexual element essential to understanding many ordinary crimes involving the use of firearms.

Political crimes, and in fact political acts of a noncriminal nature, have likewise been imputed to have an unconscious psychosexual motivation such as homosexual attacks upon a father figure. But only in rare instances is it necessary to resort to this type of symbolism in order to account for the fact that the act took place. In other words, the act is not "senseless" when the sexual motiva-

---

° This episode, which occurred in Brooklyn in the early 1970s, was fictionalized in the movie *Dog Day Afternoon*.

tion is removed although the elaboration of such a motive may aid in understanding why it took place in a certain form, at a given time, and under particular circumstances. Without a subculture of violence, political frustration, a feeling of repression, and numerous other factors, perhaps the act would not have occurred; yet given these forces, it may have required someone with specific traits, which may or may not include disturbances (the latter not necessarily sexual, unless one sees sexuality as the root of all disturbances), to have been the one "chosen" by history to carry it out.

LATENCY AND FREUDIANISM

Freud wrote of the period of "total or at least partial latency" during which one develops the psychic forces that later act as inhibitors of sexual life and narrow its direction.

> The historians of civilization seem to be unanimous in the opinion that such deviation of sexual motive powers from sexual aims to new aims, a process which merits the name of sublimation, has furnished powerful components for all cultural accomplishments.[20]

Thus, a Freudian approach to sex criminality would have to face the overwhelming problem of how to unleash and utilize the powerful sex drive for purposes of cultural accomplishments without allowing part of this energy to be diverted into destructive and self-destructive channels.

REACHING A DEFINITION

To limit oneself by definition to acts aimed at sexual gratification may entail some classificatory difficulties that can be solved if one includes such behavior as is involved in the exploitation of sexuality. In this case the act itself is illegal but not sexual; however, it is performed for the sexual gratification of others. Thus, we differ with Karpman in that we do see pimping as a sex crime although the pimp himself does not seek sexual gratification through this act. Similarly, the author, publisher, and purveyor of hard-core pornography may be wholly profit oriented while catering to a sexually oriented clientele.

Thus, we reach a definition: *sex crime is behavior that is illegal in a given jurisdiction, that is explicitly sexual, or that has been declared criminal because it exploits, caters to, makes possible, or is dependent upon explicit sexual behavior.*

Some Tangential Issues

The law on sexual behavior has been infused with moral and social issues that are often tangential, that may at one time have been relevant but are no longer so, and that generally involve not the propriety of the act or the protection of a potential victim but the consequences of the act for the victim or for society. Three such issues are illegitimacy, abortion, and venereal disease.

ILLEGITIMACY

The stigma of illegitimacy, for both mother and offspring, has evidently declined but cannot be said to have disappeared.[21] (There have not been any signs of serious stigma for the imputed father in the past, and in some societies, in fact, males have gained status in proportion to the number of their bastards.) The social concern has been with the need to provide economically for the child; in the United States this concern has led to welfare payments for mothers of dependent children, with considerable middle-class resentment of the welfare system.

Illegitimacy involves difficulties in establishing biological parenthood and with it responsibility on the part of the father; whereas a child born to a married woman is presumed, for lack of strong evidence to the contrary, to be the offspring of the mother's spouse. Finally, there is a belief held by many people, although it has been challenged by some feminists, that a child is psychologically handicapped by being socialized in a one-parent household.[22]

Despite stigma, the availability of contraceptive methods, and, since the late 1960s, the ease of obtaining an abortion in some parts of the United States, illegitimacy has not declined, contrary to the predictions that had been made by many authorities.[23] Young women account for the majority of illegitimate births, and many of them are reluctant to confide in their parents until it is too late for abortion, do not know where to obtain good medical advice, and in other ways are unable to handle premarital sex and unwanted pregnancy. The continued prevalence of illegitimacy is traceable to several other factors, including the refusal of some couples to marry despite the desire to have a child (or children); the virtual institutionalization of nonmarital sex; the inadequacy of knowledge about birth control methods; the diminution of responsibility by males for pregnancy prevention since the advent of the birth control pill; and the propaganda of various organized groups against planned parenthood, on ethico-religious grounds in some instances and in others on the ethnic strength argument. Furthermore, out-of-wedlock pregnancy and illegitimate offspring are not always unwanted. They may derive from the wish to obtain the partner as a spouse, to manifest rebellion against parents, or to escape from the boredom of school.

Forcible rape does not appear to be making a major quantitative contribution to illegitimacy. It is routine for a rape victim, if she reports the matter and presents herself to a doctor or to a hospital, to undergo medical treatment to prevent the growth of a fetus should conception have occurred. For the most part, but with some exceptions, opponents of abortion make the point that they would permit victims of forcible rape to obtain removal of a fetus.

The major criminal source of unwanted pregnancy and illegitimacy is probably statutory rape, and it is possible that the pregnancy itself results in bringing many adult-minor relationships to the attention of authorities. If the male (presumably the older of the two) is unmarried, the couple can often resolve the issue by marriage, and many states provide for such a legal binding of the two even though the female is well under the age of consent for out-of-wedlock sex.

ABORTION

Unless one regards abortion as a crime and looks at the arguments for and against decriminalization, one must conclude that here, too, the issue is tangential to sex crime. Few sex crimes, as already pointed out, result in pregnancy; for those that do, the opposition to abortion is not so strong as under ordinary circumstances. The problem of abortion is largely religio-philosophical, revolving around whether one considers the fetus to be a living human being inasmuch as our society and most other modern societies oppose infanticide. There is a pragmatic issue as well: women who have unwanted pregnancies will search out illegal abortionists if legal avenues are closed. This situation hurts the poor more than the well-to-do, results in efforts to self-abort by some women (with disastrous consequences), and leads countless others to undergo illegal abortions, often performed under unsanitary conditions and at exorbitant fees by incompetent persons who are unwilling and unable to take the risk of providing even minimal aftercare. The opponents of abortion find the moral issues overriding and urge better social services and education for the woman who finds herself with an unwanted pregnancy. By definition, we do not find this argument germane to sex crime because whether abortion is defined as criminal or legal, as immoral or proper, it is not a sexual act itself, any more than would be the suicide of a pregnant woman or desertion by her husband.[24]

VENEREAL DISEASE

Only a small proportion of reported venereal disease results from crime. Almost routinely, a woman who has been sexually assaulted, if penetration was effected, is tested and/or treated for a venereal disease, if only as a preventive measure. In the United States, public health authorities believe that neither child molestation nor prostitution constitutes a major mechanism for the transmission of venereal diseases. They are transmitted mainly by promiscuity, heterosexual and homosexual, and it is unlikely that any legal provision against fornication, adult consensual homosexuality, adultery, or seduction would be effective in controlling or reducing their spread. The specter of disease has never succeeded in keeping men from prostitutes or from casual relationships when opportunities came their way; moreover, the general knowledge that venereal infection is widespread in homosexual circles has not diminished sexual activity in the gay world. Neither stigma nor law prevents risk taking, and recourse to law hardly seems justifiable although in many countries military authorities punish the venereally diseased as military offenders, with more serious punishment meted out to those who do not voluntarily come forward when the first symptoms appear.

The venereal diseases (or STD, for sexually transmitted diseases, a euphemistic innovation of the 1970s) were thought to be within control, if not on the verge of eradication, only a short time ago. The rapid treatment developed during World War II, first with the sulfanilamides and then, even more effectively, with antibiotics, was believed to offer the possibility that the diseased would be treated, quickly placed in a noninfectious category, and soon returned to their old patterns, without jeopardizing others. For several reasons, this great hope proved to be chimerical: the declining use of the condom in favor of birth control pills and intrauterine devices removed one of the possible prophylactic mechanisms; the rise of single bars, gay bars, and widespread nonaffectional sexuality reduced the possibility that one could trace the partner from whom the disease had been contracted; antibiotics and other therapeutic measures provided a dangerous and unfounded sense of security to people who might otherwise have been much more careful about their health; and penicillin-resistant strains of syphilis and gonorrhea appeared as the use of antibiotics became widespread.

The venereal diseases can best be controlled (at least until effective immunization measures are developed) by much more thorough education so that they are quickly recognized, treated, and reported. Whether certain forms of sexual behavior are legal or illegal (teenage sexuality or homosexuality, for example), will in all likelihood have little effect on the prevalence and the incidence of these diseases.[25]

The Examination of Sex Crime and Law

We attempt in this book to look at the issues of sexuality and its relationship to crime and law with a degree of dispassion. Ideology has been rampant, both from the side of the moralists and from that of the sexual freedomists. The former have abhorred every deviation from a strict sexual code and have been ready to blame the downfall of youth, if not of civilization itself, on sexual laxity.[26] The libertarians have urged that everything (force excepted) goes, and that all forms of consensual sexuality, no matter who the partners or how many, and in some instances regardless of their age, should be treated as equally good and as free choices to be made by free people.[27] Between them there has stood a significant group, represented in American social thought by such persons as the psychologist Albert Ellis,[28] and in Britain by the influential legal philosopher H. L. A. Hart.[29] These writers contend that some forms of sexual behavior are matters of private and not public morality even if the participants are neurotic and compulsive and the conduct self-defeating. They neither condemn nor condone the acts and the participants but seek to protect them from the arm of the law. In the words of Ellis, such people have a right to be wrong.

Pressure groups have entered this fray: religious organizations, conservative political groups, educational and parent organizations, on the one hand, and, on the other, feminist, gay, legal reform, and countercultural groups. But social movements tend to be self-serving, always selective in the information that they put forth and in the interpretations that they volunteer and accept. Criminology, like other social and behavioral sciences, must make an effort to be more objective no matter what the opinions of the individual criminologists may be.

An example is seen in the still raging controversy over pornography.[30] Conservatives see pornography as an evil in itself and as generating evil. Liberals see censorship as the evil and view pornography as harmless and sometimes even helpful (helpful, it is claimed, because it deflects potentially dangerous libidinal energy into such outlets as masturbation or vicarious erotic satisfaction). Conservatives see the need for a society of moral cohesion in which the people are rallied around a single moral code; whereas liberals are more likely to emphasize the benefits of diversity. A conservative may find the new sexual morality a threat to the sanctity of the family; a liberal will see human liberation, particularly from outmoded sex roles, as emanating from the sexual upheaval of the mid-twentieth century. This is not to suggest that either would support sex criminality. The point is that the general political orientation of the individual is likely to color his attitude toward what ought or ought not to be criminal and how the offender should or should not be handled. A political view, not only tinted but also tainted, makes it difficult to develop objective data.

Thus it is not only secrecy, failure to report, fear of reporting, and shame that have clouded the issue of sex criminality and made scientific research difficult; one is also confronted with competing ideologies, often eloquently defended by people with vested interests.

Is Sex Crime a Logical Concept?

One way out of the dilemma created by the emotionalism and ideologies, the fears and the prejudices, has been suggested. One could view sex criminality with a greater degree of objectivity if one could completely abolish sex crime as a separate concept. In fact, from a jurisprudential point of view, there is not and there cannot be such a category. If there were no category of this sort in criminology and in psychology, as well as in the mass media, forcible rape would be seen as a form of aggravated assault, child molestation as a form of exploitation or of child abuse (except by the small minority who would institutionalize the behavior altogether), exhibitionism and voyeurism would be nuisances, disorderly conduct, and acts against public order. While such a move would go far toward removing the image of the "sex fiend" and would reduce the absurdly punitive sentences meted out on occasion to offenders posing little public danger, it would have the scientific disadvantage of effacing an otherwise tenable category. The category consists of the totality of forms that the conscious struggle for sexual gratification takes when contravening the norms and codified morals (especially the laws) of a society. There is an inherent logic, we believe, in an approach that studies as a single group laws pertaining to sex behavior, the relationship of the laws to prevailing norms, the offenders, their victims, the societal reaction, and other important aspects of the interaction of sex, law, crime, and society.*

---

* Despite rigorous efforts to insure the up-to-date accuracy of the materials in this study, the uneasy relationships among sex, crime, and the laws in our many jurisdictions are far from static; indeed, they are in constant flux. Thus, while the typescript was being converted to galleys, developments such as these were reported in the press: the obscenity-pornography convictions of Larry Flynt (in the *Hustler* magazine case) and Harry Rheems (in the *Deep Throat* motion picture case) were overturned and new trials ordered; the revised S–1 (U.S. Senate Bill no. 1)—codifying federal criminal laws, while retaining the controversial "community standards" criterion—limits prosecutions to the United States judicial district in which a major aspect of production-distribution took place, ending the prosecution ploy of selecting some especially puritanical community as the venue of trial; the Secretary of the Navy has ordered the "other than honorable" discharge of an admittedly homosexual ensign to be upgraded to "honorable"; as of this writing residents of the Miami area voted overwhelmingly, in the first referendum of its kind in a major U.S. city, to revoke a Dade County ordinance protecting homosexuals from discrimination in employment, housing, and public accommodation; meanwhile the New York State Court of Appeals has intimated (but not ruled) that the penal code proscription on consensual sodomy between adults in private may be unconstitutional.

2 Forcible Rape

My boys were in the army, my girl was at college, and I lived alone.
I live in the mountains at the end of a road which is completely blind.
None of my neighbors can see up that road, so someone could park up
there, and no one would ever know it. Apparently the man who raped
me had been following me and watching my habits for a long time. He
had probably tried the door on several occasions, but fortunately it was
locked.

It was a Sunday morning around noon. I had gone up the road
to get the newspaper and had come back into the house and was read-
ing the paper. Then I went into the bathroom. I opened the door to the
bathroom from my bedroom, and he was standing there with a gun.
I just froze. I went into shock.

He kept me prisoner for two nights and two days. With a gun
at my head, he made me call my school district on Monday to tell them
I was sick. I tried to get out of the bathroom window once, but he
caught me....

He was very sadistic. His sexual assaults went on constantly, and
I was forced into perverse activities—the whole ugly mess—gagging,
choking, vomiting.... I found that if I fought him very hard, he came
to orgasm more quickly, and it was over for a while, which shows
his sadism. I was wondering, "What can I do to get out of this horror?"
I would try to submit, thinking, maybe that would get it over with, but
I found that it infuriated him if I submitted without fighting him. °

If, as Kingsley Davis suggests, the sex drive is competitive and
instinctively anarchic,[1] so that every society must set up norms for
the regulation of sexual conduct, the first and most pervasive of such
norms is that sexuality must be by mutual consent: both parties
must be willing. In fact, the very term "adult consensual act" im-

° From an interview with a rape victim in Diana E. H. Russell, *The Politics of*
Rape: The Victim's Perspective (New York: Stein & Day, 1975), pp. 17–18.

plies that one partner must not be compelled to participate either by the actual violence of the other or by the threat of violence substantiated by disparity in age, size, or strength, proneness to violence, or other factors. Such disparities are usually present and mitigate against the female in an adult-to-adult heterosexual encounter that is not consensual. When one party is a child, the law finds force implicit in the age differential. However, for purposes of both law and sociological study, it would seem preferable to make a clear distinction between the use or the threat of violence and the use of nonviolent enticement or persuasion when one of the partners is a child.

There is a widespread belief that animals are sexually violent and that the male ravishes and subdues the female, the violence causing arousal of the female. Clellan Ford and Frank Beach, however, while noting that males of many species do employ violence, contend that such males "can never copulate with a female who is truly nonreceptive. The female must respond appropriately to the male, and nonestrous females fail to do so." [2] Some persons have—in our view mistakenly—extrapolated this zoological comment to apply to humans, drawing the conclusion that a woman who is "truly nonreceptive" cannot be raped. In addition to the physiological differences between human and nonhuman animals, a broad range of factors makes this argument questionable: fear of death, of permanent injury, or of threatened injury to the victim's children; the use of guns and other weapons; the male's generally superior ability to grasp, punch, and kick; the frightening and threatening nature of the language that can be employed; and the not uncommon crime of two or more males subduing one female.

In the wake of the emphasis on mammalian sexual behavior by the influential scientists at the Institute for Sex Research,[3] however, it may shed light on human sexuality to note that violent behavior during precopulatory foreplay has, in the words of Ford and Beach, an "important biological function." They write: "Many males refuse to mate with females that are too compliant and therefore fail to offer the normal amount of resistance." [4] The analogue with the human male who shows contempt for a woman too ready to offer herself may be apparent, but it is both anthropomorphic and misleading so to argue for such a man's attitude is rooted in cultural traditions (particularly the double standard). The zoological observation may well shed light on the capacity of a few males to obtain gratification only by brutally subduing a highly resistant female. However, we would find it more plausible to locate the roots of such behavior in a culture and a subculture of violence rather than in biological factors.

Problems of Definition

From a legal viewpoint, the definition of rape offers several difficulties. When the word "rape" is used by itself, it usually refers to forcible rape, and clarity is served if the concept is distinguished, as it ordinarily is, from so-called statutory rape. The latter refers to an act in which force and violence are not used to effect sexual intercourse but "consent" is not given in a legally binding sense because the person is under age (or, in rare instances, mentally incompetent) and therefore does not have the right or the ability to give such consent. Sex crimes of this type, and perhaps carnal abuse of willing children, are best studied as separate phenomena (see Chapter 3).

As defined in most penal codes, rape refers to a completed sexual assault by a male upon a female. However, an uncompleted sexual assault is a serious offense in all jurisdictions in the United States. It is generally defined as attempted rape and often is punished by a prison sentence about half that prescribed for the completed act. The public, and scholars as well, speak of homosexual rape, but legally this term is a contradiction.* By definition, and for obvious biological reasons, a woman cannot be guilty of raping a man (although she can be an accessory). If the male is young enough, she might be charged with child molestation or, more likely, with impairing the morals of a child, but clearly a woman cannot bring about sexual intercourse with a male against his will. However, under the legal rule that a person aiding and abetting a crime is guilty of its commission, a charge of rape was

---

* This is not to deny that homosexual assault exists and constitutes a severe social problem, particularly in prisons. The point is that it does not fall under the technical and legal definition of rape. Sexual assaults of males upon other males are discussed in Chapter 5. So-called lesbian rape is probably extremely rare, and no such case has come to our attention. Homosexual relations in women's prisons, as David Ward and Gene Kassebaum as well as Rose Giallombardo have pointed out, are usually not violent and forcible and in other respects are unlike the analogous sexuality in men's jails and prisons. See David Ward and Gene Kassebaum, *Women's Prison: Sex and Social Structure* (Chicago: Aldine, 1965); and Rose Giallombardo, *Society of Women: A Study of Women's Prisons* (New York: Wiley, 1966).

brought against a female in Toronto in November 1975. It was alleged that she had assisted her brother in the rape of another woman. Thus, through the fact of being an accessory to the crime, the female was accused of a crime that by definition can apparently be committed only by a male. Note, along this line, that of a very large sample of those arrested in 1975 on a charge of rape in the United States (22,000 persons) approximately 1 percent were female.[5] Without access to further information, it appears logical to assume that almost all of these women were accessories to the crime, aiding a male, as in the Toronto case.

Attempted rape is a serious crime, generally defined as an effort to commit violent or forcible rape in which the male does not succeed in effecting penetration because of the woman's resistance, interruption during the struggle, loss of erection, or fear of apprehension. For purposes of conviction under the rape statute, the act must go past the attempted state. In most jurisdictions, it requires penetration of the female genitalia by the penis; however, neither full penetration, rupture of the hymen, nor ejaculation of seminal fluid is necessary to support a charge of rape. If the man succeeds in penetrating anywhere else, whatever other crime it is (sodomy, sexual assault, carnal abuse), legally and technically the act is not prosecutable as rape. If he does not use his penis but his tongue, fingers, elbow, knee, a dildo, or some other vicarious instrument, the crime would be assault and attempt but not rape.[*] In instances of attempt, prosecution may be less difficult, as penetration does not have to be established; yet the punishments, as we have noted, are usually less severe. Indeed, in almost all crimes—homicide, for example—the unsuccessful attempt is not punished so severely as the successful crime. Nonetheless, in attempted rape, unlike homicide, the damage to the victim can be as great from the viewpoint of mental anguish, fear, physical danger, injury, trauma, and psychological aftereffects as the damage to the rape victim.

In addition to rape, statutory rape, attempted rape, so-called homosexual rape, and accessory to the act, several related terms require definition. The term "sexual assault" is often used to describe any uninvited touching of the erogenous zones of another's body, as for example the breasts or buttocks; thus, the term is not

---

[*] Ironically, the most famous rape in American literature turns out to be not rape at all but assault and attempt. In the central scene in Faulkner's *Sanctuary*, Popeye, impotent but determined, resorts to a corncob to gain entry to Temple Drake.

interchangeable with "attempted rape," in which force and violence are used but the offender is unsuccessful (however, "sexual
assault" is used not infrequently for homosexual situations). There
is room in a charge of sexual assault for ambiguity, misperception,
and error, say, if the man has falsely perceived an invitation that
was not offered.* On the other hand, in a crowded area, the touching may have been accidental, or so the man might claim. In such
instances, there is usually a hasty retreat, with or without apology,
when the woman makes her displeasure known.

Still another problem of definition (and hence of prosecution
under penal codes) arises when the male has violently and forcibly
committed a sexual act other than coital intromission (that is, other
than insertion of the penis into the vagina). Charges of so-called
sodomy rape, forced anal sex, fellatio, and on rare occasions cunnilingus have been brought with increasing frequency in recent
years, but whether this is because there has been an actual increase
in such activity or because women have become less reluctant to
describe the events and newspapers to print details, one cannot be
certain. The American Law Institute, in its proposed model law on
rape (quoted in full on pages 31–32), handles this by explicitly including anal and oral sex within the definitions offered and not distinguishing these forms from other types of sexual intercourse for
purposes of defining the crime.

It is generally accepted that a man cannot, in the legal sense,
commit rape upon his wife, a concept under attack from feminists,
libertarians, and legal scholars. The traditional law that exempts a
husband from the legal capability of committing an act of rape
upon his wife—an exemption that does not hold in South Dakota—is
based on the presumption that the woman consented to be his
sexual partner when she married him; however, an egalitarian
approach to marriage would lead many to the view that the timing
and circumstances of sexual activity should be as much her choice
as his, and indeed militant equal rights groups are positing this
principle.

Thus, if a woman offers resistance to the sexual advances of her
husband and he beats her into submission, he is technically not
committing rape although he can be (but seldom has been) prose-

* An interesting case involved a man who on St. Patrick's Day kissed a girl
wearing a button reading "Kiss me, I'm Irish." He was arrested, but the
charges were dropped.

cuted on a charge of assault. Nor is a man able to prevent his spouse from testifying by invoking the privilege that a wife cannot bear witness against her husband in a criminal proceeding: this provision does not apply when a wife is the victim of her husband's crime.

The courts have ruled that a divorced or legally separated woman can be raped in the legal sense by her husband; that is, a forcible sexual attack that meets all the other criteria for rape would not fall outside the definition by reason of their former relationship. In New York, a man was accused of rape by a woman from whom he was separated but not divorced; the separation itself had not been legally declared. With the increasing number of such de facto separations and with the current vigorous insistence by feminists and others that rapists be prosecuted, such charges may be brought more frequently in the future, and there is a likelihood that judicial decisions or legislative enactment will make clear that the protection of the man from the charge of raping his wife was not intended to cover spouses separated from each other.

The American Law Institute has suggested that a model statute on rape and related offenses (including definitions of the relevant terms) might read as follows:

Section 213.1 Rape and Related Offenses.

(1) *Rape.* A male who has sexual intercourse with a female not his wife is guilty of rape if:

(a) he compels her to submit by force or by threat of imminent death, serious bodily injury, extreme pain or kidnapping, to be inflicted on anyone; or

(b) he has substantially impaired her power to appraise or control her conduct by administering or employing without her knowledge drugs, intoxicants or other means for the purposes of preventing resistance; or

(c) the female is unconscious; or

(d) the female is less than 10 years old.

Rape is a felony of the second degree unless (i) in the course thereof the actor inflicts serious bodily injury upon anyone, or (ii) the victim was not a voluntary social companion of the actor upon the occasion of the crime and had not previously permitted him sexual liberties, in which cases the offense is a felony of the first degree. Sexual intercourse includes intercourse per os or per annum, with some penetration however slight; emission is not required.

(3) *Gross Sexual Imposition.* A male who has sexual intercourse with a female not his wife commits a felony of the third
degree if:

> (a) he compels her to submit by any threat that would
> prevent resistance by a woman of ordinary resolution; or
> (b) he knows that she suffers from a mental disease or
> defect which renders her incapable of appraising the nature
> of her conduct; or
> (c) he knows that she is unaware that a sexual act is be-
> ing committed upon her or that she submits because she falsely
> supposes that he is her husband.[6]

In this proposal, the American Law Institute makes a sharp distinction in the seriousness of the crime based upon whether the
female is a voluntary companion of the offender; if she is not, it is
a felony of the first degree, and otherwise of the second degree, with
corresponding differences in punishment. The proposal places in the
category of forcible rape all intercourse with girls under the age of
ten. If the act is buggery rather than coitus, it remains under the
classification of rape.

Then, in a new category called "gross sexual imposition" the
Institute would reduce to a lesser felony a number of other offenses.
All three listed in the section quoted are likely to arouse debate,
with many insisting that the perpetrator ought not to be entitled
to lesser punishment. The most controversial is probably the first,
in which the man compels submission "by any threat that would
prevent resistance by a woman of ordinary resolution," as distinct
from the greater crime, in which the threat must be "of imminent
death, serious bodily injury, extreme pain or kidnapping, to be inflicted on anyone." The last phrase is meant to include a threat to a
companion (particularly a boyfriend) or a member of the family
and is omitted, it will be noted, from the third-degree felony
described as gross sexual imposition.

The American Law Institute not only would exclude a husband
from prosecution on a charge of rape or certain other offenses of a
sexual nature that would be criminal if committed against someone
other than a wife but also would extend this exclusion "to persons
living as man and wife, regardless of the legal status of their relationship." Although the Model Penal Code would make the exclusion inoperative if the man and woman were living apart "under
a decree of judicial separation," it is silent, and by implication continues to exclude the male from culpability, about cases in which the

separation is de facto. There is one other statement of interest in the paragraph on spouse relationships: "Where the definition of an offense excludes conduct with a spouse or conduct by a woman, this shall not preclude conviction of a spouse or woman as accomplice in a sexual act which he or she causes another person, not within the exclusion, to perform." [7]

Cross-Cultural Information

Save for the incest taboo, which although universal exhibits infinite variations, no form of sexual activity is so widely condemned as rape. In Africa, Ford and Beach report, there has been a strong tendency toward severe corporal punishment for sexual violence.[8] In their cross-cultural study of almost 300 societies, these authors found no instances of institutionalized socially accepted activities that could be called forcible rape by modern definitions.

> Under special circumstances physical force and perhaps pain may on occasion be inflicted upon a woman by a man in an attempt to compel sexual acquiescence. But, save in rare and extreme cases, the behavior does not contribute to the sexual arousal or satisfaction of either partner.[9]

Note that in this passage the authors go beyond stating that forcible rape is not normative; they say further that it is not gratifying in and of itself. Thus, as it can be said that a man who commits rape is not acting like a beast (at least not literally), so it can be added that a civilized man who performs such an act is not behaving like a savage although the latter performing in such manner might well be accused of conduct more characteristic of a "civilized" person.

There have been instances of what can be termed institutionalized rape in which women not of one's own society were ravished. Probably the most common form of this behavior is wartime rape by the conquering army, from the most ancient depredations to a variety of scandals and rumors of the twentieth century. That the soldiers of biblical times engaged in the practice of ravishing women captured in war is quite probable, writes Samuel Glasner, but an effort was made "to meliorate this barbaric practice." The Talmud tends in the direction of leniency for the act, Glasner contends, pointing out that "even in the case of rape the initial moral resentment on the part of the woman may gradually turn into an inward, instinctual consent." [10] It is clear that this last statement,

male originated and male conceptualized, reflects the type of thinking that continues to dominate the minds of many rapists (and,
unfortunately, many police, prosecutors, judges, and jury members
in rape cases) and that has been given some support by Freudians
while under considerable attack by feminists.

In modern times, instances of mass rape by conquering soldiers
are many and are often well documented, although one must be
somewhat skeptical about the propaganda of partisans of the con-
quered people. One of the most publicized such events occurred in
Bangladesh, thousands of women allegedly having been raped by
Pakistani soldiers. What seems to have attracted the greatest attention about this event, however, was the stigma attached to the unwilling victims by their own people: the women became outcasts
because they had been defiled, no matter how much this had been
against their will.

Forcible rape has been institutionalized or at least accepted in
situations in which there is a dehumanizing attitude toward one
racial group (such as has long existed in the United States against
blacks); exploitation of the females of the other race by dominant-
group males is accepted in such a society because the victims are
defined as the latter's sexual property.[11] In some American Indian
tribes, organized rape was punishment for adultery; according to
Fred Voget,[12] sometimes a husband would turn his wife over to
twenty or more men.* Rape has also received some ex post facto
approval in Sicily and elsewhere when it is preceded by the abduction of a virgin by an unmarried male who following the defloration not only offers but insists upon marriage (a tradition
challenged in Italy in the 1950s, when a woman not only refused
the hand of her abductor in marriage but reported him to the police
and insisted—with success—upon his prosecution). Anthropologists,
many of whom espouse a concept of cultural relativism, which
postulates that there are no universals in human proscriptions and
that no acts are inherently evil, have pointed to the Gusii, a tribe
in southwestern Kenya, among whom forcible sex seems to be
approved; however, a careful reading of the documentation reveals
that what is involved is more a game of teasing and capture than
anything analogous to rape.[13]

---

* Interestingly enough, mass sexual assault as a punishment either for an offense
  committed prior to incarceration or for a violation of the inmate norms is
  frequently imposed by "kangaroo courts" in jails, prisons, and juvenile correctional facilities.

The Problem of Resistance

A great difficulty in the discussion of sexual assault is posed by the amount of resistance a woman must put up for the act to be defined as rape rather than as a response to indications that she is ambivalent about her intentions, is quite willing if the male can be sufficiently persuasive, or is pretending to resist when she is actually playing a teasing game, wanting to be begged and finally taken. Rape involves and implies resistance, but the resistance need not be physical. It might stop at a certain point out of fear, for example; in fact, if fear itself is established as having motivated a woman to comply against her wishes, it is logical to demand that the perpetrator be charged with rape. Nevertheless, lack of resistance offers a male charged with rape an opportunity to defend himself in court with the countercharge that the woman was not a victim but a willing, even an eager, participant in the act.

How much resistance must a woman offer, and at what point can her diminished resistance be interpreted as coy acquiescence? Must she "kick, bite, scratch, and scream" to the utmost, as Morris Ploscowe has asked. And what if the male interprets such behavior as sex play?

This question is especially crucial if the event involves one female and one male (not several males acting in concert) who has not used any physical blows to weaken the woman or knock her unconscious. His very presence, particularly if he is a stranger, may be sufficient to frighten her into submission. Returning to the ability of female animals to prevent insertion of the penis if there is resistance (an important matter when insertion is legally necessary for the act of the human male to be prosecuted as a rape), some scholars have been skeptical of the ability of a man to insert when the woman is unwilling. Along this line, Ploscowe writes:

> Many experts in the field of legal medicine believe "that rape cannot be perpetrated by one man alone on an adult woman of good health and vigor." Medicolegal experts therefore tend to regard all accusations of rape made under such circumstances as false. For example, Beck [1863] states in his treatise on medical jurisprudence: "I have intimated that doubts exist whether a rape can be consummated on a grown female in good health and strength. . . . The opinion of medical jurists is very decisive against it. The consummation of a rape, by which is meant a com-

plete, full, and entire coition which is made without any consent
or permission of the woman, seems to be impossible unless some
very extraordinary circumstances occur. For a woman always
possesses sufficient power by drawing back her limbs and by the
force of her hands to prevent the insertion of the penis while she
can keep her resolution entire."[14]

This position fails to take into account not only fear but also
weaponry, as well as the violence surrounding the act. Whatever
validity the point of view quoted by Ploscowe might have appears
limited to acts of sexual intercourse involving a friend, a close
acquaintance, or a relative rather than a stranger. In court, far less
resistance than that described by Beck is required, and if this has
led to some abuses on the one hand, it has led to legitimate prosecutions on the other, when the female surrendered out of fear,
exhaustion, or other reasons. Furthermore, Beck's formulation notwithstanding, "complete, full, and entire coition" is not required for
conviction; any penetration by the penis, no matter how slight, constitutes rape.

In a Connecticut case discussed by Ploscowe, the defendant
claimed that the act was not rape because the woman had not
resisted to the limit of her power and had not made every possible
effort to prevent sexual intercourse. The court rejected this defense,
stating: "To make the crime hinge on the uttermost exertion the
woman was physically capable of making would be a reproach to
the law as well as to common sense." [15] The general trend of the
1960s and 1970s, particularly as a result of the feminist outcry
against unsuccessful prosecutions, has been to deny the need to
prove that the woman physically resisted to the greatest possible
extent. (In fact, some experts advise against such resistance on the
ground that it is more likely to lead to permanent injury or murder.) On the other hand, a general trend proceeds unevenly, and
the matter of resistance is interpreted differently by different judges
and juries, taking into account such factors as the specific law in the
jurisdiction and the events surrounding a given case, not to mention
personal beliefs. In New York City, a man who brought a woman to
an apartment (not his own but one for which he had been given a
key) by misrepresenting himself as a psychologist and making
fraudulent claims about what he could accomplish for his new-
found companion was found not guilty on a charge of rape. The
judge stated that the man could rightly be denounced as a liar and
a cad, but that this did not make him a rapist.[16]

Those who insist that a man is guilty of rape only if the woman screams, bites, and kicks to her utmost, even at the risk of greater injury to herself, sometimes invoke a Freudian approach to account for an apparent lack of resistance. They suggest that the woman's restraint stems not from fear but rather from an unconscious need to be ravished or from some element of masochism or self-hate. It hardly appears that a Freudian analysis of the victim's behavior, conjectural at best, is relevant to a defense. Motivations of offenders are of interest only for therapeutic purposes, not for criminological or legal classifications of crimes. Likewise, motivations of victims are irrelevant in a prosecution: the only problem is whether the complainant has been victimized and, if so, whether the accused is the offender. Even a victim who is "rape prone" in the sense that she repeatedly takes risks that have led her to be forcibly raped in the past° is entitled to protection from men who would assault her. That she needs counseling or that she may well fit the psychoanalytic model of a nonresisting rape victim who has an unconscious need to be ravished does not exculpate the male who has victimized her.

Although penetration, however slight, is required for rape to be effected, ejaculation is not. Ploscowe quotes a complainant who was drinking in a tourist cabin with a companion who demanded sexual intercourse, which she refused. Her story continues:

> "Well, I fought just as long as I could and then I could not fight any more, and then he picked me up and put me on the bed and I still had my coat on. With reference to my pants or undergarments, Keeton didn't do anything at that particular time. I still had them on at the time he made an effort to have sexual intercourse with me. As to whether he penetrated my person . . . yes, sir, he did. He remained in that position just a minute or so and then took my pants off. I don't remember whether they were torn. . . . He succeeded in removing the garment from me. Then with reference to having or tending to have intercourse with me, he went ahead. . . . As to whether the defendant had a completed act of sexual intercourse with me or whether it was only partial, it was only partial. There was no discharge. . . . He complained because he wasn't getting any satisfaction out of it."[17]

° This description fits one of the cases described by Diana E. H. Russell, *The Politics of Rape* (New York: Stein & Day, 1975), of a young hitchhiker who was raped by four men on four separate occasions without relinquishing her practice of seeking and accepting rides from strangers on the open highway.

This is the type of borderline case that has caused great anguish in determining whether an act qualifies as rape and whether there are mitigating circumstances that reduce the enormity of the guilt, and hence the severity of the punishment if the man is indeed found guilty. The woman voluntarily joined a drinking partner in a tourist cabin, drank with him while alone, was not held prisoner or captive, and balked when he wanted to "go all the way." At this point, according to her story, he used force and she did resist, but there is little evidence that the force approached "uttermost resistance." If in such a case the accused should deny that he had made threats or used force and claim that the complainant was a willing partner, it is difficult to obtain a conviction upon her uncorroborated testimony.

Modern legal codes do not insist or even suggest that only a previously chaste woman has the right to deny a male access to her body. Even if they are close friends and have had consensual intercourse on previous occasions, she has the right at any time to say no (just as he has). However, it is more difficult to prosecute and convict when the man claims that the act was voluntary and that there was a previous social relationship of a cordial nature between the two. Much less ambiguous is the case in which the man and woman are total strangers. As rape was becoming a more and more disturbing issue in America during the quarter of a century following World War II, the fears of women were focused far more on sexual assault committed when they (the women) were indisputably unwilling, unresponsive, and uninviting to the intruder.

On Rape Statistics

Rape was one of the first serious crimes about which it was generally known that reported and published incidence did not closely correlate with actual incidence. According to the *Uniform Crime Reports*, of all the serious offenses, rape is probably "the most underreported crime." [18] The main impediment to discovering the number of rapes and their distribution among races, urban and rural centers, and age groups of both perpetrators and victims has been the frequent reluctance of victims to report the act. Rape victims have generally been stigmatized, seen as defiled, although this situation appears to be changing somewhat, at least in America, largely because of feminist influence. The stigma has been especially severe for the unmarried woman because rape makes her "impure" (meaning that she no longer has an intact hymen). Women known to have been raped claim that they are thenceforth regarded as "open territory" by other men. There have been several reports of married rape victims who were divorced or deserted apparently because their husbands suspected their innocence. Reluctance to report a rape to the police or to others may be fed by accounts of humiliating interrogations to which rape victims have been subjected (with questions about their previous sex life, sneers that suggested that perhaps they had "asked for it" and had "liked it") and by fear of embarrassment should the event become known. In addition, a woman may be frightened by the possibility of retaliation if she reports the crime, particularly if the rapist is a man she knows; moreover, she is aware that she will be denounced as a fool for having had a drink with a stranger, accepted a ride, allowed a man into the house who identified himself as a salesman, or acted in some other manner that made it possible for her to be victimized. Under these circumstances, it is understandable that many women have failed to report forcible rapes to police, family, and friends.

From another direction, a difficulty in arriving at reliable statistics on forcible rape derives from the possibility that some girls, discovered *in flagrante delicto* or finding themselves spurned by a former date, have cried rape when they had been quite willing partners to the act. Some charges of rape against black men by white women seem to be very clear examples of voluntary sex the discovery of which embarrassed the female partner (see, for instance, the well-publicized *Giles-Johnson* case).[19]

It might be thought that overreporting and underreporting balance each other out. This is a neat calculus, but it is pure conjecture; more likely, underreporting in the past has had a much greater effect in the distortion of rape statistics than overreporting. Victimization surveys conducted for President's Task Force Commission on Crime and Administration of Justice indicate that only one out of every three instances that the victim sees as forcible rape is reported to the police.[20] According to *Uniform Crime Reports*, the FBI has concluded that in the 1970s one out of every five reports to the police of forcible rape prove upon investigation to be unfounded.[21]

Distortions of rape statistics have declined, probably as a result of changing sex mores, improved crime reporting, and feminists' efforts to persuade victims to go to the police. Virginity is no longer so widely worshipped; hence a woman who has been raped by a stranger is more likely today to report this fact. Furthermore, greater acceptance of nonmarital sex means there is less pressure to invoke a charge of forcible rape when sexual activity is discovered. Finally, feminists have worked with police officers (male and female) to make them more sympathetic to complainants; they have set up specialized police rape units and treatment centers and have instituted other mechanisms for giving assistance to victims.

Figure 2–1 shows that forcible rape in the United States, according to the official statistics as published in the *Uniform Crime Reports,* increased by 48 percent from 1970 to 1975. The rate of victimization (number of victims per 100,000 inhabitants) rose during this period by 41 percent. Over the same years, all violent crime increased by 39 percent, the rate by 32 percent; all "index crimes" (seven major crimes for which reliable figures are believed to be available and that are used as an index of serious criminality) went up by 39 percent, the rate by 33 percent. These figures suggest that

FIGURE 2.1. Forcible Rape. SOURCE: *U.S. Department of Justice, Federal Bureau of Investigations,* Uniform Crime Reports for the United States, 1975 (*Washington, D.C.: Government Printing Office, 1976*), p. 23.

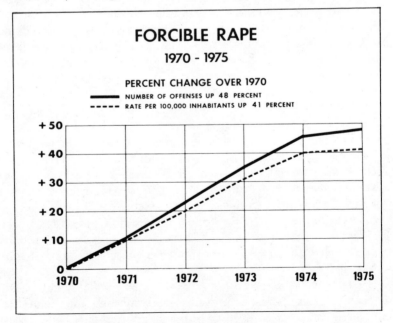

the increase in rape has been real, not an artificial side effect of the women's liberation movement, which has encouraged reporting. One can also conclude that America is faced not so much with a specific rape epidemic as with a rising wave of violence and of crime.

Table 2–1 shows the number of rapes (including attempts to commit rape) from 1960 to 1975. During this time, rape went up by 226.3 percent, compared with a rise of 255.8 percent for all violent crimes and 232.6 for all index crimes. The rape rate was 9.6 in 1960 and 26.3 for 1975, but the figures have to be doubled (or slightly more than doubled) since only females can be victims of this crime. As Table 2–1 shows, 1975 saw an estimated 56,090 cases of forcible rape (including "assaults to rape") in the United States. Assaults to rape, defined as serious assaults for which there is evidence that rape was attempted but not completed, account for about one-third of all cases. The figure does not include nonforcible statutory rape and is limited to heterosexual acts.

That murder and rape are often combined is well known; the body of almost every murdered female is examined for evidence of rape (the same is true of murdered boys, whose bodies are examined for signs of sexual assault). Murder may be combined with rape because of the amount of resistance offered by the female and the escalation of the violence by the male seeking to subdue her; if they were not strangers but known to each other, the murder may have been carried out to silence the woman. Felony rapes

TABLE 2–1. Rapes Reported in the United States, 1960–1975.

1960	17,190	1968	31,670
1961	17,220	1969	37,170
1962	17,550	1970	37,990
1963	17,650	1971	42,260
1964	21,420	1972	46,850
1965	23,410	1973	51,400
1966	25,820	1974	55,400
1967	27,620	1975	56,090

SOURCE: U.S. Department of Justice, Federal Bureau of Investigation, *Uniform Crime Reports for the United States, 1975* (Washington: Government Printing Office, 1976), p. 49.

committed during a planned burglary seem to be especially likely to result in murder.

If it is true that American society has seen a rise in violence since World War II, this trend appears to manifest itself not only in a greater number of violent incidents but also in an increased amount of "unnecessary violence," a sort of supererogatory display, during robberies, rapes, and other crimes (by "unnecessary" is meant more than required by the offender to carry out his offense). While unpremeditated murder that occurs during the commission of a rape does not appear to account for a large percentage of homicides, it is of sufficient significance to make this a major problem in the study of rape.

The Act: Time, Place, Setting

Research on rape has been handicapped by underreporting and false reporting, the general reluctance of victims to be interviewed, and finally, as is true of research on other crimes, by the necessity to rely on arrested, accused, and incarcerated men, who may or may not be a representative sample of rapists. Balancing this somewhat, rape is a crime about which some information on the offender can be known even if he is not apprehended, and it is also a crime that has attracted the attention of the public (largely through the efforts of feminists) and of research scholars. Of several research studies that have appeared, the most abundant information can be found in a study conducted by Menachem Amir [22] in Philadelphia,* and in a 1965 investigation by Paul Gebhard and his colleagues [23] at the Institute for Sex Research (the Kinsey Institute). Amir made a study of all rapes reported in Philadelphia for the years 1958 and 1960; Gebhard studied convicted and incarcerated offenders.

There were 646 reported rape cases in Philadelphia during the two years under investigation, each involving one victim; there were 1,292 offenders, including 370 instances of single rape (one rapist with one victim), 105 of double rape (two rapists, one victim), and 171 group rapes. This adds up to 580 offenders in single

---

* Amir's work has been severely criticized by many scholars and in the main received unfavorable reviews. However, we are relying on his data, not on his interpretations, and the data do seem to be reliable and unequaled except for the work of Gebhard. Amir's research is also dated, but nothing better has been produced since.

or double rapes and 712 in multiple-offender acts (three or more rapists). With 171 such events, there would be an average of slightly more than four rapists in these instances.

There is a seasonal variation in rape, although Amir finds this lacking in significance. Summer almost always brings an increase in reported rapes, and the consistency of this finding year after year cannot be overlooked and may provide some clues to this crime. Human beings, it should be emphasized, are not sexually seasonal animals; neither males nor females have periods of the year affected by temperature or chemical changes in the body or even periods of the month during which they are "in heat." For some people, sexual need is constant, for some sporadic, but there are few (if any) for whom it is cyclical. Why, then, the seasonal variation? Possibly because in summer there is more forcible rape between strangers rather than people previously acquainted with each other, and it may be that these events are more likely to occur outdoors or in an automobile rather than in an apartment. Winter may just not be conducive to a man's proceeding with activity outdoors in which he must partially undress and still retain his potency.*

Perhaps the most important single factor with regard to the setting concerns the degree of previous acquaintanceship and the nature of the relationship between victim and offender. Almost half of the identified victim-offenders were known to each other to the extent to constitute a 'primary' relationship, writes Amir,[24] and 14 percent of all the rapists had what Amir calls previous "intimate" contacts with their victims.† This does not mean that all of these victims had invited the event: the primary relationship can be with a neighbor and the intimate one, for example, with a relative.

Amir employs the logical term "victim-precipitated rape" (an

---

* This explanation is conjectural but is brought forth by the recurrent statistics that show increased rape in the summer months. Our explanation can be tested by seasonal breakdown in various parts of the country, including sections with warm winters, and by a study of the correlation between place of event and month.

† Amir himself does not define the two key terms "primary" and "intimate" and definitions in sociology are somewhat elusive. A primary relationship generally refers to one in which the persons have known each other for a long period of time, with frequent and direct contact, in a manner involving a variety of activities and common interests and not limited to one status. The intimate relationship would have all of these features but would also be warm, involving close emotional ties and a deep knowledge of each person by the other.

extension, as he notes, of "victim-precipitated homicide," a term used by Wolfgang) [25] "to refer to those rape cases in which the victim actually (or so it was interpreted by the offender) agreed to sexual relations but retracted before the act or did not resist strongly enough when the suggestion was made by the offender.* He likewise uses the term when a victim enters situations charged with sexuality.[26] With this concept, he concluded that 19 percent of all forcible rapes studied could be described as victim precipitated.

A factor often confused with victim precipitation and one that is important in studies of crime prevention is risk of victimization. Such risk occurs when a woman is attacked although she has not teased, led on, or encouraged the man, has not entered a situation "charged with sexuality," has not accepted a ride from a stranger, and has not invited a man previously unknown to her to an apartment for a drink. Rather, she has conducted her legitimate and necessary activities in a manner that made her a more likely target for the rapist. In this category is such ordinary behavior as coming home at night alone, shopping in an area not frequented by large numbers of people, and not being as prudent and suspicious as is sometimes required by modern urban living and hence walking into an elevator alone with a strange man. For example, women who return from work to deserted home neighborhoods after dark are in a high risk category. The study of risk of victimization offers one avenue for crime reduction. It does not suggest that the victim is at fault or has even made an unwitting contribution to the crime but that since crimes are more likely to be performed at certain times and places and under given conditions, these risks can sometimes be avoided.†

The study of convicted sex offenders and their offenses con-

---

* The quote from Amir is given because victim precipitation plays so large a role in his thesis. But essentially the definition fails because it contains the significant and undefined phrase "strongly enough." One is back at the argument discussed by Ploscowe and many others: how strongly must a woman resist to demonstrate that she is an unwilling partner?

† One of the arguments against crime prevention through the use of greater caution is that it does not prevent crimes but merely causes criminals to seek other targets. This claim may be true for robbery and burglary, but it is doubtful in cases of rape. Environmental protection against crime has been the subject of several interesting studies. See C. Ray Jeffrey, *Crime Prevention through Environmental Design* (Beverly Hills: Sage Publications, 1971); Oscar Newman, *Defensible Space: Crime Prevention through Urban Design* (New York: Collier, 1973); and Thomas Reppetto, *Residential Crime* (Cambridge: Ballinger, 1974).

ducted by Paul Gebhard and his colleagues places great emphasis on the borderline cases between force, suggestion, and persuasion. Gebhard writes about the "socially approved pattern for feminine behavior, according to which the woman is supposed to put up at least token resistance, murmuring, 'No, no' or 'We mustn't!'" He continues: "Any reasonably experienced male has learned to disregard such minor protestations, and the naive male who obeys his partner's injunction to cease and desist is often puzzled when she seems inexplicably irritated by his compliance." Furthermore, Gebhard et al. continue, women on occasion "desire to be overpowered and treated a little roughly," or at least some men so believe, and such men, following this line of thinking, may find themselves accused of committing rape.[27]

How pervasive among males (or females) is the outlook described by Gebhard is surely a matter for debate. Certainly many women, probably most, do not "desire to be overpowered and treated a little roughly," and it may be the cultural outlook that they do so desire that gives men a feeling of license to commit rape and then causes the tragic situation in which a woman does define the act as rape and the man is surprised by her definition and complaint. One of the problems here is the strong motivation for prevarication about the events that occurred during the hours, or even minutes, directly preceding sexual intercourse, a motivation for distortion of the truth on the part of both male and female, albeit in different directions.

An example of the thinking that has aroused a great deal of indignation among feminists is the statement by Alfred Kinsey that the difference between a "good time" and a "rape" may hinge on whether the girl's parents were awake when she finally arrived home.[28] However, such a remark, whatever its merits, can involve only a dispute over resistance or lack of it in a primary or intimate previous relationship; it is not applicable in an evaluation of stranger-to-stranger rape. Furthermore, there is a reverse situation, noted by Gebhard, in which the male insists that the female was entirely willing but "upon examining official records, we may discover that the allegedly willing female had to have five stitches taken in her lip."[29]

In the study by Gebhard's group, cases of genuine rape were uncovered, but there is an emphasis on convicted rapists who "believe in their innocence and are honestly mystified about why the woman brought charges against them."[30] These men were interviewed in prison following conviction, and the researchers are skeptical of whether their version of the story is to be readily accepted. In fact, they believe that these rapists are "victims of self-delusion and projection; they have in their minds minimized the violence and wishfully interpreted the woman's ultimate ac- quiescence as cooperation and forgiveness." [31]

Offenders and Victims

In the Amir study, most of those arrested were under the age of twenty-five, and many were between the ages of seventeen and twenty. From descriptions offered by the victims in cases that re- mained unsolved, youths were believed to be the perpetrators in the majority of the unsolved as well as the solved cases. In a na- tional sample consisting of about half of those arrested for rape, it was found that the accused were somewhat younger than those arrested for other major crimes; the average age for rapists was twenty-seven, and almost 20 percent of the defendants were un- der eighteen. However, the age factor may be misleading. What we may be dealing with here is the high percentage of forcible rapists who are unmarried, a status that increases the likelihood that the individual is spending time wandering the streets alone or with other males; that he will be invited to the homes of females or be in a position to invite women for automobile rides; or that he will be able to entice women into situations conducive to rape.

About 50 percent of the rapists who were located and identified in the Philadelphia study were found to have a previous arrest record, but only a fifth of those with an arrest record (or a tenth of all identified rapists) had committed crimes against the person, and a still smaller percentage had been arrested previously for rape or other sexual offenses. About one-fifth of the victims had an arrest record, mainly for sexual misconduct.

What do such data indicate? Most arrests are of males of low socioeconomic status, and the fact that such a high percentage of the rapists had also been arrested for property crimes would strongly suggest a ghetto or poverty background and a general orientation of disrespect for the law. More important, they are in the main not people who are psychopathically involved as over- sexualized beings or persons with uncontrollable sexual impulses. With few exceptions, they do not seem to be "career rapists," or even "career sex criminals," although they might be seen as career criminals. They commit the crime under conditions and in situations conducive to it, have insufficient inner defenses when confronted with opportunities, or feel relatively little deterrence in the form of anticipation of punishment.

As for the rape victims, women with arrest records, although constituting a minority of all victims, were nevertheless disproportionately represented in the sample. Not surprisingly, their arrests involved charges of sexual misconduct, first because this charge accounts for a large percentage of arrests for all females who come into conflict with the law, and second because it is a history of, and reputation for, such alleged misconduct that frequently acts to neutralize the restraints and identify a victim in the mind of an offender. Following this line of reasoning, one finds that about 20 percent of the victims, according to Amir, had a "bad reputation" in the neighborhood.

Like Amir, Gebhard also found a considerable consumption of alcohol related to the sexual encounter. About three-quarters of the females were strangers to the offender, and most of them were young. Some of the men complained, "It wasn't rape—she took her clothes off!" In most cases where there was resistance, the aggressor did not emerge with bites and scratches. Of the convicted men, 57 percent fully admitted their aggression, either to the authorities or to the Institute's researchers, while 14 percent completely denied their guilt. The men were usually not "sex maniacs," Gebhard maintains, although one case involved a man who "had since puberty been sexually excited by stories of rape" and who had a history of both peeping and sexual assaults.

The method of apprehension in this last instance may throw light on some of these offenders. The male, after planned aggression in which he ended by stealing a woman's purse and fleeing but without carrying out the intended and fantasied rape, continued and pursued a second possibility.

Finding the woman asleep in bed (as in the earlier instance), he put his hand over her mouth, told her to be quiet, and began to caress her. She told him she was menstruating and showed him the tampon; this caused him to lose his erection (an instance of the impotence not uncommon in this variety of aggressor) and he was unable to continue. After talking a while he left under the impression that the woman would welcome his return. He did subsequently return some nights later and was welcomed by the waiting police. This wishful self-delusion that their victims have become desirous of seeing them again is frequent among [sexual] aggressors against adults, and they seem to find it difficult to believe that the women bear them any ill will.[32]

The Gebhard team found that some rapists were of the assaultive variety (they used unnecessary violence and the violence itself was exciting to them); some were amoral men, who pay little heed to social controls "and operate on a level of disorganized and egocentric hedonism" (these include some intoxicated men); some were men who can be categorized as the explosive variety (on the surface they are average and law-abiding people who suddenly snap and who are extremely dangerous once the explosion takes place); and some were subscribers to the double standard, men who want to marry a virgin but feel little guilt when they force themselves upon "bad females who are not entitled to consideration if they become obstinate." The researchers quote a male in this last group as saying, "Man, these dumb broads don't know what they want. They get you worked up and then they try to chicken out. You let 'em get away with stuff like that and the next thing you know they'll be walking all over you." [33] With increasing modification of the double standard, there may be a diminution of this way of thinking.

Finally, some of the convicted rapists were mental defectives, some were characterized by the researchers as "unquestionable psychotics"; and many were suffering from personality defects and stresses which ultimately erupted in sex offense. A few appeared to be "statistically normal individuals who simply misjudged the situation." [34]

Race, Rape, and the Societal Reaction

In most rapes, perpetrator and victim are of the same racial group (except in situations such as war, military occupation, or slavery). In the United States, most white females who fall victim to rapists are violated by white males, and black females by black males. This may be only a matter of proximity and opportunity, for large cities have many highly segregated areas that are residentially all-white or all-black, where neither a potential rapist nor a possible victim of "the other race" is likely to be wandering the streets or standing at a bar, visibly out of place. Furthermore, the intraracial character of the event is enhanced by the considerable number of rapes in which the victim and perpetrator were previously acquainted and even on friendly terms. If these conditions were eliminated and one studied only rapes committed by strangers (including rapes that were unplanned but took place during the course of executing another crime), the interracial factor would probably take on greater weight.

This is not to say that interracial rape is a fiction but merely that there is a folklore and mythology built around it. In the South particularly, the black man as rapist, defiler of the good, pure white woman, was a specter evoked, most likely with deliberation, to give strong institutional support to segregation, oppression, and lynching. But rape of black against white is by no means unknown, and it would be difficult to locate an account of a forcible sexual assault in terms of black and white more relevant to this question than that narrated so vividly in the autobiography of Eldridge Cleaver.

> I became a rapist. To refine my technique and modus operandi, I started out by practicing on black girls in the ghetto—in the black ghetto where dark and vicious deeds appear not as aberrations or deviations from the norm, but as part of the sufficiency of the Evil of a day—and when I considered myself smooth enough, I crossed the tracks and sought out white prey. I did this consciously, deliberately, methodically—though looking back I see that I was in a frantic, wild, and completely abandoned frame of mind.
>
> Rape was an insurrectionary act. It delighted me that I was defying and trampling upon the white man's law, upon his system of values, and that I was defiling his women—and this point, I believe, was the most satisfying to me because I was very resentful over the historical fact of how the white man has used the black woman. I felt I was getting revenge. From the site of the act of rape, consternation spreads outwardly in concentric circles. I wanted to send waves of consternation throughout the white race.[35]

This account notwithstanding, the black man has little opportunity for rape of a white woman and faces frighteningly severe punishment at the hands of mobs, police, courts, and juries if apprehended. Moreover, with the rise of racial pride and militance, many blacks stigmatize interracial sexuality, voluntary or other, as a betrayal of the women of the race and of the cause. The white, likewise with diminished opportunity, at one time had little to fear in the way of prosecution, and the generally negative attitude toward both blacks and women made him see possession of the black woman as his "right." Furthermore, the socialization and education of white males portrayed black women as promiscuous and ready to welcome white lovers.

In this situation, there has been a shift away from denigration of the female partner and depiction of black women as ready bedmates for white men. At the same time, the white male cannot proceed with impunity for he faces the wrath of the women's movement and of individual women (as in the Joan Little case), as well as a civil rights movement that has had many permanent effects although it no longer has the dynamism that characterized it in the 1960s; too, he suffers at the hands of white and black officials who are compelled to bring him to justice.

Part of the mythology surrounding interracial rape may be rooted in the fantasy needs of whites, who have long believed (as have other race oppressors) in the "sexual superiority" of the oppressed, a belief that it is possible for a group to hold while still conceiving of itself as superior because the ultrasexual is equated with the savage, the beast, the criminal. According to this theme, black men are genitally bigger, more powerful, more capable, and less self-controlled; they are called, with scarcely concealed admiration, sexual athletes. The fantasy of a back man taking a white woman by force and violence gives vicarious pleasure and excitement to whites to whom "good" women are frigid, and it is a fantasy that at the same time legitimates racial hatred, scorn, and oppression. A passage in Lillian Smith's *Killers of the Dream* describes the sexual fantasies that grew around race in America, particularly in the South.

> The more trails the white man made to the backyard cabins, the higher he raised his white wife on her pedestal when he returned to the big house. The higher the pedestal, the less he enjoyed her whom he had put there, for statues are only nice things to look at. . . . Guilt, shame, fear, lust spiralled after each other.[36]

The white man, filled with this guilt, began to suspect the white woman of the sins "he had committed so pleasantly and so often." In jealous panic, Smith writes, he began "to project his own sins on to the Negro male."[37]

That interracial is more severely punished than intraracial rape is dramatically illustrated by data offered by Haywood Burns, national director of the National Conference of Black Lawyers.

National prison statistics show that of the 19 jurisdictions that have executed men for rape since 1930, almost one-third of them—six states—have executed only blacks. There have been some years in which everyone who was executed for rape in this country was black. Detailed state-by-state analysis has shown that the discrepancy in death sentences for rape is related to the race of the victim.

Blacks raping blacks is apparently less serious than whites raping whites, and certainly less serious than whites raping blacks. But the black man today convicted of raping a white woman can be as certain of receiving the harshest treatment as was a Kansas black convicted of an interracial sex crime in 1855. For example, in Florida between 1960 and 1964, of the 125 white males who raped white females, six—or about 5 percent—received death sentences (four of these involved attacks on children). Of the 68 black males in the same period who were convicted in Florida of raping black females, three—or about 4 percent—received death sentences: and this when in two cases the victims were children. However, of the 84 blacks (same period, same state) convicted of raping white women, 45—or 54 percent—received the death sentence; only one of these cases involved an attack on a juvenile. None of the eight white men who raped black women was sentenced to death.[38]

Along the same lines, Frank Hartung has pointed out that from 1909 to 1950, there were 809 rape convictions of white men in a group of southern states but not one execution; during the same period, 54 black men were executed for rape, not to mention the many lynchings.[39]

While Burns and Hartung cogently contrast the punishments meted out in crimes of white against white, white against black, black against white, and black against black, the material they cite offers a good opportunity to examine the racial composition of the sample of convicted men and their victims. To turn to the data of Burns, it would seem that of the 285 males convicted, 133 were white, 152 black; of the victims, 209 were white, 76 black. Of the rapes, 193 were intraracial, 92 interracial. However, these figures are misleading and should be interpreted with care, bearing in mind that rapists of blacks (whether the criminal is white or black) are prosecuted and convicted far less frequently than those who victimize whites.

In the Amir study in Philadelphia for the years 1958 and 1960, rape was found to be mainly an intraracial event, far more common among blacks than whites, with the potential for victimization of the black woman twelve times as great as that for the white. When these figures are recomputed for housing conditions, employment, and other socioeconomic factors, the gap between blacks and whites of similar economic and educational status would probably narrow considerably, but it is unlikely that it would disappear.

Interestingly, the relatively higher black rape rate coexisted with the lesser social sanctions against premarital sex then prevailing in the black community. Thus, one faces the apparently contradictory situation in which sex is seized by force and violence more frequently in precisely that group of the population in which it is most readily attainable without the use of force. This would seem to suggest that rape cannot invariably be understood as the desperate act of a frustrated and sexually hungry male who finds other avenues closed to him. It is more likely that rape is fostered by a cultural milieu and at the same time is highly situational in a culture in which conditions favorable to the act are likely to be encountered. In this sense, Amir sees in the black ghettos (and we find the argument convincing) what Marvin Wolfgang and Franco Ferracuti have named a subculture of violence [40] and what Walter Miller has called one of the focal concerns of lower class life.[41] This violence, taught, admired, institutionalized, becomes associated with masculinity in a people whose males have been given only limited opportunities to be breadwinners (the traditional role of the man in the family) or in other ways to assert their dominance in a normative manner and who resort to deviant and criminal mechanisms to demonstrate strength, superiority, and ability to subdue others. That a few of these men choose rape as an expression not of their sexual needs and frustrations but of their general alienation and anger, their desire to display assertiveness, aggression, and dominance, all qualities associated with being male, should not be surprising. That the black woman should be the object, or victim, is as much a matter of convenience as of choice.

Severe punishment has been meted out to blacks for the rape of whites throughout American history. In the colonies, writes Robert Frumkin, blacks were "castrated for attempting rape of a white woman, and a Pennsylvania law of 1700 provided the death

penalty to Negroes for buggery and for rape of a white woman." [42]
Rape, not merely when it was interracial but especially so, became
a capital crime in many colonies and in most states of the newly
formed union (one should bear in mind that capital punishment
was then in effect for many crimes that are considered minor
today). As the death penalty was gradually abolished for most
felonies except murder, rape, kidnapping, and wartime treason, the
number of legal executions and extralegal lynchings for rape (the
latter often in response to unfounded rumors), remained high. Between 1930 and 1967 (a period that includes a decade during
which legal executions were on the decline), 455 civilians and 53
military men were legally put to death in the United States for rape;
of the 455 civilians, 405 were black, 48 white.[*] During that period,
the number of lynchings of actual or rumored rapists was probably
in the hundreds, although lynchings had been much more frequent
in the previous sixty or sixty-five years.

In many American jurisdictions rape is punishable by death. Until the execution of Gary Mark Gilmore (for murder, not rape) in
January 1977, it was not certain whether any executions would be
carried out. Indeed, the future of the laws was unclear; the Supreme
Court in *Gregg v. Georgia* upheld the constitutionality of the death
penalty in principle but limited its application and stayed executions in a series of succeeding decisions and orders. The National
Association for the Advancement of Colored People and the Legal
Defense Fund have accumulated statistics to show that the death
penalty and long prison terms have been selectively meted out in
a considerable number of states to black offenders convicted of
raping white women but seldom to white offenders against black or
white women or to black offenders against black women.

One of the most thorough studies of race, rape, and capital
punishment was made by Donald Partington.[43] He surveyed all
executions for rape in the state of Virginia during the years 1908–
1963. In this period, there were 2,798 convictions for rape, attempt
to rape, statutory rape, and attempt to commit statutory rape
(the last two offenses constituted only about 15 percent of the
total). The black offenders outnumbered the whites 1,560 to 1,238.
Of the fifty-six men executed, all were black.

Interesting information on interracial rape appears in a study

[*] Data taken from National Prisoner Statistics, *Executions*, No. 42, June 1968.
There were no executions in the United States for any crime from June 1967
to January 1977.

by Jerome Kroll of American military personnel incarcerated for crimes committed in Vietnam.[44] Despite the fact that the percentages and in some instances the absolute number of black soldiers incarcerated for most crimes were greater than the comparable percentages and number of whites, this pattern is reversed for violent acts against Vietnamese nationals. In the case of rape against Vietnamese women, thirteen of the fourteen soldiers found guilty and incarcerated were white, one black, and with the latter, the act "appeared to occur as an afterthought to a burglary." On the other hand, the violent crimes, including rape,

> committed by white soldiers against Vietnamese people showed a disdain and disrespect for the life and sensitivity of the Asiatic victims. . . . The victims were brutalized, not necessarily in terms of torture, but in terms of violence done in their existence as human beings, as people, with one exception. This pattern was not seen in the black soldiers' violent crimes against Vietnamese people. . . . Except for the rape case, there was not in these crimes the degrading and overtly sadistic attitude toward the Vietnamese people that was present in many of the white soldiers' offenses.[45]

It is possible that this small study can throw light on the matter of interracial rape and of violent rape itself. These acts appear to involve contempt for the victim either because she is female and the rapist is disdainful of all females, or because she is of another race toward which hostility has been ingrained or developed deliberately by propaganda, as in the derogation of enemy humanity and worth.

Group Sexual Assaults

That a not inconsiderable percentage of forcible rape occurs with two or more offenders attacking one woman was made clear in the work of Amir. The mere presence of a second man, of course, makes the attack far easier to effect; the victim often perceives that struggle is likely to be futile if not potentially more dangerous to her than submission.

Attention to adolescent gang rapes and "gang bangs" was given by Albert Reiss, who suggests that "most lower-class adolescents" have been involved in such events at one time or another.[46] There is, however, an important distinction between the gang rape and the gang bang, the latter being a relatively voluntary act on the part of the female to permit a succession of males to have intercourse with her. Bear in mind, further, that Reiss is referring to situations in which no force or threat of force was employed. In an event of this type, if the female is below the age of consent, any males participating who are past the age specified in the given jurisdiction can be charged with statutory rape (discussed in Chapter 3). The female, when such events come to the attention of authorities, is often held as a delinquent; the younger males, if charged at all, are likewise defined as delinquents and hence are not held accountable for a specific crime such as rape or sexual assault.

The nonforcible adolescent gang bang has been described by Bernard Rosenberg and Harry Silverstein, who reproduce an interview between themselves and some young males who had participated in such events (however, the authors note that this is "by no means an everyday occurrence").

> "If you got a really good friend, and the girl is willing if she's really bad off or somethin', you know what she will do? *She'll pull the train.*"
>
> "Pull the train?"
>
> "Yes, that's what we call it: pulling the train. You take one chance. Then another guy takes a chance. You know."
>
> "Usually, how many guys are there?"
>
> "Two."
>
> "Not like ten guys with one girl?"
>
> "Oh, depends on what kind of a girl. . . . I been in a situation with about six guys."[47]

FREUDIAN INTERPRETATION

Adolescent gang bangs have sometimes been interpreted by Freudians as having unconscious homosexual meaning to the males. A man who inserts his penis into a woman's vagina so soon after another's penis has been removed and while the odor of his male friend is still permeating the female skin, it is said, may be seeking unconscious homosexual gratification. The latter derives, it is postulated, from the closeness of the two male penises to each other and from the sexual smell permeating the atmosphere; on a conscious level, the participant may be protected from homosexual panic by the knowledge that it is a female with whom he is copulating.

A report incorporating this line of interpretation was given by W. H. Blanchard, but the findings are inconclusive.[48] Utilizing inkblot tests and interviews in which the responses were described as "guarded," Blanchard found that in gang rapes there was a leader who was stimulated by the presence of the other males. In one case, the interviewers found a feeling of eroticized attachment so strong that it was just short of being overtly homosexual in its content.[49] But Blanchard concluded that most of the evidence regarding homosexual factors in gang rape is speculative.

GROUP FORCIBLE RAPE

A sociological analysis of group rape has been offered by Gilbert Geis. The act itself involves, he states,

> a pair or a company of men behaving in accord with well-estab-
> lished principles of collective behavior. There is generally a leader,
> who usually plans the act, and who is the first of the offenders to
> have intercourse with the victim. His associates, consigned to later
> "shares," suffer the definitional insult of dealing with already used
> and abused merchandise.[50]

Geis further reported on an unpublished study of world rape literature conducted by W. E. Lucas, of the Australian Department of Public Health.[51] Confirming and if anything adding to the evidence of Amir that multiple-offender rapes are not rare, Lucas showed that two-thirds of those charged with rape in Canada were involved with one or more other offenders. Care must be exercised in interpreting these statistics: they do not show that two-thirds of the rapes were pair, group, or multiple events—simple arithmetic will reveal that if there are exactly the same numbers of rapes with one offender and with two, half of the offenses are committed by pairs but two-thirds of the offenders are involved in such crimes. The Canadian figures also deal with rapists who were caught, and there may be greater ease of apprehension and more vigorous prosecution in multiple-offender cases. Even bearing this possibility in mind, it is difficult to understand the figures offered by Lucas for New South Wales, where for a given year he reported that 96 percent of all convicted rape offenders had been found guilty in multiple-offender cases. It is possible that, as feminists claim, men have not been successfully prosecuted in single-offender situations; whereas in multiple-offender cases, the defendants' claim that the woman voluntarily engaged in sexual activity is less likely to be made or believed. Another factor is that in cases involving multiple de-fendants, the prosecution can play them off against one another and possibly obtain highly incriminating testimony by offering one defendant, often the most vulnerable, the opportunity of turning state's evidence.

One of the interesting sidelights to be found in the statistics of Amir, although he himself does not take note of it, is that although cunnilingus was reported not infrequently by victims of solo rapists, it was not reported in a single instance of multiple-offender rape. This finding would seem to confirm an observation by Geis: "To rape a girl in company with other men presumably says something about shared concepts of maleness and shared sexuality, about camaraderie, and about the place of women in relationship to men." [52] One might add that men who seek to engage in cunnilingus probably see this activity as humiliating to themselves (not to the woman, as Amir mistakenly suggests) and do not want to display this aspect of their sexuality before male comrades.

Geis contends that "group rape is probably the most understudied behavior among those acts regarded today as serious criminal offenses." [53] A few cases are reported in depth, but little is known of the dynamics of the event itself. That group rape is not rare is attested to not only by the statistics of Amir and Lucas but also by the frequency of newspaper reports of this type of crime.

If rape is easier to carry through to the desired end when two or more males are present, it likewise places would-be rapists in greater jeopardy. When only one person commits an act of rape, and when he is a stranger to the victim, he alone knows the identity of the offender although she may be able to give clues that will lead to his apprehension. But when two or more persons know who committed the act, it is no longer a tightly held secret, as the history of all areas of criminal detection will attest. Thus there is greater likelihood of apprehension, and there is a chance that one of the assailants will turn state's evidence, plead guilty, and assist in obtaining convictions of the others. In this sense, as well as in a broader psychological meaning, one can agree with Geis that "group rape may also create among its perpetrators a sense of shared guilt and, perhaps from this, a sense of entwined fate." [54]

Problems of Legal and Social Policy

Forcible rape and carnal abuse of children are probably the only sex crimes about which social policy cannot be seriously debated

Even this statement requires modification for on rare occasions a voice is heard defending adult-child sexuality. The pedophile sometimes invokes pity or compassion, the rapist only a sense of outrage. The act of rape or sex without consent is intolerable, no matter what the ages, relationships, degree of force, cultural pressures, racial heritage, miscues and misunderstandings of the persons involved, the previous sexual history of the woman—her chastity or promiscuity (with other men or with the offender), and the numerous miscellany of factors may be. None of these factors excuses the act although they often account for it and for the reaction thereto.

It is difficult to research the extent to which the source of the drive in some males to rape can be explained by thousands of years of history in which females—except those worshipped and idolized for their chasteness—were seen as the sexual property of males.[55] That there has been such an orientation cannot be denied; the long tradition of bride capture, which is so similar to rape, attests to this. Nevertheless, such a heritage does not explain the personality and situational conditions associated with rape or the increase in the rate of victimization in the United States. It throws no light on interracial rape of black against white: certainly black men have not regarded white women as their property, and the need for revenge, the expression of hostility and anger, would appear to have more explanatory value. While the very aggressive campaign against the view of women as the sexual property of men is unlikely to reduce the incidence of rape, it can have important effects in arousing the indignation of the public, in reorienting police and detectives so that rape victims are interviewed with all the compassion shown to the survivors of other brutal crimes, and in offering therapy as well as punishment to those males who are, one might say, career rapists. However, the research evidence clearly indicates that such persons constitute a small percentage of all rapists, so that a campaign to assist them in their personality problems, while desirable, can hardly be considered an important contribution to the reduction of this crime.

Understandably, there is tremendous anger and frustration among women because of the relatively poor record of apprehension and prosecution of rapists. Nationally, 51 percent of the forcible rapes in 1975 were reported "cleared by arrest"—a figure lower than that for other violent crimes against the person but far higher than that for any serious crimes against property. In a very small national sample of persons charged with the crime, 51.2 percent were found guilty of forcible rape, 9.1 percent of a lesser charge, 24.2 percent acquitted or dismissed, and 15.5 percent referred to juvenile court.[56]

Many cases of rape are reduced to misdemeanors, but this information should be placed in the total context of plea bargaining, whereby persons who have been charged with major crimes commonly plead guilty to a lesser offense and are rewarded for their cooperation with more lenient sentences. This hardly permits us to speak of a certainty of punishment, a fundamental prerequisite for effective deterrence. Nor is the celerity factor in deterrence demonstrably more evident with the time span from arrest to sentence in rape cases exceeding a year and the serving of sentence frequently further delayed by appeals.

Men who have been accused of rape and who have denied their guilt have offered two types of defense: they say that they are being mistakenly identified (this defense is often accompanied by an alibi);* or that they did indeed participate in sexual intercourse with the complainant but that the woman had been willing. It seems to us important from a social policy standpoint to separate these two arguments.

As for the former type of defense, no civilized society would want the wrong man to be prosecuted. Certainly, if the woman is not convinced that her identification is correct beyond a reasonable doubt, and perhaps in her mind beyond any doubt, it would be preferable to see an accused man go free than to imprison an innocent man. For not only would this be a gross miscarriage of justice in which he would be victimized severely, but the case would be considered "solved" while a rapist was still at large, free to prey on other women. In a defense of this sort, we see no justification for the pursuit by a lawyer for the accused, or the permitting of such pursuit by a judge, of a line of cross-examination into the moral and sexual life of a complainant. Such information is entirely irrelevant given the defense the accused has chosen. It does not matter whether the accused had been chaste or promiscuous—she should not be discouraged from appearing in court and, while there, should not be humiliated, exposed to public ignominy, or subjected to traumatic cross-examination. Yet such types of questioning have

---

* The word "alibi" is here being used in the legal sense, meaning that one seeks to establish presence in another place at the time of the commission of an act. The layman frequently uses the word as a synonym for excuse, and a lame and contrived excuse at that.

been permitted, and they have undoubtedly contributed to the reluctance of some women to report a rape, to identify a man in a lineup, and then to appear in court to testify.

There are further problems in a case of this kind. They involve the fact that often there is little evidence except for eyewitness identification by the victim. Quite naturally, when a rape is committed by one offender, he usually does not act in the presence of witnesses.* Eyewitness identifications of complete strangers, in all types of criminal cases, are fallible.[57] This is especially so when the victim and the offender are of different races. It is true that proximity offers the woman an opportunity to get such a good look at the offender that her identification ought to be unimpeachable, but this factor is counteracted by the traumatic conditions under which the crime takes place. Furthermore, it is not rare for the rape to occur in the dark.

In New York City, in a period of only a few months during 1972, two men were arrested on different rape charges and both were unhesitatingly identified in lineups; in each case the accused adamantly refused to admit guilt and would not plea bargain. Each case ended in the same manner: a so-called look-alike was found, and the indicted man was freed with profuse apologies. In an even more bizarre case, two look-alikes were separately identified as multiple rapists, only to have a third man, almost identical in appearance to the other two, arrested and convicted.[58]

The only manner of preventing such instances—and even worse, the prosecution and conviction of innocent men because of mistaken identifications—is careful police, prosecutorial, and defense investigations aimed at uncovering the truth, meticulous examination of alibis, and the honoring of the fundamental concept of Anglo-American justice that conviction can take place only if a case against the accused has been established beyond a reasonable doubt. That some guilty men will go free is a danger in all criminal cases, but in rape this danger becomes greater not because of the enormity of the crime but because it is so difficult to locate corroborating witnesses or other corroborating evidence.

The problem of prosecution and conviction becomes even more serious when the accused admits that he had sexual intercourse with the woman but insists that the act was mutually voluntary. We believe that some of the traditional guidelines (such as those quoted

---

* The exception is the case in which a husband and other family members are held at gunpoint, bound, and then obliged to witness the rape itself.

by Ploscowe and given earlier in this chapter) are unrealistic and rooted basically in antifemale ideology. Many experts are urging women not to resist so as to avoid physical injury; certainly if a rapist has a club or gun, it would be folly to attempt resistance. Yet, a woman may find herself in the position of not having physically resisted and hence having no cuts, bruises, or other marks, not having screamed because she was frightened and had in fact been propagandized not to scream, and then being confronted in court with her inability to produce evidence that she had been an unwilling partner.

There would be an easy way out of this dilemma if there were no rational explanations for a woman, under any conditions, to call an act rape when she was in fact eager to have the sexual encounter. Unfortunately for law and justice, there are explanations and there is an abundance of documented instances of such conduct: pregnancy, revenge, anger because of some fraud, apprehension in an interracial affair, or jealousy. It goes without saying that there are rational explanations for a man to have committed the act forcibly and then to state that the woman was willing, even as there are motivations for her to be the willing partner and to charge that she was forced into submission.

Cases are usually more complex than merely balancing a complainant's charge and a defendant's denial. One must delve into the nature of their relationship before the act, the behavior of each of them immediately thereafter, their possible motivations for lying, and the like. In cases of admitted copulation in which the question of consent is at issue, both the complainant and the defendant might be requested to submit voluntarily to polygraph examination. In the absence of any other evidence that would show whether the sex act had been a willing encounter or a rape, some have asked, "Why isn't her word as good as his?" This is a logical question, and if the persons were meeting in a family gathering, a social group, a therapy session, or elsewhere, one would say that her word must be as good as his, and sometimes—if she is a person who has shown herself to be believable—it may be better. But in a criminal case, when the evidence is neatly balanced, one cannot convict solely on the contested word of the victim. If the jury feels that complainant and defendant are equally believable (although one must be lying), it has no choice: it must find the man not guilty. To act otherwise would erode the principle of presumption of innocence and abandon the concept of guilt beyond a reasonable doubt, and no fighter against crime and violence has made this suggestion seriously.

Finally, and perhaps most controversial of all, what can be said in open court of the previous sexual history of the victim and the accused? So far as the latter is concerned, there are special problems. If the defendant brings character witnesses, and if he decides to take the witness stand in his own behalf, then it is possible for him to be questioned, within the limits of the rules of evidence governing what is relevant and material, about previous sexual, criminal, and violent activity. However, if he chooses not to use such a line of defense, offers no character witnesses, then it would be a contravention of his basic rights, guaranteed by the fifth amendment, to bring forth such evidence.

More important is the issue of the questioning of the complainant, particularly on cross-examination. It has been suggested that she be examined and cross-examined in camera in order to protect her from fishing expeditions and from embarrassing and irrelevant questions that do their damage merely by being asked. Then, only such cross-examination as had been deemed relevant would be heard in open court. Another possibility would be to attempt to obtain from the press and other media the type of voluntary agreement not to report embarrassing details, similar to the agreement that has generally prevailed in cases involving blackmail. Furthermore, it is possible that the changing sex mores, in which being an unmarried virgin is no longer synonymous with being virtuous, and a woman with an active sex life is not brought into public disgrace, will reduce the victim's fear of having disclosures of previous sexual experiences, or even of arrests and convictions, made in court.

It is not only the defense but the prosecution as well that has been responsible for eliciting embarrassing information in court about the prior sexual history of the complainant. If the defense has often attempted to portray her as wanton and promiscuous, the prosecution has sought to show her as previously chaste. On this matter, the American Civil Liberties Union has laid down excellent guidelines.

> There is in many rape cases a potential conflict between the right of the defendant to a fair trial and the complainant's right to have his or her claim to protection of the law vindicated without undue invasion of sexual privacy. In many cases this conflict may be irresolvable, and when that is the case the right to a fair trial should not be qualified, no matter how compelling the countervailing concerns. However, careful application by trial judges of the proper standards of relevance of testimony, control of cross-examination and argument, and elimination of prejudicial in-

structions unique to rape and similar cases could do much to preserve rape complainants from unnecessary imposition upon their
rights to sexual privacy, without detracting from the fairness of
the trial. Closed hearings should be used to ascertain the relevance of any proposed line of testimony or cross-examination that
may involve a witness' prior sexual history. The determination of
relevance or irrelevance should be stated by the court on the
record along with its reasons for so holding.

A determination as to the relevance of the prior sexual history
of either the complainant or the defendant in rape* cases is acceptable only if it is administered fairly and free from sexist assumptions. Subject to special evidentiary rules designed to protect defendants for reasons other than relevance, the criteria for
admitting evidence of prior sexual history employed in rape cases
must apply equally to the prosecution and the defense. Similarly,
any pre-trial screening process must apply equally to the prosecution and the defense.

Some aspects of some current rape laws clearly do not meet
minimum standards of acceptability. Even where the defense is
consent, the prosecution should not be permitted, as a matter of
course, to introduce evidence of the complainant's prior chastity;
neither should the defense, without more, be permitted to prove
the complainant's prior unchastity. 'Unchaste witness' instructions
which permit an inference of lessened credibility from the fact of
prior sexual activity are based on no rational inference and violate
a complainant's right to sexual privacy—just as a 'chaste witness'
instruction would violate a defendant's right to a fair trial if invoked by the prosecution. A statute, for example, which makes
admissible evidence tending to prove that the complainant had
been convicted of a prostitution offense, or even evidence concerning prior consensual sexual relations between the complainant and
the defendant, without the necessity of showing a particular relevance, unconstitutionally infringes on the right to sexual privacy
of such complainants.

* While sexist assumptions and practices cause harm most often to victims of rape or attempted rape, their rights can be protected if rape
  is treated as but one form of sexual assault by statutes and courts. We
  therefore urge that standards and procedures be developed to apply
  to all forms of sexual assault and that the phrase "sexual assault" be
  used instead of "rape" in policy statements, laws, etc., in order to
  remove special legal disabilities from rape complainants.[59]

In our view, the struggle against rape must be conducted without violating the constitutional rights of the accused in the administration of criminal justice. The most important single factor in
a campaign against rape is that it be part of an effort to diminish

violence in the country as a whole. So long as there is an ambience of violence, it will manifest itself in numerous forms, not excluding forcible rape.

It is to be hoped that the changing sex mores will help to diminish the incidence of rape, but all the evidence shows that it is not the unavailability of consensual outlet that accounts for this crime.[60] Environmental defense and greater care on the part of women will result in some diminution. While a change in the attitude toward women, in which the sexual property concept is eradicated, will make a contribution toward lowering rape rates, it is doubtful that such rates will as a result drop precipitately. The same can be said of interracial tensions: if they are reduced there may be less rape, but not a major decline.

One encouraging sign, deriving from the new sex morality, is that women are not so ashamed of having been victimized by this crime as they once were. Rape is more likely to be reported than hitherto, and this fact can act as a deterrent. Other than that, the outlook is as optimistic or as grim as it is for any other form of violent crime in the United States.

The convicted rapist has been punished severely in most societies. Draconian penalties, largely retributive though rationalized as deterrent, have been his lot; death, corporal punishment and long-term imprisonment have been meted out to both first offenders and those whose guilt was at least in question. Although incapacitation by castration and other measures have been tried in past centuries and more recently for multiple rapists (over 900 castrations during a thirty-year period in Denmark) and voluntary castration in lieu of long-term imprisonment has been authorized in Canada by the Ontario Supreme Court in 1976, and proposed by offenders in California and Michigan without acceptance by the courts during the past several years, there seems little public or professional support for this approach. The almost equally militant opposition to the use of the more rigorous behavior modification techniques and the very minimal success achieved with less intensive therapeutic interventions would seem to leave society with no other recourse than long-term imprisonment of those convicted of rape and/or attempt to rape. With this outlook, it becomes all the more important to protect the accused from being unjustly convicted, and to work toward reduction of rape by sex education, environmental protection, and particularly reduction of violence in the entire society.

3 Sex Between Adults and Minors*

Like rape, sexual contact between adults and children receives little or no institutional support in most societies. The strength as well as the prevalence of the condemnation is usually in inverse relationship to the age of the child and in direct relationship to the presence of force, the age differential of adult and child, an incestuous element, completion of a sexual act rather than advance or suggestion, and, for an older minor, a resultant pregnancy.

Nevertheless, not all societies have been punitive toward all sexual relations between adults and children. Charles McCaghy found that adult-child sexual contacts are institutionalized in some preliterate societies and in others only lightly sanctioned.[1] References to this phenomenon in the anthropological literature, writes McCaghy, following a very thorough study of the subject, are scarce.

According to Clellan Ford and Frank Beach, in some societies adults take "a completely tolerant and permissive attitude toward sex expression in childhood," but upon examination this toleration turns out to be toward masturbation, fondling, and other forms of sex play between children, sometimes manipulation of the genitals of a child by an adult, and even very early sexual intercourse.[2] However, the latter almost always involves a boy and a girl, not an adult and a child. An exception is found in an Asiatic Indian

---

* The authors wish to thank Charles McCaghy for helpful comments on an earlier version of this chapter.

group in which "older men occasionally copulate with girls as young as eight years of age. Instead of being regarded as a criminal offense, such behavior is considered amusing by the Lepcha." [3] This would appear to indicate an attitude short of approval; it might even suggest that the older person is subject to mild ridicule.

Even in modern societies, adults are not unanimously condemned for sexual contact with children. For example, René Guyon,[4] a French jurist and philosopher and a campaigner for a new sexual ethic and for sexual freedom (but not unrestricted libertarianism), suggested that a society without antisexual biases would see an adult's sexual overture to a child not as an "abuse" but as an opportunity to further the child's range of pleasures. A few voices have occasionally been heard in America calling for abolition of all age restrictions on sex,[5] and there has been a small organized movement in Holland dedicated to that goal,[6] but advocates of this view are usually denounced by those who are struggling for liberalization of sex laws and mores.

Definitions of Terms

A technical term that describes the erotic and libidinal love of a child is pedophilia, and a person having such interests is said to be a pedophile.[*] Some authorities would restrict the term "pedophile" to those whose major and exclusive or near exclusive interest is in children, whether male, female, or both (perhaps undifferentiated).[7] While pedophilia as a psychological category might best be analyzed in that manner, as a legal-behavioral category it is the act itself that is of interest, not the nature of the drive behind it.

In criminal law, in the social and behavioral sciences, and in journalistic and other nontechnical accounts, a number of other terms can be found. These include "child molestation," "carnal abuse" of a child, "child abuse," "impairing the morals of a minor," and "statutory rape." Like other crimes, these are defined in a

---

[*] An interesting definition is offered by Money and Ehrhardt, except that they limit the word to interest in a male child: "The condition of being responsive to or dependent on sexual activity with a prepubertal or early pubertal boy, in order to maintain erotic arousal and facilitate or achieve orgasm. A pedophiliac may be a male or a female, though typically a man." See John Money and Anke A. Ehrdhardt, *Man & Woman, Boy & Girl: The Differentiation and Dimorphism of Gender Identity from Conception to Maturity* (Baltimore: Johns Hopkins Press, 1972), p. 306.

variety of ways in different penal codes and in various jurisdictions of the United States and elsewhere in the world.

"Child abuse" is a general phrase that is not specifically related to sexuality and is most often used to refer to the battered or brutalized child and sometimes to the neglected and undernourished child. "Statutory rape" usually refers to nonviolent sexual intercourse of a male over the age of consent with a female under the age of consent, a consensual act in that both parties agreed but one legally regarded as a form of rape because the age and presumed immaturity of the female did not give her the legal right to offer consent.*

Whereas "statutory rape" legally includes only sexual relations in which intercourse takes place or penetration is effected, the same is not true of "child molestation" and "impairing the morals of a minor." These are general terms usually covering any sexual contact at all between an adult and a minor, from touching the buttocks of a little boy or girl to completing a sexual act. Some people have objected to the term "child molestation" on the grounds that it is not sufficiently "neutral" and that the behavior it covers could be more accurately described as adult-child sexuality, but against this there is the argument that because of the age of the child any sexual contact with an adult is ipso facto molestation, even if the child is a willing or initiating partner. Whereas statutory rape is generally applied only to heterosexual acts, the other terms are both heterosexual and homosexual.

The law often speaks of "impairing the morals of a child" or "of a minor." This is usually a lesser offense, and hence offers an opportunity for plea bargaining; furthermore, although it is most frequently used for matters pertaining to sex, this term can be and has been applied to such nonsexual matters as introducing a minor into crime by encouraging theft, although this would more likely be prosecuted as "contributing to the delinquency of a minor." To impair the morals of a child in a sexual event, one need not have made overtures to, or have had contact with, the child; the impairment can be through teaching, encouraging, or making possible

---

* In rare cases, this term is used for the prosecution of an older female who has had sexual relations with a younger male (a French case along such lines attracted international attention in the early 1970s), but whatever the frequency of such events they are seldom reported to the police. In the United States, such a situation, if prosecuted, would be under a charge of contributing to the delinquency or impairing the morals of a minor.

such sexual contact with others or even through permitting and encouraging the child to witness such events. Showing pornographic films or other such materials to a child, taking a minor to a brothel, gay bar or obscene exhibition, or in at least one prosecution to a nudist camp, administering an aphrodisiac, selling or giving contraceptives to a child below the age for sexual consent, are all subsumed under "impairing the morals of a minor."

Age and the Law

The key question in the determination of an offense of a sexual nature under the rubric of child molestation involves the age of the child; as a secondary question, the age of the offender is also relevant.

In this century, when vital statistics are kept on almost all individuals in Western societies, sharp lines of distinction are made in law along chronological age. On reaching a given age, one may legally vote, get married, be accused of committing certain crimes, be held accountable for them as criminal offenses, enter school, leave school, drink alcohol, gamble, smoke cigarettes, and become eligible (or ineligible) to use public transportation at reduced fares. Similar legal distinctions along age lines are made with regard to the right to engage in sex. Nonliterate societies distinguish between child and adult primarily on the basis of appearance, progress in the development of visible secondary sexual characteristics, menarche (for a girl), occupational abilities (for a boy). "Some [preliterate] peoples," write Ford and Beach, "make a sharp distinction between socially immature and mature persons with respect to permissible sexual activity. These societies take the attitude that sexual intercourse before adulthood must be avoided; but once the person is mature by these standards, considerable freedom in sexual matters may be allowed." [8]

In modern societies, legal authorities have often urged that the chronological age difference between the older and the younger in a sexual encounter be taken into account. Inasmuch as youthful offenders under the age of sixteen in New York State, for example, are treated not as criminals but as juvenile delinquents, so sexual solicitation by a fourteen year old or a nine year old would not fall within the rubric of sex crime. What adult-child sexuality concerns, then, is some form of sexual confrontation between a person over the age of sixteen (usually over eighteen) and a child much younger than the age of consent and hence a more aggravated offense than statutory rape. There are instances of an adult woman being charged with impairing the morals of a child for having made physical contact of an indubitably sexual nature with a boy, but complaints to the police of such occurrences are most infrequent, and subsequent prosecution still more so. There is almost universal agreement by researchers that pedophilia is unusual in females; women may have not infrequently been involved with adolescent boys but there is little statistical evidence of their involvement with prepubertal children.

The concealment of age by the younger of the partners in a willing relationship generally has been unacceptable as a defense in sex cases involving minors (i.e., teenagers) and especially unacceptable in cases in which one partner is a child (usually defined as under twelve years old).* However, the American Law Institute has made a reasonable suggestion that the defense, "I didn't know that she (or he) was that young," should not be accepted in court if the child is under ten but is permissible between ten and the legal age of consent provided that it is substantiated by the general appearance of the minor and other relevant evidence.

These two points—the age difference between offender and victim and the presumption that the offender knew that the victim was a minor—are incorporated into the Model Penal Code of the American Law Institute.

Section 213.2. Corruption of Minors and Seduction.

(1) *Offense Defined.* A male who has sexual intercourse with a female not his wife, or any person who engages in deviate sexual intercourse or causes another to engage in deviate sexual intercourse, is guilty of an offense if:

(a) the other person is less than [16]† years old and the

---

* Frederick Ludwig offers an excellent discussion of the varying ages mandated from state to state and also of each sex for age of consent to sexual relations, marriage with or without parental consent, purchase of alcohol or cigarettes, criminal responsibility, and other matters. See Frederick Ludwig, *Youth and the Law* (Brooklyn: Foundation Press, 1955).

† The numbers shown in brackets are suggestions for which individual jurisdictions are expected to make substitutions if other ages or other age differentials seem more appropriate. Note, further, that contrary to the Wolfenden Report, the American Law Institute does not recommend a lower age of consent for heterosexual than for homosexual acts. The matter is discussed later in this chapter. See *Report of the Departmental Committee on Homosexual Offences and Prostitution* (London: Her Majesty's Stationery Office, 1956).

actor is at least [4] years older than the other person. . . .

Section 213.6. Provisions Generally Applicable to Article 213.

(1) *Mistake as to Age.* Whenever in this Article the criminality of conduct depends on a child's being below the age of 10, it is no defense that the actor did not know the child's age, or reasonably believed the child to be older than 10. When criminality depends on the child's being below a critical age other than 10, it is a defense for the actor to prove that he reasonably believed the child to be above the critical age.[9]

Offenders and Victims

There have been two important empirical studies of adult-child sexuality, any number of psychoanalytic and psychological studies (mainly of individual case histories, some highly speculative, one of which is reported in book-length detail), interesting analyses of two homosexual pedophile cases in the sociological and legal literature, and some follow-up studies of what happens to the victims as they grow into adulthood.

In the Gebhard work, the interviewers had direct access to the offenders (who were incarcerated) and also to court records and other information about the victims. These were defined as prepubescent: "They had not developed pubic hair, breast enlargement, and other adult sexual characteristics that are sexually attractive to ordinary men." [10] This is primarily a matter of defining the area of study, and the line of demarcation between child and minor, at age twelve, largely places into the former category those who fit Gebhard's description. But, more significantly, the description implies that the offenders did not err, were not expressing an interest in youthful girls who they mistakenly thought were teenagers, but were deliberately involving themselves with children.

Despite the public stereotype of these offenders as dirty old men, most of them were far below an age qualifying them for that category: the average age was thirty-five, with only one-sixth over fifty. It is difficult to know whether young adult offenders (in their twenties and thirties) are more likely to be reported to authorities, whereas older ones are ignored, avoided, or perhaps handled with "psychiatric compassion," thus giving these figures a certain bias, or whether the figures accurately reflect the age distribution of offenders. Whatever answer future research may bring forth, one can be rather confident in denying that most men committing these offenses are in their later or even, for that matter, their middle years.

There is a relatively high rate of recidivism in these cases: 40 percent had at least one previous sex offense and nearly 20 percent more than one, but these previous offenses were not always child molestation. Again, the figures may be distorted because only those incarcerated at the time of the study were in the sample. It is possible that the recidivism accounts in part for their receiving prison terms rather than suspended sentences and that if all convicted, or possibly all known, offenders in the "child molestation" category were studied, recidivism would be relatively low. There seems to be evidence that many of those incarcerated with a record of previous offenses are psychiatrically disturbed people, often compulsive, with poor inner controls that had led to difficulties in a variety of areas. Many of the men claimed to be under the influence of alcohol at the time of the offense; in fact, 20 percent claimed to be completely drunk and not just moderately intoxicated. As will be seen when we discuss the work of McCaghy, a figure of this sort is not always reliable and must be interpreted with caution.

Many of the offenses took place in a home, and the majority were committed by men previously known to the girls as friends, casual acquaintances, neighbors, or relatives.° The offenders who knew the children and hence were aware that they could be identified by their victims were in all likelihood either drunk or compulsive; furthermore, they did not think that the child would talk about the event or that she would be believed.

Of those offenses not between a man and a child previously known to each other, some were outdoor encounters; some took place in school buildings into which the man wandered, there meeting the girl; some in automobiles in which the child had been offered a ride; others, in parks, playgrounds, and vacant lots. There is petting in theaters: a man sits down next to an unaccompanied girl and, if she rebuffs his advances, moves to another seat to find a more willing neighbor, an activity that is called "playing checkers." † To avoid such encounters, some movie houses take

---

° Relatives constituted a higher percentage of those studied in the research by Gebhard et al.; note, however, that such cases were categorized as incest.

† A short story based on this kind of a child molester is "Hard Candy" by Tennessee Williams.

precautions, seating unaccompanied children in sections from which adults are excluded and watching from the back of the theater for seat-changers (who often include molesters of adult women, pocketbook thieves and pickpockets, exhibitionists, men who masturbate while watching a film, and hair fetishists who cut the hair of women seated in front of them).

In the successfully prosecuted cases (which would make up the entire sample of Gebhard's group), the girls were of an average age of eight, and the activities usually consisted of fondling, heavy petting, exposure, masturbation, some mouth-genital contacts, and, in a relatively small number of cases, attempted coitus. In about 2 percent of the instances under study, there was successful coitus. Note, however, that minors were studied separately by Gebhard and hence were not part of the sample of children.

Research on child molestation conducted by Charles McCaghy was not limited to incarcerated offenders but included all persons who had been found guilty—under any law or any section of the penal code—of a sexual offense with a child in certain counties of the state of Wisconsin over a given period, whether the persons were incarcerated or on probation. McCaghy studied the records of persons convicted under all statutes, ranging from disorderly conduct to rape, which might logically be applicable when convicting a child molester. His final sample consisted of 181 persons: 124 incarcerated at the time of the study, the remainder all on probation, none yet on parole.[11]

The McCaghy study differs from the work of Amir on rape in that it does not include cases reported to police but not solved (an unlikely avenue for investigation in child molesting); it goes beyond the study by Gebhard, inasmuch as it includes persons on probation and those convicted of other offenses although the behavior falls within an understanding of what is meant by child molestation. In various respects, the McCaghy and the Gebhard works complement and verify each other. The offenders were not old men; in many instances they were not strangers to the children. Those involved with the very young frequently denied the sexual content of the event; with older children, the offenders more frequently denied culpability on the ground that the child had "wanted it." This finding may reflect in part the use of a higher age cutoff for legal purposes in Wisconsin than that in the study by Gebhard (age twelve).

As in the study done by Gebhard, the Wisconsin offenders frequently claimed that they were intoxicated at the time of the act.

It is difficult to know to what extent these statements were accurate or were intended to reduce the stigma and mitigate the punishment. By claiming drunkenness, a man is saying in effect that he is not the sort of person who in a sober state would become involved in an act of this type. He is claiming not only a different morality for himself but a different problem, one that is ostensibly easier to handle and far easier to empathize with because it is shared by so many others. He does not need psychiatry, punishment, and rehabilitation, he is saying, but only an effort on his own part to control his drinking. The claim of having been intoxicated is difficult for the prosecution to refute, and a child's interpretation of the adult's behavior is hardly likely to carry weight in this aspect of the case.

Characteristics of the Offenders

Who are these offenders? In addition to the stereotype of the dirty old man, two other, almost contradictory, views appear in the literature as well as in the public mind. One sees them as oversexed, the other as extraordinarily timid: but these two themes can be reconciled not only by applying one to some offenders and the second to others; in fact, the same persons can be both highly sexed and terribly timid. The timidity is supposed to explain the male who is fearful of approaching adult females lest he be rebuffed; the oversexuality explains the compulsive person for whom the sex drive is beyond control, who will approach anyone at all.

While there are drunkards, psychotics, mental defectives, and senile deteriorates among child molesters, from a social policy view most important would be the group that Gebhard labeled pedophiles, who constituted between one-quarter and one-third of the offenders. The term "pedophile," Gebhard writes, "is somewhat unfortunate since these men evidently did not consciously prefer children as sexual partners, but simply found them acceptable." [12] Some of these pedophiles were repeaters; many had been making passes at children for twenty or more years. For those who find children acceptable but not preferable as sex partners and who are certainly not driven toward children in an exclusive and compulsive manner, therapy, whether in prison or out, has been said to be especially successful. Many of these men can be convinced that they are capable of finding gratification elsewhere, that sexual approach to a child is self-defeating and is easily controlled; they then may simply decide to avoid this behavior.

The child molester, both in prison and out, lives with a stigma that goes far beyond that of most other offenders. No matter what effort is made by prison authorities to conceal records and what account the prisoner himself gives of his crime, the nature of his offense will probably get around (although in one instance we know of it was effectively concealed throughout a rather long prison sentence). Murderers, burglars, check forgers, and even rapists are outraged by the child molester and look upon him as an abomination unworthy to associate with the likes of themselves. If he is himself reasonably young, the nature of his crime may become a justification in their minds to commit gang rape upon him: give him a piece of his own medicine. In the play *Short Eyes* the incarcerated child molester is murdered by fellow inmates.

General statements about molesters and molestation are still difficult to make. McCaghy was deeply interested in the meaning children have for molesters and in the molesters' extreme resistance to accepting responsibility for their offense (including resort to the claim of drunkenness as the justification or excuse). All research seems to suggest that offender stereotypes (the senile and the highly sexed, particularly) tend to be oversimplified. It appears that there is a high degree of personality maladjustment, neurosis, and psychosis among persons whose interests are directed to the extremely young, but that most so-called child molesters are in fact drawn to teenagers and other young people, sexual contact with whom would not be defined as child molestation.

In a study of Canadian pedophile offenses, Alex. Gigeroff referred to these as cases involving male adults or adolescents with prepubertal children and stated that they were among the most common types of sex offenses brought before the courts.[13] Inasmuch as most offenses of this nature probably never come to the attention of the police or courts, this finding would indicate that such events are not infrequent. Of the heterosexual cases, most did not involve rape or sexual intercourse but were limited to fondling, showing, and looking. The victims were for the most part between the ages of six and eleven; they were somewhat older when the offense was of a homosexual nature. The offenders were not old men but fell into three groups: an adolescent category; men in their mid-to-late thirties; and some men in their late fifties or early sixties.

A PSYCHOANALYTIC REPORT

A book-length, largely psychoanalytic study of a heterosexual child molester (who had some homosexual encounters in his own childhood) is presented by Alan Bell and Calvin Hall. Norman had been sexually assaulted by his father when he was four years old; in addition, he had an extraordinarily strong dependency on his mother, with whom he had, the authors state, a "detested" relationship. He had had an antisexual education and was brought up in close proximity with a sister about whom he displayed considerable curiosity, described as "voyeuristic."[14]

Norman had been convicted and institutionalized many times for molesting children, spending about seven years in five different institutions between the age of twenty, shortly after receiving an honorable discharge from the army, and age thirty-seven. As the case history draws to its close (he is forty-two years old when the last is heard about him), he has made some important adjustments, mainly with the assistance of an unusual form of psychoanalytic therapy (particularly dream analysis, but without free association and transference). He seems to be capable of channeling his interests in socially more acceptable directions, and he has remained free of committing offenses, so far as the readers and authors know, for an encouraging period. He has developed a relationship with an adult woman "based more on fantasy than fact," and the authors conclude with what appears to be a dim but ambiguous outlook.

> If he experiences rejection by [the adult woman] before the range of his other social contacts is greatly enlarged, it is quite likely that he will once again turn to a child, even as his father turned to him. Norman's present situation is most precarious, and given all that has happened in the past and that accounts for a psychological status that had once been more apparent in his dreams than in his waking life, it is difficult to know the "worst" that can be anticipated.[15]

The case of Norman would appear to illustrate two points: that sexual urges toward children seem to be accompanied by other serious psychological disturbances; and that the immediate problem of controlling molestation appears to be easier to solve than long-range problems of life adjustment.

Resistance and Acquiescence

Child molestation sometimes is and sometimes is not a violent act; in his sample, McCaghy found violence to be present in about 20 percent of the cases. Thus, to classify it with other nonviolent sex offenses, like exhibitionism and incest, as was done by Don

Gibbons,[16] is no more correct than to classify it, under the heading of violent personal crime, with homicide, forcible rape, and aggravated assault, as was done by Marshall Clinard and Richard Quinney.[17]

With regard to the degree of resistance or encouragement by the child, there is a considerable difference between the official record of the case (based primarily on the victim's story) and the offender's description of the event to the investigators of the Institute for Sex Research (in interviews conducted under sophisticated conditions, with assurances of confidentiality, and long after adjudication of guilt and incarceration). The difference between the two versions is shown in Table 3–1.

TABLE 3–1. Resistance of Female Child to Adult Male Sexual Aggression (Percent)

	RESISTED	PASSIVE	ENCOURAGING	N
According to record	75.4	8.2	16.4	61
According to offender	14.6	36.9	48.4	157

SOURCE: Paul Gebhard, John H. Gagnon, Wardell B. Pomeroy, and Cornelia V. Christenson, *Sex Offenders: An Analysis of Types* (New York: Harper & Row, 1965), p. 72.

For several reasons, these figures can be misleading. One must not forget that these are cases that did not fall within the purview of forcible rape (only because, as a matter of analysis, the latter cases were studied as a separate category by Gebhard and his research team). Hence, the percentage resisting is far lower than would be apparent if all cases of sexual offense against children had been included.

But what is more important is the discrepancy between the record, given primarily by the child, and the version related by the offender. Both are suspect. The child is old enough to understand that she will exonerate herself if she claims resistance or lack of encouragement; since she is a prosecution witness, she is prodded in that direction by the prosecution in order to obtain a conviction. Courtroom procedures in America, furthermore, have given rise to an etiquette whereby one seldom attempts to impeach the testimony of a child for such an effort, it is believed, antagonizes jury or judge and does the defendant more harm than good. On the other hand, the defendant is anxious for the court and the researcher to believe that he was led on. Gebhard concluded that the court records often contain additional confirming evidence of resistance, passivity, or lack of encouragement and found that consequently "we tend to rely upon them more than upon the offender in forming our overall impressions." [18]

Guilt and Innocence

There were some offenders (as high as 20 percent) in Gebhard's sample who denied their guilt, not only in court, but to the investigators as well; that is, they maintained "their innocence in the face of ample testimony and evidence to the contrary, and one often felt that they could not admit the truth even to themselves. Their explanations were generally unconvincing and frequently contained a paranoid theme concerning their having been 'framed.'" [19] Again, this statement should be read with caution for the researchers were here dealing only with persons who had been found guilty in a legal trial in which conviction supposedly occurs only if guilt is established beyond a reasonable doubt (at least to the satisfaction of an admittedly fallible jury). Thus, many of the falsely accused or the borderline cases had already been eliminated by nolle prosequi, by findings of innocence, by hung juries, by failure to prosecute because of weakness in the state's case, by plea bargaining, or even by suspension of sentence because of a lingering doubt in the mind of a judge. In all such instances, the person was not part of the Gebhard studies, which were conducted in prison.

While the image that has been conjured up by numerous novels and films of a prison system filled with innocent men is an exaggeration, some innocent people have gone to prison only later to be exonerated (a phenomenon examined by Donal MacNamara in a study of innocent persons who had been convicted). [20] It is difficult to imagine that there might not have been one or two completely guiltless among those in the study by Gebhard who most stoutly denied their culpability although they had been convicted and had nothing further to gain by this denial save the psychological reward of saving face. For the fact is that in sex cases generally, and particularly in those in which the accuser is a child, there is a long tradition of pretrial prejudice and of conviction on relatively slight evidence. While the courts always emphasize that a person cannot be convicted on the uncorroborated testimony of the victim, the degree of corroboration used is sometimes so miniscule as to be almost worthless.°

Few types of cases lend themselves to revenge, reprisal, and frame-up so readily as one in which a child accuses an adult of sexual advance, particularly if the two were alone and together for legitimate purposes. No alibi can be established; as the cliché goes, it is his word against hers. Male teachers, doctors, dentists, and others are particularly vulnerable: the accusation itself does great harm even when there is insufficient reason for prosecution or when the accused is eventually exonerated.†

The Therapeutic Outlook

When subjected to therapy, the offenders in the McCaghy sample seemed particularly adept at manipulating the situation to gain early release from incarceration. They learned the language of therapy; they soon learned that denial of the act, placing the blame on the victim for enticement, and similar mechanisms would prove of no avail. The molester had to learn that he had (or had to say that he had) deep problems, often of an unconscious nature. He had to know the language, often the clichés, by which he could convince the world that he now knew how to deal with his problems in a socially acceptable manner. Inasmuch as many a molester had an indeterminate sentence and had an interest in terminating his stay in prison as quickly as possible by parole, his problem be-

---

° There is a special irony in the disbelief shown by Gebhard and his colleagues to the replies of the respondents. This work was conducted by the Institute for Sex Research, founded by Alfred C. Kinsey, and one of the arguments leveled against Kinsey is that people would not tell him the truth about their sex lives. Kinsey and his co-workers insisted that the truth could be obtained; in the Gebhard work, they admitted that they did not, in their own opinion, manage to obtain it.

† From 1951 to 1960 Donal MacNamara participated in a study of accusations of fondling, solicitation, and sexual abuse of girls ranging from four to eleven years against building service employees (janitors, elevator operators, and doormen); approximately a score of these accusations were established beyond a reasonable doubt as false and malicious. The motivation was usually minor; in one case girls were stopped when roller-skating in the lobby; in two cases the charge was made as an excuse for a late return from school; and in another case a slap on the backside of a girl who spit on a doorman was interpreted by her parents as "fondling." In all instances, polygraph examination of the alleged molesters supported their protestations of innocence, and no criminal prosecutions resulted. A strong union, protecting the rights of its members, made this result possible. Had such charges been levied against unprotected individuals, a miscarriage of justice might well have occurred.

came one of learning how to express himself in a manner that would convince staff members that he was making progress toward his release date. This does not in itself prove the ineffectiveness of therapy; it simply suggests that therapy can turn into a mutual put-on in which the therapist may very well see through the presentation of self being made by the molester but may find it necessary to play the game. The therapist, let it be recalled, is always faced with a great dilemma: who is his client? Is his first obligation to the patient (the convicted offender) or to the institution that has hired him and is paying him? Piously, one responds that the primary obligation is to society, but this begs the question of role conflict rather than answering it.

Therapy frequently consists in teaching the offenders prudence. For the sake of self-interest, they are urged to reorient their drives toward the slightly older in order to avoid conflict with the law. That this is a less serious and difficult change than is a reorientation from homosexual to heterosexual, for example, is evident from the high degree of success claimed in such cases.

> Society's attempts to alter molesters' motives are on the whole successful. Under conditions in which accepting responsibility for the offense is a prerequisite for release, molesters come to embrace new, and presumably socially acceptable, explanations for their conduct.[21]

Do they accept these explanations or do they play the game of impression management? Perhaps they start with a presentation that will be acceptable to others and in the effort to delude (or convince) therapists, researchers, and social control agents come to accept as real what they had originally offered as pretense. Once accepted, the new motives seem to become guides for new modes of behavior. More draconian therapeutic interventions, behavior modification, aversion therapy, hypnotherapy, chemotherapy, narcotherapy, and even neurosurgery, have been experimented with or, more frequently, recommended, but there is bitter controversy over the desirability, legality, ethics, and effectiveness of such approaches.

Statutory Rape

Sex criminality insofar as it refers to the age of the parties (particularly that of the younger of the two, almost always the female) cannot be discussed without a review of the rational age of consent. The age of consent has been set as high as twenty-one and as low as sixteen in various jurisdictions of the United States; it is still lower in many other parts of the world. In England, it was traditionally set at twelve, then raised to thirteen and later made considerably higher. While a girl under the age of consent could frequently marry, with or without consent of parents (depending again upon state marital laws), and marriage legalizes sexual intercourse with one's husband, she could not legally engage in the same sexual behavior without benefit of marriage. This differs from the female's complicity in the violation of laws prohibiting fornication in that the offense if she is under age is exclusively the responsibility of the male and involves statutory rape, an offense far more serious than fornication.

The term "statutory rape," although unfortunate in that it suggests similarity to another type of behavior outrageous to victim and public, is not without its rationale. Rape itself is nonconsensual sexual behavior; a minor, it is reasoned, no matter how willing or eager, has not given consent because she is below the age at which she has the legal right or the social maturity to offer it. Nor is this right vested, as are certain others, in parents or guardians. No one has the right to consent to the act as agent of, or in behalf of, the female.

Ralph Slovenko contends that convictions for statutory rape far outnumber those for forcible rape, and it is possible that they may account for the largest number of arrests, convictions, and incarcerations or probations of any sex crime except prostitution.[22] If one accepts the view that the minor, however willing she may be, is nevertheless a victim, then there is little doubt that statutory rape accounts for the majority of prosecutions in sexual matters except for the "victimless crimes" of prostitution and homosexuality. For this reason alone, it warrants greater attention than it has hitherto received. According to Slovenko, the statistics indicate that

> approximately 80 percent of so-called rape convictions are of the statutory rape variety. In one ten-year period in New York City, 82 percent of all rape convictions were for statutory rape. For the same period, 59 percent of all convicted sex offenders were charged with statutory rape. A five- to ten-year maximum sentence is a typical provision of laws proscribing such behavior.[23]

Note, however, that Slovenko is writing of convictions, not frequency of occurrence. Most so-called statutory rape, it is assumed, is never reported to the police.

The line that distinguishes illegal sexual behavior with a minor from child molestation is a matter that, before the law, involves the age of the younger person but as a matter of the dynamics of the behavior usually involves her appearance, previous sexual behavior, and affectional interests in the older partner, as well as the willingness with which she entered the relationship. The law may be able to state that at age twelve a female ceases to be a child and becomes a minor, and at age sixteen (or some other) she ceases to be a minor and for purposes of making decisions about her sexual life is a young adult. But at fourteen she may be very much a child, undeveloped, timid, sexually hardly more advanced or interested than girls two or three years her junior; at the other extreme, she may be highly experienced and may have the appearance of a female in the late teens. It is when she is close to but still legally under the age of consent, when she has the behavioral patterns, interests, and appearance of someone much older, and particularly when her partner is himself not much older than she that borderline cases may ensue, resulting in conviction of a young man who in pattern and potential is hardly a sex criminal. By contrast, men in their late twenties or thirties who involve themselves with girls in their lower teens are probably exploiting the young for their own sexual gratification, perhaps sometimes with the object of preparing them eventually for a career in prostitution. Against such a man, able to spend money that schoolboys cannot, flattering the girl with his attentions, the law offers the protection of the statutory rape provisions.

Because the age of consent is the crucial factor, not the willingness of the younger partner, the previous chastity of the female is legally not relevant although many judges take it into account as a mitigating factor in determining the punishment to be imposed on the male. Here there is an interesting parallel with, and a departure from, cases of forcible rape. Although a woman's previous promiscuity cannot be used as a defense by the accused rapist if it can be shown that he did indeed use force, violence, or threat in inducing her to have sex (she is entitled to say no even if she has voluntarily said yes to him on many previous occasions and even if she accepts all other males and is in fact a prostitute), the defendant can invoke her promiscuity to establish the fact that he would not need to employ force and in fact did not do so. The minor girl, whom the law is designed to guide and protect, is likewise entitled to that protection no matter how unchaste she may have been. But the defendant cannot invoke her sexual history as a defense precisely because the only points at issue, from a legal view, are her age and whether the sex act took place. Some further issues—how old she presented herself as being and what the motives and intentions of the male were—have been raised, but for the most part these are more significant in determining the severity of the punishment than in the adjudication of guilt or innocence. Cases involving child prostitutes present complex problems for which equitable solutions are difficult to find.

This problem has come before the courts on many occasions, but it is doubtful whether it has been discussed in stronger or more colorful language than by a 1923 Missouri court quoted by Slovenko.

> There are not a few sober-minded fathers and mothers who feel that the statute is more drastic than sound public policy requires. The purpose of the lawmakers in its enactment is manifest. Experience has shown that girls under the age of sixteen, as the statute now reads, are not always able to resist temptation. They lack the discretion and firmness that comes with maturer years. Fathers and mothers know that this is true for boys as well. It is too true that many immature boys do not have the moral fiber and discretion of a Joseph. A lecherous woman is a social menace; she is more dangerous than TNT; more deadly than the "pestilence that walketh in darkness or the destruction that wasteth at noonday. . . ."
>
> We have in this case a condition and not a theory. This wretched girl was young in years but old in sin and shame. A number of callow youths, of otherwise blameless lives so far as this record shows, fell under her seductive influence. They flocked about her, if her story is to be believed, like moths about the flame of a lighted candle and probably with the same result. The girl was a common prostitute as the record shows. The boys were immature and doubtless more sinned against than sinning. She was a mere "cistern for foul toads to knot and gender in." Why should the boys, misled by her, be sacrificed? What sound public policy can be subserved by branding them as felons? Might it not be wise to ingraft an exception in the statute? But that is a question solely for the lawmakers; courts must construe the statute as they find it.[24]

Statutory rape often involves a male not more than a year or two older than the female, and the difference in age is taken into account in many of the new penal codes that are being adopted or proposed. The offender may not have any sexual problems or manifestations of psychopathology, although the victim, so to speak, if she is a very young girl already involved in extreme promiscuity or prostitution, might have such problems. Unlike most other sex crimes, then, there is and can be no question of rehabilitation or therapy for the offender.

The study by Gebhard and his colleagues, to which we have frequently referred, was limited to persons convicted of nonforcible sexual relations with girls between the ages of twelve and fifteen and to men in prison at the time.[25] A small proportion of pedophiles and others with grave problems were found, but this proportion might be exaggerated because of the nature of the sample, for such people would be more likely to be arrested, prosecuted, convicted, and imprisoned for lawbreaking activity. The most significant finding of Gebhard, in our view, was that the bulk of the offenders could be divided into two groups, which he termed "subculture offenders" and "near-peer offenders."

> The subculture offenders are those who belong to a portion of society, a subculture, which regards as a suitable sexual object any female past menarche, or even a prepubescent female if she is of adult size. In envisioning such a subculture one at first thinks of the rural mountain people, but this same low age limit may be found among the lower socioeconomic stratum in big cities. The existence of this subculture is clearly indicated in a tabulation of the ages of the wives of offenders against minors at the time of marriage. . . . Half of the brides were aged sixteen to eighteen; about a tenth were younger. It is obvious that a man who married, say, a sixteen- or seventeen-year-old is not going to regard a fourteen- or fifteen-year-old as too young for a sexual relationship. . . .
>
> The near-peer offenders are simply males who are so close in age to their "victims" that a sexual relationship is psychologically and socially appropriate although illegal. A classic case is that of a seventeen-year-old boy and a fifteen-year-old girl. In prison, where the boy was serving six months for statutory rape, the psychologist described him as ". . . an embarrassed male of seventeen who had intercourse with a girl fifteen. He says she offered no protest and he thought there would be no legal complications."[26]

The distinction made here is useful, and it calls attention to the fact that there are adult males (in their twenties and thirties) whose chief libidinal interest is in girls considerably younger than themselves. That a comparable phenomenon characterizes homosexuals is widely believed; males having interest in adolescent boys are known in the homosexual argot as "chicken hawks." Note, further, that males having such interests in very young girls do not, in Gebhard's description, constitute a subculture; rather, they come from a subculture, often rural, in which such heterosexual behavior is not strongly condemned.

Adolescent sexuality seems to be one of the major sources of venereal disease, and this may be due in part to lack of sex education as well as fear of reporting symptoms to authority figures, including parents. Despite the dissemination of information on birth control and the relative ease of obtaining abortions, unwanted pregnancies among unmarried adolescents continue to be a grave problem. Some scientists contend that after menarche but before complete maturity the human female is in a low fertility state. "Relatively few girls are capable of reproduction before 15 years of age," write Ford and Beach, "and even then their reproductive capacity is not as great as it will be later." [27] The many exceptions to this general statement have resulted in legal and personal difficulties. It is likely that a research study would show that most fathers of the children of unwed teenage girls are not much older than the girls themselves, and some may be slightly younger. Under many new or proposed penal codes, such males would not be guilty of any crime. As a separate, noncriminal legal and social problem, there is concern that these young males seldom contribute to the support of the children and are reluctant to marry the child-mother and assume paternal responsibility.

Adults with Young Males

The involvement of men with young boys presents a problem in some ways similar to, and in other ways quite different from, that encountered in studies of men with female children and minors. Some of the offenders against children studied by Gebhard were primarily oriented toward males (they made an identification of self as homosexual) and had a great deal of activity with and interest in other males, not particularly with children. [28] Some were youth oriented, especially toward teenagers. However, some of the offenders had sexual interests in children who had not yet developed the secondary sexual characteristics that cause obvious differentiation between the clothed boy and the girl. So that a pattern emerges in which on the one hand the desire is for males who are young and on the other for young people who may or may not be males.

The study by Gebhard demonstrated that the median age of the male child victim was slightly higher than that of the female (in both cases, those over the age of twelve were excluded because they were studied as minors not children). It appears that the offenders in these cases were homosexuals interested in "chicken," or very young boys, and that those men who were apprehended had explored slightly lower age levels. Seldom was force or threat used, and some of the youths were apparently willing partners if not actually the "aggressors." Some, even at the tender age of eight or nine, were active boy prostitutes, selling their favors for money, meals, or entertainment denied them in their economically deprived homes, or in response to a show of interest or affection they had seldom or never experienced in a fatherless home or from emotionally cold parents.[29]

Like offenders against male children, not all "seducers" of male youths are "dirty old men." The average offender had just passed his thirtieth birthday, was unmarried, and presumably could easily locate homosexual partners of his own age but generally had an interest in partners far younger than himself. The extent of the child's encouragement is indicated by the fact that the official records and the offender's report were in agreement that 70 percent of the boys were either passive or gave encouragement; in another 19 percent of the cases there was agreement that the boy had resisted. For an understanding of the phenomenon of adult-child homosexual relations, these figures should be interpreted with great care, taking into consideration that the possibility of apprehension and eventual arrest is far greater when the boy has resisted. Thus, it can be assumed on the basis of some evidence, but awaiting further proof, that in an overwhelming percentage of homosexual relations between a man and a young boy, the latter is either passive or encouraging. Only a few of the boys reported the cases; most instances were discovered by checking of automobiles, police surveillance of suspicious persons, and a variety of other ways. While not reported by Gebhard, quite a few of the adult-child, and even more of the adult-minor, homosexual cases involved a monetary transaction.

McCaghy found molesters of boys to be more candid than molesters of girls, and they less frequently used drunkenness as an excuse for their behavior.[30] The homosexual molesters, it appears, had already accepted their deviant role in society. Since these people, in identifying themselves with homosexuality, had made "a drastic departure from the sexual norms of conventional society," the accusation of child molestation "does not constitute a threat to the present self-concepts as sexual deviants." [31] Nevertheless, for reasons that pertain to the struggle of organized homosexual groups against discrimination and for legal change in their status, the homosexual child molester is likely to be denounced quite vociferously by gay liberation and sexual freedom groups, which would say that he has indeed made a new "drastic departure from the sexual norms of conventional society" in approaching a child and that this constitutes a threat to others who deviate from social norms in somewhat more acceptable fashion. [32]

For a single, detailed case history of the relationships of a homosexual with a number of boys in puberty and early adolescence, the reader is referred to the story of a man called Dr. Martin, narrated by Richard C. Donnelly and his colleagues. [33] This case brings to the fore certain problems involving homosexuality and child molestation or the seduction of male minors. Dr. Martin was a school physician with the best credentials, a rather youthful bachelor whose sexual interest in boys was combined with dedication to their medical and general welfare. He was not a drunkard, nor did he display signs of psychopathology (unless his sexual interests in the male youths are so interpreted), and he offered the boys who came under his tutelage what might be called "loving care." When finally apprehended, because a child let fall an almost innocent remark in speaking to his mother, Dr. Martin pleaded nolo contendere on the ground that he refused to subject his wards to whose interests he was so deeply committed to the trauma of courtroom testimony and examination. Following his client's plea, the attorney for the defendant insisted that leaders of the society should have an open mind on admittedly unorthodox approaches to difficult problems and that Dr. Martin was, in a manner that might some day be looked on with far less disfavor, offering these boys therapy and perhaps doing them a great deal of good.

A second case of homosexual child molestation has been presented in great detail by Livingston Hall and his colleagues. [34] J. W. was a married man, described in many of the official documents as "a bisexual," who was repeatedly arrested on homosexual molestation charges over a period of many years. It was not quite clear whether he was guilty on each charge, and it is possible that the arrest record followed him and militated against his obtaining a fair trial with a presumption of innocence. Nor was the evidence against him, on the other hand, weak. Caught up in the indeterminate sentence system that develops into a virtual life sentence for some sex offenders, he was resistant to therapy, did not appear to be able to control his interest in young boys, and gave all signs of being a "career pedophile."

EFFECTS OF THE ADOLESCENT HOMOSEXUAL EXPERIENCE

Much of the problem concerning homosexual molestation of prepubertal or adolescent boys has centered around the question of the effect of initiation into such behavior on later life patterns.[35] Actually, little is known on this question. Assuming, to take one not uncommon type of case, that the boy was not resistant and might even have been quite willing, there is still little known about what will happen to him and others like him, as contrasted with a group of youths at a similar stage of psychosexual development and with similar interests who do not engage in homosexual behavior.

Peculiarly, and almost contradictorily, the seduction of a girl by a male has been blamed for that girl's turning away from men and toward other women—that is, she is said to become a lesbian after and because of an earlier heterosexual event—while the seduction of a boy has been blamed for that boy's being inducted into the world of homosexuality and turning toward men. Some contend that this thesis is illogical: you can't have it both ways. On the surface, it appears to be more moralistic than scientific and designed to arouse the public against adult-child sexuality.

There may be no contradiction here, however, for it is possible that two entirely different types of phenomena are under study. A young girl who is seduced may be unwilling, and the entire episode may be a frightening and distasteful one to her (as has been reported of girls seduced by stepfathers, for example); even if she was not forcibly raped and was not highly resistant, the incident may leave her with a feeling of repulsion against men as lovers or as sex partners. The boy who is seduced, particularly if he is a minor and not a child, is often responsive; he is in a polymorphous state seeking sex outlet and discovers it in what may have been at first an unexpected and later an easily obtainable, even profitable, form.

The effect of homosexual experiences during the prepubescent, pubescent, and adolescent stages of life on the future sexual life of the male is a matter on which little information is presently available and that has been obscured by both the moralistic denunciations of the law enforcers and the ideological explanations of those struggling for homosexual rights. Some of these youths no doubt "outgrow" their homosexual experiences and make satisfactory heterosexual adjustments in life; yet there is evidence that many do not. Of the latter, were they "destined" to develop in a more and more homosexual direction, and would this development have taken place without homosexual experiences during the early and formative years? While the answer cannot be stated in any definitive manner, there is some evidence that homosexuality is a learning experience, that some males learn to enjoy and to adjust to this life-style during their early years while at the same time they find their bisexual leanings difficult to handle and repress the heterosexual component.[36]

Some writers, such as the authors of the well-known Wolfenden Report,[37] have suggested that the age of consent for the younger partner in a heterosexual encounter be lower than that for the younger partner in a homosexual encounter, a view predicated on the belief that great damage may be caused by adolescent homosexual experiences with an older person. The Wolfenden recommendation was put into law in the new code established in England. To this, some homosexual spokesmen, demanding complete equality and asserting that their way of life should be seen as on a par with the other, have protested strongly. Certainly it is discriminatory, but is it unfair discrimination, is it irrational? The English lawmakers would contend that so long as homosexuality does not offer so wide a range of fulfilling potential to the individual as heterosexuality does, such a rule is completely rational and in the best interests of society. One might posit another question: Is consensual adult-child homosexual experience more traumatic or less, more potentially harmful or less, than peer homosexual experiences?

Incest with Child or Minor

Incest is contrary to the mores of all societies. The type of incest that comes to the attention of the public most often is that between an adult and a child or a minor, although incestuous behavior between two consenting adults is not unknown. The latter is usually not regarded as a serious offense from the viewpoint of penal law; the former is a special, often aggravated, instance of child molestation or statutory rape. Some European jurisdictions have made a further distinction between what might be called "true incest" (a phrase used by Herbert Maisch) [38] and "statutory incest." The former involves a genetic tie between the partners, the latter a legal, affinal, or contractual one developed particularly as a result of marriage.

If one is going to speak of the incest taboo, this concept as used in the anthropological and psychoanalytic literature hardly seems applicable to people linked to each other through marriage to a third person. That is to say, sexuality in the absence of a genetic tie does not arouse in a considerable portion of the populace a sense of instinctive repugnance. Only true incest seems able to elicit such repugnance, although sexual contact between a stepfather and a young stepdaughter would bring forth strong indignation. Sexual relations with first and second cousins, prohibited in some penal codes and by canon law, are debatably incestuous in a criminological sense.

So far as official records are concerned, incest itself seems to be rather rare. It is only when the younger partner (almost invariably female) is a child or minor, and usually as the result of pregnancy or, less frequently, a marital crisis between the parents that the matter comes to public attention; hence the overwhelming majority of known instances involve father-daughter situations. Of these, Hector Cavallin writes:

> We make no difference as to whether the relationship of the participants is a "blood" relation or a "contractual" one (a stepbrother, stepfather, stepmother, etc.) since what is relevant is that they are members of the same direct family. It is possible that incest occurs more often among "contractual" relatives. In that case, a rationalization that "no real relationship" exists may ease the breaking of the prohibition.[39]

Most instances of father-daughter incest reported in the literature do not specify whether the relationship was genetic or contractual. Gebhard, for example, describes incest offenders as "adult males who have had sexual contact with their daughters or stepdaughters" and then goes on to speak of the very small sympathy for the offender "especially if the girl were a stepdaughter rather than a genetic daughter."[40] The "small sympathy" may reflect anger that a man took advantage of his wife's child, as contrasted with a situation in which a man has seduced his own child, which brings forth the rather sympathetic feeling that he, the father, is mentally ill to have committed such an act.

In a situation in which a man marries a woman with an adult daughter, the potential for incest may be quite strong. Gebhard notes that such a man "can scarcely look upon the girl as a true daughter," and for him to be in the same house with her and to see her "without any thought of sex entering his mind is a virtual impossibility." [41] Any sexual liaison between such a man and his stepdaughter would almost invariably arouse jealousy in the wife and perhaps disrupt the new marriage.

A similar situation, with only slight legal distinction, may involve a form of statutory rape or even child molestation having a pseudo-incestuous character, reportedly on the increase in the United States during the 1960s and 1970s. This involves the rape or seduction of the daughter by the mother's boyfriend, a man who has neither the permanence nor the legal status to be termed the stepfather but who has a surrogate father role, at least to a limited degree, in the household. Situations such as this occur when the man lives in the same apartment or house, has free access to it without actually domiciling there, or is simply an extremely frequent visitor. The increasing number of arrangements like this may make pseudo-incest a more common occurrence during the years to come. Some of these mothers are more jealous of their daughters, it is claimed, than they are angry with the boyfriend; some who do experience such anger may suppress it (or punish the daughter rather than complain against the perpetrator), because of the investment that they have in the continuity of the relationship with the male.

Of the seventy-five cases of heterosexual incest studied by Maisch (homosexual incest is probably rare or at least is seldom reported although there are instances of fathers who have made sexual overtures to both a son and a daughter), sixty-six were of the father-daughter variety. [42] Mother-son situations constitute only a minuscule proportion of the reported incest cases, and almost nothing reliable is known of sibling cases except that they seldom become matters for police and court action. Of the sixty-six father-daughter cases, thirty-two offenders were stepfathers, thirty-four biological fathers. If these figures are indicative of a distribution (and it is the only reported study known to us that has made this distinction), it appears that the likelihood of a stepfather-stepdaughter relationship is far greater than a father-daughter one. In the Maisch data, approximately half of the cases were of each type, but the number of households in which there is a father and a daughter is surely many times greater than that in which there is a stepfather and stepdaughter. On the other hand, one can postulate that stepfathers are more likely to be reported to police by a family member (victim or other) than are fathers under otherwise similar circumstances.

Ambivalence marks the relationship among all the members of a family in which a father-daughter (or stepfather-stepdaughter) incest has occurred. Other than murder attempted between couples living together in intimacy, writes Hedwig Wallis, "there is hardly any other set of legal circumstances which bind offender and victim so closely together in such a tight, often tragic, network of affection and distance, fear and fascination, care and lack of consideration." [43] That there is a high incidence of undiscovered and unreported father-daughter, sibling, and perhaps uncle-niece incest among low socioeconomic level families, those living in overcrowded conditions, or heavily dependent on alcohol and drugs, or in isolated one-family settings in "backward" areas of the country, is accepted as fact by many sociologists. We do not disagree with statements to this effect but merely point to the paucity of confirming data.

Adult-Child Sexuality and Social Policy

Study of the effect of any sexual act between adult and child or adult and minor on the future sexual pattern and general well-being of the younger person is important to guide social policy. There are at least four separate types of activities: forcible rape, incest, homosexual, and consensual heterosexual. Each of these can differ according to the age of the younger person, and incestuous and homosexual activity can be consensual or forcible. The varieties are many, and the available findings thus far are meager.

Some authorities have stressed that the victims of incest (children particularly), and indeed of other sexual experiences may not be injured by the event as much as by the public, familial, or court reaction to it. Along this line, Franco Ferracuti writes as follows, summarizing the work of others on this question: *

---

* The specific reference is to incest, but the questions raised have been extended to other types of child molestation.

According to Allen, the psychological effects of the discovery of incest are more serious than the biological; if the victim does not realize she has violated the incest taboo, the effects should be almost nil. It seems necessary, however, to point out that the same degenerate causal factors which have led to the incest can frequently induce such sexual behavior. According to Weiner, the daughters who are objects of incest are characteristically precocious in their learning and are anxious to assume the adult role. They are especially gratified by paternal attention, and they use the incestuous relationship to express their hostility toward the mother. Rarely do they resist the sexual act or feel guilty about it. Frequently they become sexually promiscuous after the end of the incestuous conduct. Nevertheless, it is hardly proved that participation in incest, particularly before the onset of puberty, results in psychological disturbances.[44]

Ferracuti balances this by citing Sloane and Karpinski, who refer to "the persisting neurosis and sexual conflict present in the victims of incest." [45] Ferracuti continues:

Schultz, in an article on the technique of interviewing victims of sex crimes, discusses, among other cases, a victim of incest. He notes all the evidence of harm occasioned by the judicial interrogation of the victims of sex crimes, and he reports the special Israeli legislation prohibiting the direct interrogation of underage victims, which is in keeping with Reifen's recommendations for the protection of child victims.[46]

Many writers, including McCaghy, have stressed the trauma suffered by the child as a result of the discovery of a sexual episode with an adult, and these researchers suggest that the child might escape such trauma if the episode is not pursued. The act itself, McCaghy declares, might not be traumatic, but the disclosure of it very well could be.

Parents must realize that despite their precautions their child may be molested, but a great step will be made toward peace of mind and proper handling of the situation when parents also recognize that an incident of molesting is not likely to be traumatic for a child unless the parents themselves make it so.[47]

Against this position, one could also postulate that the child might be adversely affected by the failure of parents and authorities to react against the offender and further that even without any immediate trauma there may be damaging long-term effects on the child's psychosexual development.

While protecting child victims must be a major concern in any judicial proceeding, this goal has to be pursued without violating the constitutional rights of the defendant, his presumption of innocence, and his right to cross-examine the complainant. Children are indeed victimized, and prevention of the act and prosecution of the perpetrator are necessary; however, children can err in identification, have flights of fancy, be spiteful or vengeful, misunderstand a situation, or in other ways incriminate an innocent person. Stuart Finch has placed this question in focus.

> Once a sexual seduction has been suspected, there is the problem of how much further emotional trauma to impose on the child in court procedures to convict the presumed sex offender. The accused has the right to defense counsel and due process. If he invokes them the child may suffer still more emotional turmoil. Yet if the offender is not prosecuted he may harm other children. Anyone accused of an illegal act should have the protection of the legal system. But if the accuser is a child and the offense is sexual, the whole matter becomes quite complicated.[48]

One of the interesting research problems often preceding investigations leading to the formulation of social policy is determining the percentage of persons involved in a particular type of activity. In arriving at the incidence of preadolescent sexual contacts with adult males, Kinsey and his colleagues studied 4,441 females.

> For the sake of the present calculations we have defined an adult male as one who has turned adolescent and who is at least fifteen years of age; and, in order to eliminate experiences that amount to nothing more than adolescent sex play, we have considered only those cases in which the male was at least five years older than the female, while the female was still pre-adolescent.[49]

Using these criteria, Kinsey and his co-workers found that 24 percent of the females "had been approached while they were preadolescent by adult males who appeared to be making sexual advances."[50] Approximately half of these approaches were by strangers (neither relatives nor friends/acquaintances); about 85 percent reported that only one male had made such an approach and 62 percent were either verbal approaches or genital exhibitions.*

---

* Donal E. J. MacNamara, in a series of anonymous classroom surveys of college students regarding crimes committed against them during childhood and adolescence, found that half of the males and one-third of the females had been approached sexually by men over the age of 21.

It is probably true that there is a general public antipathy to explicitly sexual approaches to preadolescent females by adult or even adolescent males although studies on such attitudes are not available. Despite the failure to back up his statements with scientific evidence, it is likely that Kinsey was accurate when he wrote:

> Most persons feel that all such contacts are undesirable because of the immediate disturbance they may cause the child, and because of the conditioning and possibly traumatic effects which they may have on the child's sociosexual development and subsequent sexual adjustments in marriage.[51]

Whatever may have been the attitude of the public earlier in the twentieth century, it is doubtful that his concern today extends strongly to the protection of the underage female who is a consenting partner in what turns out to be statutory rape. Modern societies do require a sharp line of demarcation for chronological age of consent; whether this age should be fourteen or eighteen or somewhere between is matter for further study. We would strongly endorse the American Law Institute proposal, implicit in the Kinsey work, that would limit criminal prosecution to cases in which there is an age gap of at least four years between the male and the female (the latter younger). Whether age of consent should be higher for homosexual activities, as recommended by Wolfenden and put into law in England, or the same, as recommended by the Model Penal Code of the American Law Institute, is worthy of further study. It would appear to us that if the age differential suggested here is adhered to, there will be sufficient protection of young males and females. For slightly older adolescents, in their later teens, for instance, it is unlikely that the law can be effective in diminishing consensual activity, and legal constraints may result in blackmail, shakedowns, or fear of counselors and social workers.

What still remains is the problem discussed by Ferracuti and the many scholars whose work he cites of the effect of interrogation and prosecution on the child and, further, the effect of the sexual act itself (or approach, or whatever form the experience may have taken) on the later life of the preadolescent.

That a courtroom appearance, with the difficulties of cross-examination, will be traumatic and will often produce shame at the disclosures far beyond that which the child previously had felt appears indisputable. One may regard the argument of Dr. Martin's lawyer that it was for love of the children that he pleaded nolo contendere, in order to save them from the dire effects of having to testify in court, as the ruse of a clever lawyer. But it contains more than a grain of truth. One can imagine these boys, twelve or thirteen years of age, required to describe fellatio and other homosexual acts before a court that even if the sessions were in camera neverthless included a judge, some attorneys, the defendant (toward whom they may have felt affection even while articulating the details of his crimes), and their own parents.

Nonetheless, as in rape cases, social policy may require prosecution and measures to reduce the difficulties for the victim while at the same time demanding that the constitutional rights of the accused not be abrogated. Compassion and counseling shown to the victims, pretrial testimony to determine just how far courtroom examination and cross-examination might go, and other measures can be taken to assist a child. It hardly seems reasonable that notwithstanding the law prosecutions should be abandoned and criminal activity be permitted to continue with impunity because there is no method of helping the complainant avoid psychological harm.

As to the effects on later life patterns, the fact is that little is known. Many experts have contended that the sexual contact may not be so traumatic as has often been believed. This would depend not only on the age of the child and the circumstances but on the nature of the experience. There is considerable feminist literature in the opposite direction, placing responsibility for tragic life patterns and for consequent suicide on the ineffaceable memory of having been raped as a child. Furthermore, the effect may be not traumatic but perverting in a slow and insidious manner. Yet even this claim is difficult to substantiate because many children who have had such experiences, especially with a relative or close family acquaintance, may be growing up under disturbed and disorganized home conditions. What contribution to adult maladjustment is made by the childhood sexual experience is difficult to estimate under such circumstances.

Lauretta Bender and her colleagues did follow-up studies on small samples of children who had had sexual experiences (homosexual and heterosexual, including incestuous).[52] In one group the children had "deep confusion" over their sexual (gender) identity. She stresses that the child very often sought the contact and received pleasure from it and further concludes that "overt sexual behavior of the several kinds described did not necessarily forecast maladjustments specifically rooted in such experience." This work has been summarized by William Reevy,[53] who contrasts it with the traditional view that "the psychological effects of adult seduction have always been presumed to be harmful," an orientation, Reevy finds, that has received strong support from psychoanalysts. The columnist Ann Landers, whose correspondents frequently reflect significant problems, has published a considerable number of letters from women who as adolescents (or earlier) were sexually abused by fathers, male relatives, or boarders, and many of these women reported long-term traumata.

Studies of the effects of adult-child sexuality on the child have often been rooted in ideology and inflamed by emotion. There is a need for much greater research on the long- and short-range effects on the child both with regard to the sex act itself, and with regard to the willingness or unwillingness of parents and other adults to report the matter to authorities. There may well be a difference depending on whether the act is heterosexual or homosexual, consensual or forcible, committed by a relative or friend or a stranger. Public policy based on speculation can be disastrous, whether such speculation be motivated by moralistic indignation against the offender or compassion and recognition of his difficulties. Since publication of the original edition, California has threatened a film producer with fifty years in prison for consensual sexual relations with a 13-year-old female; an appellate court in New Mexico has ruled that an adult woman who had intercourse with a fifteen-year-old male was not contributing to his delinquency but rather furthering his sex education and development; and a judge of New York City's Family Court, in freeing a fourteen-year-old prostitute, ruled that such sexual relations were "recreational" and that New York's statutes on consensual prostitution and consensual sodomy were unconstitutional.

4   Prostitution

Like many other illegal acts, prostitution is defined somewhat differently in the penal codes of the fifty states and in the District of Columbia, as well as in other countries of the world. Furthermore, the definitions used in the behavioral sciences (particularly sociology and psychology) do not always coincide with those found in the law.

Morris Ploscowe describes prostitution as "the indiscriminate offer of one's body for hire, for the purpose of sexual intercourse or other so-called lewdness," [1] a definition repeated and endorsed by Samuel Kling.[2] Ploscowe, however, specified that it is the offering of the body of a woman (presumably to a man); whereas Kling, writing a decade and a half later, no longer found it desirable to make this distinction. The two key concepts here are that the action is indiscriminate and that it is "for hire"—that is, for money. Ploscowe points out, in fact, that a single act would not be prostitution and that both higher and lower courts have so decided. Nevertheless, a careful reading of many laws would indicate that a single act of solicitation, interpreted as part of a pattern, would fall within the legal purview of prostitution. While the indiscriminate person is more likely to come into conflict with the law, penal codes certainly do not exempt discriminating prostitutes. The entire matter of discrimination is meant to emphasize that under the law the "kept woman," the "paid mistress," or the "golddigger" are not defined as prostitutes; however, to qualify for this term or to be in violation of the law, it is not necessary that the woman offer to sell her sex services to *all* buyers indiscriminately.

A rather different orientation to the interpretation of the law was taken by Isabel Drummond, writing in 1953.

> In its restricted legal sense prostitution is the practice of a female offering her body to indiscriminate sexual intercourse with men. . . . It is a popular misconception that the element of money remuneration is essential to the crime. It is not an element in it unless specifically made so by statute.
>
> If a woman submits to indiscriminate sexual intercourse which she invites, she is a prostitute regardless of whether the intercourse was for hire or not, unless the statute otherwise provides. There is considerable diversity in the statutes, about twenty-nine of them furnishing no definition of the crime. Three of these—Georgia, New York and Virginia—include the for-gain element in their interpretation. Sixteen statutes have a two-way stretch in defining prostitution to be the offering of or receiving of the body for sexual intercourse for hire, and the offering or receiving of the body for promiscuous and indiscriminate sexual intercourse without hire.
>
> Pennsylvania, Maryland and Louisiana specifically limit the crime to sexual intercourse for hire only. The District of Columbia, in its vagrancy statute, makes "fornication or perversion for hire" the crime, thus encompassing homosexual prostitution.[3]

Note here Drummond's point that the concept of lack of discrimination is the sine qua non for the act to fall within the laws governing prostitution, but that monetary gain is not determinative unless specified in the law. There has been some liberalization since her writing, but it is still true that there is a diversity of definitions as well as frequent lack of definitions.

The penal code of New York State reads: "A person is guilty of prostitution when such person engages or agrees or offers to engage in sexual conduct with another person in return for a fee," but in a commentary it is pointed out that the emphasis is placed upon loitering.[4] Furthermore, the law specifies in New York that the recipient of the fee can be a male or a female and that the payer can be of either sex,[*] thus not only including homosexual prostitution but also defining as a prostitute a man who receives payment from a woman for sex.

The documentation offered by Drummond notwithstanding, it is doubtful that a prosecution under the prostitution laws could be

---

[*] The New York law, particularly as it applies to loitering, is discussed in greater detail later in this chapter.

initiated and upheld if the charge involved indiscriminate promiscuity without pay. This is not to deny, however, that police might be able to harass, and local officials successfully to prosecute, a woman engaging in such behavior, under a variety of laws such as vagrancy, public nuisance, public disorder, lewd conduct, or disorderly conduct.

Sociological Definitions

Some sociologists have used the themes of indiscriminate sexual behavior and sex for hire and elaborated on them. For example, Kingsley Davis specifies that the prostitute is promiscuous, sells her favors, and is emotionally indifferent: "the prostitute's affront is not that she trades but that she trades promiscuously and with emotional indifference." [5]

Ned Polsky, however, finds that the important element defining a person as a prostitute is the "granting of nonmarital sex as a vocation." [6] We suggest that Polsky may here be erring in the opposite direction from those who stress only unlimited promiscuity and that he is placing too much stress on the lack of an official marriage contract (which he might well modify if there were a quasi-marital relationship such as more or less permanent nonmarital cohabitation). Nonetheless, the vocational or occupational aspect is important. The various elements of Davis's and Polsky's definitions could well be combined and prostitution seen as the pursuit of sex as a vocation or occupation (this would encompass the idea of "for hire" or monetary gain) with sufficient lack of discrimination, emotional indifference to the partner, and inconstancy so that there is no one-to-one relationship, even for a short period. The kept woman, common law wife, and even relatively temporary noncommercial affairs of convenience, are thus excluded from the definition, but it is recognized that some discrimination is practiced by certain prostitutes (e.g., many reject interracial sex, others will not service the young or the old, some specialize in soldiers or sailors, and some seek out other highly specialized clienteles).

The Nature of Prostitution in America

In all American jurisdictions except some counties of Nevada, prostitution is a violation of the criminal code. However, the numbers of such violations and of the men and women involved in them are difficult to estimate. Prostitution is not an offense reported by a complainant or by one who could be called a victim, and hence the best statistics, based on arrests, are not clear indications of the extent or frequency of the activity. Arrests are sporadic, and the difference in the number of arrests from one city to another may reflect the degree of protection and corruption in a city or the vigor with which local police enforce the law.

THE CHANGING SCENE

The nature of prostitution has changed over recent decades, and there is every likelihood that further changes will be seen. Shortly after World War II, Edwin Lemert was able to write that prostitutes were, in the aggregate, "primarily a one-sex female group," although he added that a small number of homosexual male prostitutes were found in American society.[7] No one would make this mistake today for male prostitution is rampant in all American metropolises and in many small cities as well.

In the early decades of the twentieth century, there was some streetwalking, but most transactions with prostitutes were conducted in houses where sex for hire was the sole business.[8] These houses were usually owned and/or managed by an older woman, often a former prostitute, and the employees (i.e., the prostitutes) worked, ate, slept, and lived there.[*] The houses of prostitution served regular clients as well as itinerants and strangers who heard of their location; they probably had police protection; and they existed in a state of quiet but uneasy tolerance from neighbors. In some cities, there were red light districts, or areas in which such houses were permitted and clustered; whereas in other areas they were prohibited (little red lights were indeed used to indicate that these establishments were open for business).

Bawdy houses declined in America between the first and second world wars and almost but not quite disappeared following the second world war.[9] At least they were no longer visible, and those that remained went underground, no longer advertised, and were not the common knowledge of every resident; they were more like

---

[*] It would make an interesting exercise to compare the employees of such houses with inmates of prisons, soldiers in armies, and others living in what Erving Goffman has called a "total institution." See Erving Goffman, *Asylums: Essays on the Social Situation of Mental Patients and Other Inmates* (New York: Doubleday, 1961).

the speakeasies of Prohibition days, known to their clientele and protected by the police.

A DIVERSITY OF PATTERNS

In a major city on the eastern seaboard, a male entering a taxi alone or registering alone at a hotel is asked if he wants to meet a girl; often two or three males, unaccompanied by women, are likewise solicited by the driver or hotel bellhop. The latter are not easily dissuaded, and if the man declines, he is asked if he is interested in a masseuse; declining this, he is asked if he wants to go to a bar where there is a lot of "action." The steerer is of course given a percentage for all the customers he brings, and he is in little danger of punishment, for in the unlikely event that a complaint is made, it is simply filed, if it is not mislaid.[10]

In another city, the newspapers have published articles about open streetwalking, reporting the names of the streets, the time of day and night, the method of accosting, the nature of the interaction, the price, where the participants go, and how long they stay—only what happens there is not detailed.

In still another city, boys with tight pants, some of them as young, or so it seems, as fourteen, stand at designated places waiting for a likely score.[11] Thousands of men and women go by, oblivious to what is occurring around them; a youth seldom makes the error of approaching an innocent man although he may occasionally solicit a vice squad plainclothesman. In the summer a slightly older youth, a boy in his late teens, may wear a T-shirt, exposing a hairy chest and muscular biceps; in other seasons, black jacket, thick leather belt, and dangling chains. But always the tight pants. Even younger boys are made available to a pedophile clientele at a notorious quick-food outlet in the Times Square area of New York City.

TYPES OF PROSTITUTES AND THEIR ACTIVITIES

There is a stratification system in prostitution. At the lowest end of this scale, from the viewpoint of esteem, style, mode of operation, and income, are the streetwalkers.[12] They solicit on the street, usually in a place where a girl unaccompanied by a male is suspected of being a prostitute. In addition, their style of approach and their appearance and demeanor have become less and less subtle in the United States. At one time, the streetwalker's activities were largely confined to the night hours (prostitutes have been known as "ladies of the night"), but daytime solicitation has today become common and blatant. In large cities, such females are almost always attached to, or working for, a pimp (whose role will be examined presently). When a street solicitation results in agreement to engage in sex, the man and woman generally go to a room in a cheap hotel or to the prostitute's room or apartment. If they go to a hotel, the manager or room clerk is fully aware of the purpose, embarrassment is reduced to a minimum, and the room is often rented several times during a single day. More and more, streetwalkers in American cities are recruited from the minority populations, the drug abusers, and young female runaways.

Somewhat higher than the streetwalker is the bar girl. She works out of a bar, usually by arrangement with the owner or manager.[13] She induces the customer to buy drinks for both of them, sometimes receives a return from the bar owner, but more frequently is tolerated by him because of the business she develops. Such women meet competition from "amateurs" and sometimes must make it explicit that their sexual offering is for hire, which the streetwalker does not find it necessary to do. The charge to the customer is generally higher than the streetwalker can command, and the sexual encounter often takes place in less seedy surroundings and under less hurried conditions than encounters after a meeting on the street (often, in fact, in the home or hotel room of the customer).

On a fairly even level with bar girls are the women who subtly and unobtrusively meet prospective customers in hotel lobbies. The hotel management and detectives may pretend not to know what is occurring, in return either for payoffs or for the business that such women bring to the premises. The hotel management is mainly concerned that the activity not be blatant, that female guests be unaware of what is occurring, and that males not be openly solicited. Hence, the women conduct themselves more like male than like other female prostitutes in the sense that they attempt to send out cues and vibrations to those who are "tuned in" on their wavelength. Almost invariably these hotel pickups end up in sexual activity in a hotel room rented by the male.

Bar prostitutes and hotel prostitutes do not make up entirely separate categories; many women meet their customers ("johns") at bars one day and hotels on another. These two categories seem to account for a relatively small percentage of the total prostitution business; if the two groups can be separated, it appears that more women are working the bars than the hotel lobbies. Furthermore, these are women who seem to operate without pimps.

A group that has grown considerably in size and in visibility during the 1960s and 1970s consists of what might be called "store prostitutes," women employed by massage parlors and other businesses that are thinly veiled fronts for houses of prostitution. One such type of business is called M&M, meaning "massage and masturbate." Oral sex is allegedly frequent in these businesses, as is coition. The businesses are advertised by fliers and other methods that promise plenty of girls, lots of action, esoteric decor and entertainment, but do not explicitly mention prostitution.

Still another type is the convention prostitute.[14] These are women hired to entertain at conventions, and the entertainment can take the form of being available for delegates and visitors, being at the beck and call of those running the convention, or putting on exhibitions before a limited, specially invited audience. The same women may be involved in both the exhibition and the private sexual relations, or there may be a division of labor. The exhibitions themselves are sometimes stripteases and dances and frequently involve lesbian activities (which appear to appeal to all-male heterosexual audiences). If they are heterosexual, a hired male ("stud") may be supplied, or one of the male audience may volunteer, or be urged, to participate. Convention prostitutes may also be call girls, and those who perform or exhibit often have a pimp, who acts very much like a booking agent.

The highest echelon of the stratification system is the call girl, whom Harold Greenwald calls "the elegant prostitute."[15] She does not work the streets or out of a seedy hotel but out of a plush apartment, and her pimp is often a business manager in the junior executive image. Because her customers are middle-to-upper class, her prices are high, and her prospective clientele is screened, she cannot be said to be indiscriminate for not "all" males are welcome. Solicitation is often by telephone. New customers are found, and new customers locate her, by word of mouth and reference. It is widely believed that many corporations and such government agencies as the State Department and the CIA utilize the services of call girls at conventions and conferences, for visiting diplomats, informants, customers and personnel, particularly if the visitor is a purchasing agent for a governmental agency or for a large company, or one whose cooperation or support may be deemed valuable. It is widely rumored, although this claim is not subject to verification, that many governments have such women as well as young men available for visiting diplomats and dignitaries. Occasionally situations like these erupt into major scandals. In the *Profumo* case in England, the issue was possible espionage: one of the girls in the prostitution ring was known to have had an involvement with a Russian diplomat, and the use of prostitutes for such purposes has a long history. In Elizabeth Ray's case in the United States, at issue was the illegal use of government funds to keep a mistress on the payroll for government work that she claimed she was not performing, a violation that appears to be acceptable when the congressman has a wife, sister, nephew, or niece collecting a government check but impermissible when the woman is a mistress and hence an implication of prostitution surrounds the relationship. These important instances notwithstanding, much of the scandal may be traced to the inclination of journalists to write about, and the public to read about, the debauchery of the rich, the powerful, and the lordly. In the subterranean world of international intelligence activity, it is not unknown to have male or female sex partners provided, and then have subsequent activity photographed.

In addition to the various types of prostitutes, there are those who, while not selling their own sex services, are engaged in one way or another in the occupation.[16] There are probably few madams, or women managing brothels, left in the United States if for no other reason than that in most jurisdictions (certain counties of Nevada excepted), brothels themselves are no longer common. Today the major category living off the services of the prostitute is the pimp, and in New York, as well as in many other states, the punishment for pimping is much more severe than that for prostitution (although few are arrested and prosecuted). Until recent years, the pimp was almost always male and white; later, black and Hispanic males and white and black females, often lesbian, entered the field. The pimp generally has more than one woman working in his stable. Some commentators have taken a rather positive view of the role of the pimp, emphasizing that he offers the prostitute protection, is quick to find lawyers and bail money in case of her arrest, recruits clients, arranges abortions, and in other ways handles necessary matters for her. The truth, to the extent that a generalization can be made, is hardly so rosy. The pimp has sometimes recruited, coerced or enticed the woman into the field; insists that she work long hours to bring in a minimum amount of money; protects her from outside assaults but is himself brutal to her; and, if he supplies her with narcotics, is also partly or entirely responsible for her addiction. For streetwalkers, he does no recruiting of customers, but it is said that for bar and call girls, these business managers often work to drum up business. For all of this, the pimp is well paid, taking a considerable share of the prostitute's earnings. Those who have worked toward decriminalization of prostitution have not proposed that pimping be made into a legal occupation.[17] Living off the proceeds of prostitution or, worse, coercing a wife or daughter to engage in prostitution for one's own profit, excites little sympathy even among those who find it possible to rationalize, explain, and understand the perpetrators of very serious crimes.

The Law and the Process of Arrest

Prostitution, as we have noted, is illegal in all states of the United States except Nevada, which permits county autonomy and which as a result has legal houses of prostitution (but not legal solicitation in public and semipublic places) in several counties.* Other than this Nevada situation, there are many variations in the legal definitions of the act, the efforts at enforcement, the courtroom procedures, the allowable and actual sentences, and the types of law under which the prostitute, customer, pimp, madam, or some other associated person can be arrested.

PATRONIZING THE PROSTITUTE

Although patronizing a prostitute is illegal in many states, arrests on this charge are relatively rare. In New York State, the law is very specific.

A person is guilty of patronizing a prostitute when:

1. Pursuant to a prior understanding, he pays a fee to another person as compensation for such person or a third person having engaged in sexual conduct with him; or

2. He pays or agrees to pay a fee to another person pursuant to an understanding that in return therefor such a person or a third person will engage in sexual conduct with him; or

3. He solicits or requests another person to engage in such conduct with him in return for a fee.[18]

---

* New York State and many other states have defined "public place." For the definition of the American Law Institute, see page 122.

In New York, patronizing a prostitute is a violation (that is, an offense lesser in penalty than a misdemeanor). It is a relatively new provision of the New York law, but it is found in the Model Penal Code of the American Law Institute. In a commentary on the New York law, the reasoning behind the law is given: namely, that it is unjust to penalize the prostitute and not the patron and that such legislation will help curtail prostitution and venereal disease.

The New York law notwithstanding, there are many states in which patronizing the prostitute is not illegal, which may well be a result of the fact that legislators are mainly males. However, this situation may reflect the ambivalent attitude of members of society (particularly males) toward prostitution: it is not the act that is reviled but rather the woman who participates in it. Kingsley Davis suggested that prostitution is functional for the family and for a family-oriented society in that it offers the male (presumably in need of, or having the desire for, a variety of partners) outlets that are nonaffectional and not threatening to the continuity of his relationship with his spouse.[19] In all-male circles, confessions (or perhaps boasts) of encounters with prostitutes are often recounted without hesitation or shame; on television, male customers have often shown no reluctance to be interviewed as they entered or left a "massage parlor."

The stigma of prostitution, harassment, and arrest appears to be the domain solely of the woman. A few ex-prostitutes admit their activities, but this is usually because they can capitalize on their past by making public appearances or writing books.[20] There does not seem to have been a "coming out of the closet" even among former prostitutes, and the few sociologists who have done participant-observation work with such women have been participant-observers, not participants-as-observers (i.e., they were not prostitutes while observing, but only observers). By contrast, however, is the somewhat recent phenomenon of the emergence of national or local unions of prostitutes, possibly inspired by the decriminalization movement or the women's liberation movement; these unions have surfaced in the United States, England, France, and Japan, and one held a national convention in a major New York hotel.

Another reason that arrests of male patrons are infrequent is that it is difficult to apprehend a male without the use of policewomen as decoys. In Detroit, a policewoman assigned to such a task found it distasteful and insisted that it was degrading to her to pretend to be a prostitute even in the course of duty. In Salt Lake

City, civilian women have been hired for this purpose, much to the dismay of some men (including a member of Congress) who have been entrapped, and also to the dismay of some prostitutes whose business in solicitation has declined precipitously. There is no evidence of strong public or judicial support for decoys or other persons in plainclothes acting to apprehend either prostitutes or patrons at a time when crime rates are high and there is an outcry for the deployment of police personnel for the arrest of muggers, rapists, and other serious criminals.

LOITERING AND THE LAW

Laws against prostitution are directed mainly against loiterers and hence streetwalkers (there are of course special provisions against forcing women into prostitution, having prostitutive relationships with very young persons, living off the proceeds of prostitution, maintaining a "disorderly house," and pimping). One of the most stringent laws against loitering for the purpose of engaging in prostitution was passed in New York in 1976, just in time to take effect when the Democratic National Convention was gathering in that city to nominate a presidential candidate. The new law, entitled "Loitering for the purpose of engaging in prostitution offense," reads as follows:

1. For the purposes of this section, "public place" means any street, sidewalk, bridge, alley or alleyway, plaza, park, driveway, parking lot or transportation facility or the doorways and entranceways to any building which fronts on any of the aforesaid places, or a motor vehicle in or on any such place.

2. Any person who remains or wanders about in a public place and repeatedly beckons to, or repeatedly stops, or repeatedly attempts to stop, or repeatedly attempts to engage passers-by in conversation, or repeatedly stops or attempts to stop motor vehicles, or repeatedly interferes with the free passage of other persons, for the purpose of prostitution, or of patronizing a prostitute as those terms are defined in article 230 of the penal law, shall be guilty of a violation and is guilty of a class B misdemeanor if such person has been convicted of a violation of this section or of section 230.00 or 230.05 of the penal law.*

3. Any person who remains or wanders about in a public

---

* Section 230.00, defining the prostitute, and section 230.05, the patron, are the basic laws which the quoted statute on loitering was intended to amend.

place and repeatedly beckons to, or repeatedly stops, or repeatedly attempts to stop, or repeatedly attempts to engage
passers-by in conversation, or repeatedly stops or attempts to
stop motor vehicles, or repeatedly interferes with the free
passage of other persons, for the purpose of promoting prostitution as defined in article 230 of the penal law is guilty of a
class A misdemeanor.[21]

In a New York City Police Department memorandum on this
law, police were instructed to fingerprint all persons arrested. The
police department issued the following guidelines for arrests:

To preserve the integrity of this new statute in the face [of]
court tests, it is important that arrests for loitering for the
purposes of prostitution, patronizing a prostitute or promoting
prostitution be based on substantial facts which indicate probable cause. In order to be sure this probable cause exists, the
following points should be noted:

(1) There must be at least *two* incidents observed involving beckoning, stopping or attempted stopping of passersby or
motor vehicles. An attempt should be made to have as many
specific observations as possible.

(2) You should indicate a pattern of activity by the defendant which points to the commission of the crime, i.e., prostitution, patronizing a prostitute or promoting prostitution:

   a. You had the defendant under observation for a rea-
      sonable period of time. Specify the time, e.g., from
      0115 hours to 0130 hours.
   b. The location. Is it a place where prostitutes are
      known to hang out or where there have been many
      arrests in the past month, six months or year?
   c. Was she/he seen in conversation with various men/
      women or seen approaching and leaning into auto-
      mobiles to converse with men/women? Obtain times
      when she/he was observed in conversation, the num-
      ber of men/women she/he approached and/or the
      license plate and description of autos involved. Did
      you hear her/him make any propositions? If so, what
      were her/his exact words?
   d. If possible, speak to the people who were stopped,
      etc., and find out what was said to them. Also, if
      possible obtain their names and addresses as possible
      witnesses.
   e. Was she/he seen in conversation or associating with
      known prostitutes or pimps?

     f. Is the person a known prostitute, pimp or john?

     g. Does her/his general deportment indicate to the arresting officer that she/he is probably engaged in illegal activities?

     h. Observations involving pimps should show connection between the pimp, the passerby or motorist and the prostitute, e.g., a suspected pimp stopping and speaking to motorists and beckoning or calling a suspected prostitute to the vehicle in question. Again, more than one observation is required.

(3) You should keep a detailed written account of all observations from start to finish in order [to] assist you when required to testify.[22]

Many have questioned the priorities that bring about a deployment of police personnel for such purposes as this. Others have noted that visitors from out of town, people seeking directions or looking for a taxi, sightseeing conventioneers, for instance, could be arrested under the loitering law and the accompanying guidelines, particularly if the law were to be enforced against males as well as females. Aside from its questionable constitutionality and the problem of protecting the civil liberties of those who walk, wander, gaze, and loiter, there are two further problems: such a law can result in the arrest, fingerprinting, and general humiliation of a lonesome male seeking to meet a willing female for sexual purposes but without any intention of paying or being paid (known as "cruising" for a pickup); and the crackdown is directed only against the street prostitute, usually of a lower social class than the call girl.

Not that the call girl is completely free from the attention of the law. But she is often allowed to function without harassment and constant conflict with the law and sometimes, it is said, with the protection of corrupt law enforcement personnel. She comes to public attention and into conflict with the law, if at all, usually upon complaint of neighbors who do not relish the traffic of strange men and women entering and leaving at all hours of the night. Occasionally police vice squads conduct visual and electronic surveillance of call girl establishments, attempt to insinuate undercover officers as customers, make payments to building maintenance personnel for information and in general exhibit a degree of investigative perseverance and technical skill that some believe might be far better devoted to the apprehension of dangerous criminals. For all their time, energy, and expense, the police officers see a criminal court judge impose a nominal fine and probation, and the call girl operation resumes very quickly in the same or similar plush location.

One of the responses of civil libertarians, feminists, and other opponents of the antiprostitution drive in New York was a campaign in which women pretended to be prostitutes in order to lure the police into making arrests and then threatened the city with lawsuits on the grounds of false arrest, defamation of character, humiliation, and various other forms of suffering. Women dressed in what has come to be a "hooker's uniform" would stand suspiciously on street corners, ogle men passing by, pretend to be making approaches to strange men, and in other ways behave in a manner designed to give the impression that they were soliciting. The police claim that the ploy did not work, the disguise was transparent, and that the prostitutes actually arrested were well known to them.

While the activities of the women attempting to invite false arrest point up the danger of antiloitering laws, in which innocent persons can be drawn into a police net (particularly black women and especially black women meeting or accompanying white boyfriends), many legal and ethical problems are aggravated by such methods. Not uncommonly, dishonest persons have attempted to be arrested in order to gain the benefits of a false arrest suit or monetary settlement (not rare when someone pretends to be shoplifting). If such behavior is not itself criminal, it is ethically suspect and involves entrapment, which is as reprehensible when conducted by citizens' groups against the police as the reverse. Such tactics, too, might well boomerang. One would need strong faith in the American criminal justice system and in one's own ability to cope with its complexities to be certain that playacting as a prostitute did not result in an actual conviction and sentence under the law.

PROSTITUTION ARRESTS: NATIONAL DATA

Arrests do occur for prostitution although they are often a better reflection of the pressures on police than the extent of this activity. In 1975, according to the *Uniform Crime Reports*, 50,229 persons were arrested in the United States for crimes in a category called "prostitution and commercialized vice," of whom about one-fourth were males.[23] There is no information of a reliable nature on who these males were and what charges were made against them; one can only conjecture that they included male homosexual prostitutes, their clients, a few (but very few) clients of female prostitutes, some pimps, some procurers (men soliciting on behalf of women), men recruiting women into prostitution (particularly in violation of the Mann Act), some hotel owners and brothel owners and employees catering to and facilitating the acts of prostitute and client, and, finally, men engaged in the manufacture, distribution, and sale of pornography. This is a catchall figure, which leaves the number of arrests of females at about 35,000. It can be assumed that almost all of these were prostitutes, and the overwhelming majority, streetwalkers. This point is brought out in an article on the economic impact of crime, in which the Task Force on Assessment, part of the President's Commission on Law Enforcement and Administration of Justice, reported:

> This illegal service [prostitution] was once an important source of revenue for organized crime. Changes in society and law enforcement techniques, however, have rendered it much less profitable, and today organized crime is no longer interested to the extent that it was formerly. Although diminished, commercialized vice has not disappeared from the scene. In 1965 there were an estimated 37,000 arrests nationally, male and female, for prostitution and commercialized vice. These arrests touch mainly the most obvious cases. Expensive call girls are rarely arrested. Like arrests for gambling and other illegal goods and services, it is clear that the arrest figures understate the number of persons involved in prostitution. If it were assumed that the total number of persons associated with prostitution and commercialized vice were about 45,000 and that the average annual income was around $5,000 the total would be about $225 million. It is not clear how much of this would wind up in the hands of organized crime.[24]

Prostitution and Concomitant Crime

In and of itself, prostitution is often considered a matter of personal morality, something that should not be regulated by legislation or punished by law. However, the nature of prostitution as a marginal occupation, the secrecy and anonymity surrounding not only the prostitute but her customer, and the hostile social climate in which the act takes place all create a situation in which crime and other antisocial transactions may thrive.

Criminality involving prostitutes falls into three major categories: crimes by the prostitutes (or their pimps, madams, and conspirators) against would-be or actual customers; crimes by the customers, real or pretended, against the prostitutes; and crimes by police officers against the prostitutes, on rare occasions against the customers, and in many instances against "the public." There is also the negative economic and social impact of prostitution and its related pathologies on the viability of neighborhoods and on commercial enterprises.

CRIMES BY PROSTITUTES

Of crimes by prostitutes, robbery, assault, and rolling are the most frequent. One need not be intoxicated to be victimized. It is reported that at one time special closets were built in prostitutes' rooms so that after a man had hung up his clothes, shut the closet door, and was deeply occupied with other matters, another door leading to the same closet could be opened from an adjoining room and money and various valuables removed.[25] Old-fashioned brothels, depending as they did on repeat business and a "good reputation," provided some element of protection against this type of crime. More prevalent today is surreptitious or direct theft by the prostitute or assault or threatened assault by her pimp.

Prostitutes, their colleagues, and their co-workers have blackmailed customers who did not wish it to become known to family and others that they were patrons. However, ordinary streetwalkers, themselves anonymous, difficult to locate, and, if found, hard to prosecute for blackmail, have been more likely to rob customers.

Customers have also been known to pass money on to a steerer or pimp who was to make arrangements with a prostitute, only to be left impatient and angry while the pimp disappeared with the money. When such matters are reported to the police, the customer often pretends it was for another purpose that he paid in advance and in cash for services not rendered, but the facts are usually apparent. More frequently, such swindles are not reported. This is an example of "short con" or "little con" and may not involve an actual prostitute at all.

THE PROSTITUTE AS VICTIM

The victimization of deviant people has often been noted: they are stigmatized, discriminated against, and sometimes considered "fair pickings" for extortion, rolling (in the case of alcoholics), blackmail, and other crimes.* The prostitute has not been an excep-

---

* This problem is discussed in greater detail in Chapter 5 in the section on the victimization of homosexuals (pp. 156–160). Much but not all of the material in that section is applicable to prostitutes as well.

tion. Prostitutes have been assaulted in the course of their work, some have been badly beaten, and many have been murdered. Furthermore, a reputation as a prostitute, even when undeserved, has served to diminish the restraints on some men and has given them the excuse, justification, or rationalization for demanding sexual favors, even to the point of committing forcible rape.[26] In other instances, prostitutes have not been paid for their services, and in some cases they have been robbed of what other money and belongings they might have had. At one time, the social organization of prostitutes through brothels, madams, and others served as protection against this type of victimization; more recently, the pimp plays a similar role in exchange for a considerable percentage of the prostitute's earnings.

The prostitute is seldom subject to blackmail. Her anonymity, alienation from family, failure to hold down any other job of significance (with some exceptions), have made her immune to this type of exploitation, and there have been few cases of blackmail of ex-prostitutes because of a threat of revelation of their past. However, bribery, extortion, and shakedowns undoubtedly play a big part in the life, and take out a considerable portion of the earnings, of prostitutes, at least in some cities. This type of payoff is seldom demanded by policemen in uniform, and hence it is difficult to know how much of it goes to men pretending to be police officers and how much to corrupt members of the force.

Life is precarious for the prostitute because her activity is both illegal and stigmatized. Thus, the call girl is harassed by hostile neighbors, who see her occupancy as a threat to their safety and their real estate values. The street girl is chased from corners by police or by local businessmen. Because she is a prostitute, she has little standing and influence before the law. Because she is stigmatized, she can seldom turn to family or counseling services for aid.

In the 1960s and 1970s, victimization took on another form, with the wide introduction of narcotics to prostitutes.[27] It is likely that some female addicts turned to prostitution to support what had become an expensive habit, but it is also true that some women already involved with selling sex were deliberately made addicts by co-workers and particularly by pimps, who saw this as a further means of exercising control over them.

Finally, there is the matter of extreme victimization in the form of forced prostitution. Although it is our belief that this situation is largely a matter of the past, it is by no means unknown today.

The Problem of White Slavery

The term "white slavery" seems originally to have referred to Western European girls (English, Irish, French, German) who were kidnapped or enticed by offers of jobs as entertainers and transported to the Orient, the Middle East, and North Africa to serve as prostitutes in local brothels.[28] White slavery now refers specifically to compelling women—their color is irrelevant—to be prostitutes.* In the United States, particularly in the nineteenth and early years of the twentieth centuries, poor girls from the coal fields of Appalachia and Pennsylvania were recruited by procurers ("cadets") for similar purposes and brought to New York, San Francisco, New Orleans, and other port cities. There was traditionally no trading in black girls and probably little in boys.†

In the eighteenth and nineteenth centuries, there were widespread rumors that girls were held in brothels against their will, unable to communicate with anyone except customers, who were unlikely to report this crime to the authorities.[29] Often they were imprisoned with the connivance and knowledge of police and other local officials. It is said that some of these girls had been abducted and sold, but it is difficult to confirm such statements. However, the selling of children into prostitution by impoverished parents (in eighteenth- and nineteenth-century England, for example, and in Naples during World War II) has been documented. Other children—runaways, war orphans—drifted into a slavelike prostitution. Earlier in European history, white slavery was probably the fate of thousands of those who rallied to the banner of the children's crusades.

In addition to abduction and sale, contracts or promises of contracts for entertainment careers in foreign countries have been used to lure girls abroad. Once there, the girls find that there is no contract, no fee; they are penniless, held in a hotel room to which men make visits for sexual purposes. The girl is confined to her room, meals are brought to her, and the customers are not interested in

---

* Because all the victims of this practice at certain periods were not white and because some white persons have been literally enslaved (not in the sexual sense of the word), the term "sex slavery" has been coined and is used by the United Nations and by others, but "white slavery" continues to be spoken of in the popular press.

† The controversy over white slavery has focused almost entirely on female victims. The possibility of there being traffic in boys is discussed in Chaper 5 in the section dealing with homosexual prostitution (p. 147).

her tale of woe (even if she is able to communicate with them across the language barrier). If she does confide in someone, she may find herself yet more maltreated—because her confidant informed the master, pimp, or procurer. Even if the girl succeeds in leaving her room or the premises, she has no place to go, no money for food or transportation, no passport or evidence of identity. After her experience, she often does not wish to return to parents and friends because she defines herself as good for no man except as a prostitute.

In a scholarly study published in 1914, Abraham Flexner contended that white slavery had once flourished but had declined, particularly in Europe.

> Beyond question, an innocent girl might be entrapped, enticed, and immured in a European brothel; but if so, the instances would be an isolated crime, like a mysterious murder or robbery. Under existing conditions, there is absolutely no reason to think that such cases occur frequently, though there are those who would be quick to take advantage of any relaxation of vigilance. . . . On the other hand, there is evidence to suggest that European cities and ports are utilized for purposes of transit to South American ports where the trade still flourishes.[30]

Later, the matter of "trafficking in persons" held the attention first of the League of Nations and then the United Nations. In fact, prior to the formation of the League, there was an International Agreement for the Suppression of the White Slave Traffic in 1904; [31] six years later, an international convention for the achievement of the same goal.[32] The documents coming out of these meetings, however, must be read carefully for their intent reaches far beyond their titles. They demand the punishment of anyone who hires for immoral purposes a female under the age of twenty, even with her consent. In 1921, the League of Nations called the International Convention for the Suppression of the Traffic in Women and Children, which extended the legal age of consent to twenty-one, and also for the first time recommended that its restrictions apply to minors of both sexes.

In 1959, the United Nations, continuing the work of the League, published its *Study of Traffic in Persons and Prostitution*. While this document repeated many former statements against white slave traffic, it concluded, among other things, "that there is reason to believe that in many countries today the prostitute is a freer person [than formerly], less regimented and in general less subject to coercion." [33] In still another document, no evidence that traffic in women was a reality was revealed by a United Nations study.[34] It is possible, of course, that diplomatic considerations made it difficult for such an international body to name countries, places, and incidents. Instead, it may have been necessary to discuss these matters in generalities and simply express pious hopes that whatever evil existed would be eradicated. Furthermore, the United Nations, by its nature, must restrict its studies primarily to traffic crossing national borders. At the Mexico City International Women's Conference, a delegate from UNESCO charged that girls "are virtually imprisoned in brothels . . . in rich, poor and very poor countries" but when asked to name where said, "We don't know." [35]

WHITE SLAVERY IN CONTEMPORARY AMERICA

In the United States, it is most unlikely that more than a handful of women are being held involuntarily in a sexual relationship that can be described as prostitution and servitude. However, under the Mann Act (also known as the Federal White Slave Act), it is illegal to cross a state border with a woman not one's wife, or to arrange for and facilitate the crossing of the border by such a woman, for the purpose of engaging in what is called immoral behavior. At times the law has been invoked against a man whose companion was not his wife but a woman affectionately involved with him, and such an anachronism serves only to show the dangers of legislation against victimless behavior. But even if the male were "transporting" the woman for the purpose of having her engage in prostitution, this activity would not be white slavery unless she were being abducted or coerced. Furthermore, the "state line" is socially irrelevant and was made part of the law so that the federal government could enter a situation that is constitutionally the prerogative of the state. The Mann Act has also been invoked at times as a basis for the blackmail of male drivers who picked up hitchhikers at tunnels and bridges leading from New York to New Jersey. In addition, prosecutions under this law have been used to punish offenders suspected of more serious crimes, for which law enforcement agencies were unable to develop a strong enough case for conviction, or even in some instances for indictment.

Nevertheless, individual stories do turn up from time to time that appear to go beyond enticement into prostitution and involve actual capture. The American war in Vietnam led to an occasional newspaper story suggesting true sex slavery and not the volunteer prostitution so widely discussed in the American press, which appeared to have been common and open in Saigon.

THE EVIDENCE FOR WHITE SLAVERY

The matter of determining to what extent white slavery is a false issue raised by crusaders against prostitution is complicated by rumors of abduction that have been frequently linked with titillating fantasies and also with anti-Semitism and other forms of racism.[36] Nevertheless, some take a skeptical view of the position that white slavery is negligible in the contemporary world. Sean O'Callaghan and Stephen Barlay,[37] both journalists, have written books filled with harrowing tales that might well be true, but there is little or no evidence to substantiate their charges. Here and there one finds a case that has come to court or a newspaper story that names names. Barlay's work, although compiled with the cooperation and assistance of the Anti-Slavery Society for the Protection of Human Rights, has been denounced by a United Nations delegate from one of the countries named as ill-founded and malicious. Like others, Barlay tells of dance contracts as well as physical abduction but states that sex slavery in its classic forms is slowly disappearing under international pressure.[38]

A study conducted by the International Criminal Police Organization (Interpol) dealt in part with the international traffic in women under the cover of employment exposing them to prostitution. A number of instances were recorded, including the enticement of Canadian girls into the United States for work as nightclub hostesses. Although these women were compelled to perform in a manner that they had not expected and that was not in accordance with their wishes, the actions stopped somewhat short, according to Interpol, of prostitution. Instead, Interpol charged the existence of a conspiracy among the representatives of certain theatrical agencies in Canada, certain theatrical unions, and the underworld of organized crime.[39]

A NECESSARY DISTINCTION

Many women (and a few males) are held in prostitution by ties to others, by dependence on drugs, by lack of other opportunities, by feelings of worthlessness, by unresolved emotional problems, even by threats from pimps, usurers, and madams; still, their activities are sufficiently voluntary to distinguish these individuals from the sex slaves who are held captive. That some instances of white slavery exist is undisputed. However, most prostitution can be better understood as not involving sex slavery, and most involuntary servitude can best be understood as not involving prostitution. If the two are confused, if prostitutes are generally thought of as white slaves, then no understanding of either phenomenon, prostitution or slavery, can be expected.

Legal and Social Policy

It is a cliché that prostitution is "the world's oldest profession." Aside from the objection of some sociologists that it does not qualify as a profession, the expression does attest to the antiquity of prostitution and suggest that legal and social efforts to eradicate it will no doubt end in failure.

That prostitution is strongly condemned by large numbers of people in the United States one can hardly deny. If prostitution itself is not denigrated, then at least the prostitute is. However, T. C. Esselstyn finds that public outcry has diminished and is directed mainly against open solicitation.[40] The days of the moral crusades seem, at least for the moment, to be over. Nonetheless, Esselstyn finds that although few people are dedicated to a cause of saving "fallen women," prostitution is definitely being discouraged, and the prostitute herself is seen as someone who ought better to be rehabilitated. The reason for the hostility to prostitution, he points out, is that society "senses the seeds of social collapse in promiscuous, commercialized, and uncontrolled sexual congress" and as a result develops "a folk wisdom [that] commands that no one should make love for money. . . . All other arguments [against prostitution]—vice, crime, disease, white slavery—are important, but actually they are disguises." [41] Exempt from the ignominy heaped upon the prostitute is the female who marries solely or principally for money or social status. Evidently, marriage legalizes, institutionalizes, and even sanctifies her action; although, of course, marriage removes the promiscuity and indiscriminate nature of sexuality that is a hallmark of prostitution. However, to return to the statement of Esselstyn, a woman is allowed to "make love for money" so long as it is not in the form of "promiscuous, commercialized, and uncontrolled sexual congress."

Prostitution has not always been illegal, nor has it always been condemned. In addition to being seen as providing stability to the family (the argument of Kingsley Davis, which in fact goes back to St. Augustine), the prostitute has been a courtesan in some societies, a religious person (called the temple prostitute) in others.[42] However, it is difficult to compare such women and the settings in which their acts occurred with the indiscriminate women involved in commercialized sex in industrialized and urban societies. However, there are many countries where various forms of prostitution are legal, licensed, taxed, and even encouraged.

Although almost all Western cultures have condemned prostitution and the prostitute, relegating the woman to an outcast status, calling her a whore and the act "the vice," some have attempted to suppress it, others to regulate it, others to be tolerant and permissive without offering approval. The debate over the best stance toward prostitution, particularly in American society, continues. This debate involves not only such matters as concomitant criminality and enforceability of the law but social, public health and legal policy affecting a considerable number of people directly and indirectly.

Charles Winick, who studied the prostitution scene in America during the late 1960s and early 1970s, suggests that at any one time there are approximately a third of a million women in the United States who earn all or most of their money from prostitution.[43] Some prostitutes may hold other jobs as well (modeling, entertainment, and restaurant work are said to predominate); and some undoubtedly are involved in marginal and illegal activities such as drug dealing. Newspaper reports frequently refer to girls as young as ten or eleven years of age walking the streets in search of men who will pay them for sex, but arrest statistics and other reports indicate that this situation is relatively rare. Whether common or not, child prostitution poses another problem for sex and the law, that of adult-child sexuality, and a suppressive attitude toward child prostitutes and their customers is not incompatible with a permissive one toward adult consensual prostitution.

The clients of prostitutes have been studied only on rare occasions; perhaps the best known research is an investigation by Winick, who found that clients derive many symbolic and emotional gratifications from prostitutes, in addition to a physical release.[44] Kinsey and his colleagues found that "about 69 percent of the total white male population ultimately has some experience with prostitutes." [45] However, many of these men have only one or two such experiences, while others visit prostitutes quite frequently. With so many males indulging at least on one or two occasions (and the percentage is undoubtedly large even if one discounts the figures to allow for the exaggerations and errors in the work of Kinsey), it is little wonder that the male customer is seldom condemned.

It can be said that like many other so-called victimless crimes prostitution exists because there is a market sufficiently strong that offers will be made to tempt people into the act or the career. The heterosexual market (the customers, or johns) is varied: single men without regular sexual outlets or singles unable to find an outlet readily or unwilling to devote the time and attention necessary to obtain affectional sexual gratification; some who believe in the double standard and in the concept of good and bad girls, who do not court a good girl for the purpose of sex, and who find the professional prostitute naturally equipped to gratify "the devil in the flesh"; married men who seek a variety of partners and who prefer nonaffectional sex so that no involvement or entanglement develops; men desiring the excitement of interracial sex; men who need to pay for sex in order to obtain gratification (a small and little studied group); and, finally, a group believed by some to be a most important category, men who seek a type of sex that they cannot obtain or would not request from a wife or girlfriend. In addition, and not to be overlooked, there are members of the military, both married and single, far from home and from women other than prostitutes; and others whose work involves considerable absence from home. Also of interest is the fact that in many countries a young man's introduction to sex is more frequently with a woman in a house of prostitution than with a female peer. Thus, the motivations of men are diverse; they may vary with race, social class, occupation, age, and other factors.

In looking at motivations, one may note that prostitution seems to be flourishing although the changing sex mores, it would have been expected, might have diminished the demand. The "good girl/bad girl" dichotomy is made less although it has not disappeared. Research indicates that by the 1970s, premarital or nonmarital sex among young people affectionately involved with each other seemed to have increased and to have become almost taken for granted.[46] Noncoital sex, which Ned Polsky emphasized as a major factor accounting for men's going to prostitutes,[47] is more frequent in marital and affectional relationships than before and is being taught and urged by many marriage and sex counselors where once it was denounced. Even practitioners of sadomasochism, flagellation, and other such activities can be located in most of the larger cities of the United States through bars and other social gathering places; thus, seekers after this type of sex can hardly account for more than a very small proportion of prostitutes' customers.

One returns to the contention of Kingsley Davis that males presumably seek a variety of outlets, including those that do not constitute a threat to their family and other affectional relationships.[48] If indeed this is the explanation for prostitution, then one confronts the question of whether there is any justification for its continuation in a modern society in which the equality of the sexes has become a major goal. For prostitution offers the male a degree of sexual license not offered to his spouse, and the protection given to the wife is at the expense of her toleration of his sexual liberties. In a sense, she purchases continued support from her husband because she is not his equal as breadwinner. Furthermore, women (or girls) may be drawn to prostitution because they can thus earn more money than other jobs promise.

This is the same enticement that is used to lure people into any field for which there is a need in the economy, but at the same time those who fill this need are reviled, stigmatized, and held up as examples of degradation.

One of the arguments of social hygienists and moral crusaders against prostitution is that it spreads venereal disease. One might expect this assertion to be true, but investigations have failed to verify it.[49] With the high incidence of venereal disease in the United States and in many other parts of the world since World War II, experts estimate that not more than 5 percent, and possibly less, can be traced to heterosexual prostitution. This is because the prostitute is probably highly adept at taking measures that by reasons of hygiene, cleanliness, and prophylaxis make her a far less likely target than an amateur promiscuous female or a promiscuous male involved in homosexual relations.

The brothel has virtually disappeared, the red light district is virtually unknown, but some people see a greater social problem, linked to urban decay, in the appearance of massage parlors, health clubs, and other fronts for houses of prostitution. While many observers insist that these businesses do no harm to anyone and that both employees and customers are willing participants (furthermore, that they are a boon in that they attract tourists), others contend that they lure marginal characters, foster concomitant crime, repel as many or more tourists than they bring, and accelerate the decline of urban areas. It has sometimes been suggested that businesses of this kind, and those that sell pornographic material and offer pornographic performances, should be restricted to one area of a city. In fact, many cities have streets or areas known under such revelatory names as "sin strip," "skin alley," or "the combat zone." Civil libertarians may question whether this type of zoning is legal, although a Detroit zoning ordinance has been upheld by the courts, and New York has proposed similar legislation. In fact, residents and businessmen often do not object until they learn that it is their area that has been set aside for this purpose. The problem remains debated and unresolved.

THE PROPOSED MODEL PENAL CODE

The Model Penal Code of the American Law Institute has a section dealing with prostitution. This act is not grouped with sexual offenses (forcible sex, corruption of minors, indecent exposure) or with offenses against the family (polygamy, incest, abortion) but rather it is part of a category called "public indecency," itself part of a larger class of crimes labeled "offenses against public order and decency." Public indecency consists of open lewdness, prostitution and related offenses, loitering to solicit deviant sexual relations, and obscenity. The proposals of the American Law Institute with regard to prostitution and related offenses read as follows:

Section 251.2 Prostitution and Related Offenses.
(1) *Prostitution.* A person is guilty of prostitution, a petty misdemeanor, if he or she:
    (a) is an inmate of a house of prostitution or otherwise engages in sexual activity as a business; or
    (b) loiters in or within view of any public place for the purposes of being hired to engage in sexual activity.
"Sexual activity" includes homosexual and other deviate sexual relations. A "house of prostitution" is any place where prostitution or promotion of prostitution is regularly carried on by one person under the control, management or supervision of another. An "inmate" is a person who engages in prostitution in or through the agency of a house of prostitution. "Public place" means any place to which the public or any substantial group thereof has access.
(2) *Promoting Prostitution.* A person who knowingly promotes

prostitution of another commits a misdemeanor or felony as provided in Subsection (3). The following acts shall, without limitation of the foregoing, constitute promoting prostitution:

(a) owning, controlling, managing supervising, or otherwise keeping, alone or in association with others, a house of prostitution or a prostitution business; or

(b) procuring an inmate for a house of prostitution or a place in a house of prostitution for one who would be an inmate; or

(c) encouraging, inducing, or otherwise purposely causing another to become or remain a prostitute; or

(d) soliciting a person to patronize a prostitute; or

(e) procuring a prostitute for a patron; or

(f) transporting a person into or within this state with purpose to promote that person's engaging in prostitution, or procuring or paying for transportation with that purpose; or

(g) leasing or otherwise permitting a place controlled by the actor, alone or in association with others, to be regularly used for prostitution or the promotion of prostitution, or failure to make reasonable effort to abate such use by ejecting the tenant, notifying law enforcement authorities, or other legally available means; or

(h) soliciting, receiving, or agreeing to receive any benefit for doing or agreeing to do anything forbidden by this Subsection.

(3) *Grading of Offenses Under Subsection (2).* An offense under Subsection (2) constitutes a felony of the third degree if:

(a) the offense falls within paragraph (a), (b) or (c) of Subsection (2); or

(b) the actor compels another to engage in or promote prostitution; or

(c) the actor promotes prostitution of a child under 16, whether or not he is aware of the child's age; or

(d) the actor promotes prostitution of his wife, child, ward or any person for whose care, protection or support he is responsible.

Otherwise the offense is a misdemeanor.

(4) *Presumption from Living off Prostitutes.* A person, other than the prostitute or the prostitute's minor child or other legal dependent incapable of self-support, who is supported in whole or substantial part by the proceeds of prostitution is presumed to be knowingly promoting prostitution in violation of Subsection (2).

(5) *Patronizing Prostitutes.* A person commits a violation if he hires a prostitute to engage in sexual activity with him, or if he

enters or remains in a house of prostitution for the purpose of engaging in sexual activity.

(6) *Evidence*. On the issue whether a place is a house of prostitution the following shall be admissible evidence: its general repute; the repute of the persons who reside in or frequent the place; the frequency, timing and duration of visits by non-residents. Testimony of a person against his spouse shall be admissible to prove offenses under this Section.[50]

It is interesting to note that the act of prostitution itself is reduced in the Model Penal Code to a petty misdemeanor, which carries a maximum sentence of thirty days, except in special cases such as those of persistent offenders. Furthermore, the definition of prostitution offered has essentially two aspects: engaging in sexual activity as a business; and loitering (which is equivalent to streetwalking) for the purpose of finding a partner who will pay for sexual activity. This definition would appear to exclude entirely the client from culpability; moreover, it might well exclude someone who accepts money, or even seeks it, but not as a regular business and not in a public place. Finally, and most important, the greater penalties are visited upon those who live off the earnings of prostitutes, who promote the occupation, recruit, and procure, rather than upon the women themselves.

The American Law Institute has reported that the proposed law "no longer purports to reach every engagement in sexual activity for hire." [51] However, the proposal leaves dissatisfied proponents of complete decriminalization. Prostitutes, homosexuals, drunks, gamblers—categories that are not meant to be similar in other respects— are, it is contended, at most petty offenders against the social mores. They are the major victims of "revolving door penology": either repeated short sentences that neither deter nor rehabilitate and involve short-term incarcerations that are costly to the taxpayer and a wholly unnecessary burden upon the criminal justice system or the deliberate ignoring of the law, with its occasional unpredictable and capricious invocation, which has social consequences inimical to the society at large.

REGULATION, ABOLITION, DECRIMINALIZATION

What can be done about prostitution other than to condemn it or approve it? The police, it is pointed out, have several alternatives. Prostitution can be ignored while it remains illegal; it would be given sufficient police surveillance to reduce to a minimum the victimization, in a violent crime, of either the prostitute or her client. But this is a policy that gives to the police the judgment of deciding what laws to enforce and how vigorously and has the concomitant evils that always accompany unenforced criminal laws (graft, payoffs, protection, and the like). Alternatively, the police can pursue the eradication of prostitution with the utmost vigor, which would almost certainly drive the prostitutes to a neighboring state, county or even to another part of town and could hardly serve as a model type of expenditure of police effort at a time in American history when "ordinary crime" and "upperworld crime" are rampant. Or the police can harass, with occasional arrests and what amounts to "justice without trial," by holding the accused for several hours or a night, then releasing her without charge (for which she is grateful and makes no complaint unless, as is the case in rare instances, she is an innocent woman, outraged by what has taken place and by the net into which she has been unwittingly drawn). This whole practice of arresting and releasing prostitutes, Wayne LaFave points out, is of doubtful legality: "Most of the arrests [in the state of Michigan, where the study was made] fail to meet the probability of guilt requirements as those are customarily defined." [52] Furthermore, in some states (but not in Michigan), the courts "have said that a release following an arrest otherwise proper makes the arrest and detention illegal." [53] LaFave contends that the harassment policy has resulted in the arrest of black women merely because they were in the company of white men. In this respect, note that the great majority of prostitution arrests in New York City are rejected for prosecution by the offices of the district attorneys. All in all, harassment hardly seems to be the answer, and few would openly endorse it as a matter of public policy.

When prostitution is legal and regulated, as has been the case in many parts of the world at different times, it is said to give a sense of false security to customers and community, particularly insofar as the spread of venereal disease is concerned. In regulated cities, most prostitutes never register; studies made in Paris, Bremen, Hamburg, and elsewhere have found that only about 10 percent of all women regularly walking the streets or in other ways soliciting customers are registered with the police and have a license to pursue their occupation.[54] Where legal red light districts are established, the legal and other problems of dealing with prostitutes who solicit outside the designated areas are little different than the difficulties involved where prostitution is totally illegal.

Why the low percentage of registration? Social stigma makes prostitutes fear being thus officially branded. Moreover, there is reluctance to undergo the compulsory health examination: without a clean bill of health, the woman will be unable to work.

A further argument against registration and regulation is that it gives a stamp of social approval to the commercialized sexual transaction and takes away the onus of transgression, particularly from the young. Finally, it permits the open flaunting of the activity in certain parts of the town, where it is offensive to residents and passersby. The restriction of prostitution to those parts of a city, on the one hand, does not succeed in eliminating prostitutes from other sections; on the other hand, it attracts to the segregated areas a host of undesirables on the fringe of criminal activities. Against the argument that legalized prostitution diminishes forcible rape and other sex crimes, the opponents cite studies conducted in Hawaii and elsewhere demonstrating that rape declined following the illegalization of prostitution. Yet without even a speculative explanation for this fact, it seems hardly more than coincidence or perhaps the result of faulty or misinterpreted statistics.

A proposed alternative to regulation and segregation is abolition. Toward this end a commitment everywhere to suppress prostitution, a moral campaign against it, and a police policy of arresting not only the prostitute but also the customer are required. The history of prostitution abundantly demonstrates the futility of such an approach.

There seems to be a third route—not regulation but decriminalization. It is pointed out that illegal prostitution brings with it police corruption because of the protection, the abortive arrests that are bought off, and the concomitant criminality that would be reported more frequently if prostitution itself were not criminal. Prostitution can be discouraged without being suppressed. Potential participants should be warned of the dangers (as secondary criminality) and offered as many alternatives as possible to make the activity infrequent (education, better employment opportunities for women, a single sexual standard, the building of self-esteem for the woman, and destigmatization of premarital affectional sex). But after this, if two people—the argument for decriminalization goes—of proper age and by mutual consent want to have sex of an impersonal nature, with an exchange of money, let it be.*

---

* Male prostitution, mentioned briefly in this chapter, is discussed more fully in Chapter 5.

5   Homosexuality

The routine arrest of a homosexual in a Dallas restroom last year has wound up in the Supreme Court as a challenge to all state laws making "unnatural sex acts" a crime.*

What is involved in the news item quoted above is a confusion between two distinct but related matters. "Unnatural sex acts" is a vague phrase, in this instance probably referring to fellatio involving two males; it can, however, refer to a variety of other types of sexual contact between two persons of the same or different gender. Although there is a strong movement to decriminalize such activities between consenting adults, the restroom "routine arrest" could still be upheld even if the sex act were legal and the concept and phraseology of "unnatural sex act" were to become an anachronism, for many would contend that such activities, or any other overt sexual behavior, should not be permitted in a public or semi-public place. These are interrelated issues when the subject of homosexuality and the law comes under scrutiny.

The Nature and Incidence of Unlawful Homosexuality

In general, it is easier to define homosexuality than a homosexual, but both definitions have complications. One can say that homosexuality is an erotic act consciously engaged in between two persons of the same sex; that is, body contact or embrace between

* Associated Press dispatch from Washington, D.C., in the *New York Post*, 10 July, 1970.

two males or two females is homosexual if the participants interpret it as such and impute erotic meaning to it. However, on rare occasions, one of the parties may not know the sex of the other (in the case of fellatio performed by an undetected transvestite); or the aggressor-insertor may define the act in his own mind as being homosexuality for the other but not for himself (a mechanism that is used by some prison rapists and some male prostitutes); or there can be borderline instances such as mutual masturbation by two adolescent males, in which the meaning is entirely masturbatory, at least on a conscious level.

As for the term "homosexual," it would seem best to reserve it for people who have a strong and chronic preference (sometimes but not necessarily exclusive) for erotic satisfaction with a partner of the same gender, regardless of the physical nature of the act preferred or accepted by that person. Sagarin has suggested that people would have more freedom to choose their patterns of behavior if they did not label themselves and were not labeled by others as heterosexuals, homosexuals, pedophiles, and the like but thought of these as forms of doing rather than of being.[1]

Homosexuality has become a serious and important part of the study of sexual criminality for several reasons: the number of people involved, the pressure by organized gay liberation, sexual freedom, and other liberal forces to change the law, the numerous concomitant problems (disease, blackmail, extortion, stigmatization, and the victimization of the homosexual by criminals), the high incidence of adult homosexual interest in teenagers, the use of homosexuality as an almost ideal-typical example of victimless crime, and the difficulty in distinguishing between the concept of consenting adults in private and consenting adults in public.

On the number of people engaging in homosexual behavior sporadically or exclusively, a good deal of authority is imputed to the famed statistics of Kinsey and his colleagues, gathered primarily in the 1940s.[2] There is considerable reason to believe that Kinsey came up with exaggeratedly high figures on the incidence of homosexuality among white American males; in fact, Paul Gebhard, his collaborator and later head of the institute that Kinsey founded, has suggested this himself.[3] Nonetheless, Kinsey established at least two points that are relevant to a study of homosexuality and the law: that this type of behavior is extraordinarily prevalent and that it is not followed exclusively by most of those participating in it and in fact may be completely abandoned by some after years of participation and embraced by others who had previously led a heterosexual life.[4]

On the question of homosexuality as crime and the related question of homosexuality *and* crime, there is a considerable amount of confusion. Homosexuality between consenting adults is said to be a classic example of a crime without a victim, meaning that no one is hurt by the act unless it be the willing participants, that there is no complaint, and that it involves—if anything at all—nothing more than an affront to the mores (and in the opinion of some people the mental health) of other members of the society.

The term "consenting adults" would itself not be difficult to define and involves little more than setting an age of consent for the persons committing the act. In England, this age is lower for a heterosexual than for a homosexual relationship; as we saw in Chapter 3, the American Law Institute suggests that the age differential between the participants be taken into account, as well as the age of the younger of two partners, whether the sex act be between members of the same or different sexes.

Following many years of agitation as a result of scandals involving persons of the upper class, those in high political office, prominent and well-liked celebrities, and officers of the armed services, and the publication of the Wolfenden Report,[5] in which a parliamentary commission investigated the matter and suggested that homosexual relations between consenting adult males no longer be subject to criminal sanctions (similar relations between adult females had been legal for many years in England), the British law was changed. In the United States, Illinois was the first state to repeal its laws against this type of behavior and even against street solicitation for "immoral purposes" but did not legalize prostitution. In fact, the Illinois penal code is actually more lenient toward males who solicit other males on the street and in public parks than males who publicly solicit females. But this is surely not so peculiar as the repeal of the British antihomosexual law, which left it perfectly legal for an adult male to commit buggery (anal intercourse) with another adult male, in private and with his consent, while the law against sodomy, unnatural acts, crimes against nature, and other so-called abominable and unmentionable acts between a male and a female remained intact.

Several American states followed Illinois in the decriminalization process, but most states continue to have laws against homosexual relations between adults both in public and in private.[6]

According to these penal codes, one may be subject to a lengthy term in prison for violation of such laws, but there are few arrests and fewer long sentences and actual confinement. Those arrests that do occur are usually for activity in public or semipublic places.

The homosexual is subject to harassment on the job, in social relations, and in numerous other ways, including discrimination by official governmental bodies. Despite the fact that a high court has officially stated that "it is not a crime to be a homosexual," [7] the implication being that the crime is to commit the act and not to occupy the status or have the desire, it is doubtful that a person who admitted to homosexuality would be accepted on most police forces, for example. However, as of the end of 1976, both the San Francisco and the Washington State police departments had opened their ranks to avowed homosexuals. In 1975, a Texas court awarded custody of a child to his father on the sole ground that the mother was an admitted lesbian and shared a home with her female lover. However, the extralegal social sanctions are relaxing, and a school-teacher of admitted homosexuality won reinstatement, with the support of his union, after he was fired. The Episcopalian church in early 1977 ordained a minister who was an avowed lesbian, with some but not a great deal of protest; and an openly avowed homosexual was elected as a delegate to the 1976 Democratic National Convention. The U.S. Civil Service Commission, largely because of the aggressive efforts of Frank Kameny, an astronomer and a militant fighter for civil rights for gay people, has relaxed its traditionally discriminatory policies.

Arrests for violation of the law with respect to homosexual acts between consenting adults almost invariably involve either open solicitation of another person on the street or in some public place for the purpose of repairing to a private place to commit the act or apprehension during the commission of a homosexual act in a public place, such as a washroom, a park, or an automobile.

The first type of arrest is usually effected by a police decoy or plainclothesman who may or may not have initiated the conversation but who certainly encouraged it. In a series of decisions, the courts have ruled that a defendant should not be convicted on the uncorroborated testimony of the police agent and that an agent who goes under false pretenses to the home of a man suspected of homosexual activities is inviting the action and is guilty of entrapment. Furthermore, when the agent "invites" or "encourages" a homosexual to "make a pass," the latter can hardly be accused of a sexual assault for this phrase suggests an unwilling partner.[8] Certainly the law that makes it illegal to solicit on the street may occasionally protect the visitor from out of town who is shocked by such practices or the unsuspecting resident who wanders into the "tenderloin" or "sin strip" area, but it does little to protect society. Such legal restriction does not contain the spread of venereal disease, does not prevent homosexual practices, which some nonparticipants find deplorable, and does encourage blackmail and shakedowns. Furthermore, the law results from time to time in the arrest and subsequent ruination of a man who, indiscreet as he may have been in the search for a sex partner, has otherwise made a reasonable effort to adjust his life pattern to his sexual proclivities. As a mechanism for diminishing the practice or the spread of homosexuality, such laws are patently ineffective.

However, the call for repeal of the antihomosexual laws is an issue all too often obscured by partisans on both sides; the fact is that these laws for the most part are unenforced and unenforceable and that arrests are almost completely limited to public solicitations and sex in public places. This was not always the case; at one time there were raids on gay bars, which accounted for a proportion (albeit a small one) of arrests of gay persons in the United States. In fact, the raid on the Stonewall, a gay bar in New York, became the catalyst for a "fight back" movement on the part of gay organizations and their supporters—probably a turning point in the gay liberation movement.[9]

Nonetheless, although most states outlaw adult consensual homosexual acts in private, the overwhelming proportion of arrests and prosecutions are for homosexual solicitations and/or activities in public and semipublic places.* While few people defend such activities, it is argued that they occur only when an area is deserted except for willing participants and a concealed voyeur (a policeman or perhaps a sociologist, the latter not necessarily concealed in fact). It is doubtful whether the number of homosexual arrests would diminish in cities like New York, Philadelphia, or Washington if the proposals for legalization of adult homosexual acts were enacted (following the suggestions of the American Law Institute), unless

---

* To some extent, the problem is to define what is meant by "public." In Chapter 4 this question was discussed in some detail as it relates to prostitution. However, a public place for homosexual solicitation, and particularly for performance of a sex act, would not necessarily be the same as such a place for heterosexual solicitation.

in this new situation the social climate called for police to ignore transgressions in public places. The issue is whether public restrooms and sections of parks should be declared virtually off limits to the "straight" population, or even to homosexuals who find sex in public offensive, in order to accommodate the needs and desires of a special group. On the other hand, there are some businesses that operate only under the most transparent veneer; their advertisement as Turkish baths or massage parlors for males is so unconvincing that even an unsophisticated man is unlikely to wander in by chance. Tolerance of such gay spots therefore seems to pose little hardship.*

The problem of social control over homosexual activity in public or semipublic places or between people who meet each other as strangers and proceed somewhere for the purpose of erotic gratification involves many questions. One of them is whether people can be recruited into homosexuality not in the sense of being urged "to join" (although this does happen) but in the sense that they may begin in an experimental way and develop a growing inclination. Consider, for example, the following excerpt from an interview conducted by Laud Humphreys.

> "Well, I started off as the straight young thing. Everyone wanted to suck my cock. I wouldn't have been caught dead with one of the things in my mouth! . . . So, here I am at forty—with grown kids—and the biggest cocksucker in [the city]!"[10]

Many people believe that homosexuality is not something determined or destined from birth or from early childhood, that it is a learning and accommodation process; such people say that opportunities to learn should not be given in the form of tolerating easy-to-find sex in semipublic places for "the straight young thing." Persons with such a point of view prefer to discourage sex in public places, but they do not necessarily favor criminal prosecution of those who participate in such acts.

The concept that consensual adult sexuality is the free right of each individual has been gaining strength. Decriminalization has become a fact in several states and, even more important, destigmatization has proceeded along with it. There is a danger of a back-

---

* Establishments of this sort have come to be openly advertised in homosexual newspapers such as the *Advocate,* published in New York. While it is not suggested that a heterosexual would be aware of this advertising, we do wish to illustrate the openness of the appeal.

lash, of course. There have been attacks on headquarters of gay organizations, for example.

In 1976, the U.S. Supreme Court, by a vote of six to three, upheld the constitutionality of state antihomosexual laws. The Court did not pass on the wisdom or propriety of such legislation but only on the right of the states to regulate the private consensual activity of adults; it found that the laws did not contravene any guarantee of freedom under the Bill of Rights of the U.S. Constitution. This meant, in effect, that further efforts to decriminalize adult consensual homosexual acts would have to be made in state legislatures (unless the Supreme Court were to find occasion to review the matter again and reverse itself).

To achieve decriminalization through the state legislatures and state courts is a long, tedious and difficult process, with the likelihood of success dim in many areas. However, campaigns of this type are useful for those involved in the struggle for broadening homosexual rights and against employment and general public discrimination and stigmatization because they serve as a rallying point around which adherents, friends, sympathizers, and many parts of the general public can be mobilized. Funds are collected, rallies held, lectures given, letters sent to newspapers and often published, unfairness exposed, organizations built—all around an issue of a change in the law. In New York City, a campaign of this type raged for several years as organized groups sought to enact legislation banning discrimination because of sexual predilection.

The case that came before the Supreme Court is itself interesting. Two males filed a civil suit in federal district court in Richmond in which they challenged the Virginia law as unconstitutional. The law in that state, like many other state statutes, forbids "crimes against nature" and covers not only homosexual but also some heterosexual acts. In a lower court, the challenge to the law had been rejected by a vote of two to one, the court ruling that the law did not violate the right to privacy, the right to due process, freedom of expression, or freedom from cruel and unusual punishment.

The Virginia law, which carries with it a maximum penalty of five years in prison, was challenged by "John Doe" and "Robert Roe," fictitious names used by the applicants for litigation purposes. While the necessity of using such names is an indication of a highly charged social atmosphere, the discretion with which the matter was handled, preserving the privacy and anonymity of the litigants, is an indication of a condition more liberal than would have been found some years earlier. The men, represented by counsel cooperating with the American Civil Liberties Union, claimed that it was only by acts in violation of this law that they could obtain sexual fulfillment, that the law made it difficult for them to meet people like themselves, and that it violated their privacy. The failure of the Court to hear oral argument or to issue an opinion was a grave disappointment to many of those who had followed judicial trends in such matters over a period of years. The three dissenting judges (William J. Brennan, Jr., Thurgood Marshall, and John Paul Stevens) expressed a wish that the case had not been acted on until such argument had been held.

Although a decision ruling unconstitutional the laws against private consensual homosexual acts would no doubt have been a dramatic step forward, obviating the need for state-by-state legislative action, there have been some liberal reinterpretations by state courts. For example, in Massachusetts, where efforts to change the penal code have not been successful, the highest state court declared that the antihomosexual law (prohibiting, in this instance, "unnatural and lascivious" sexual acts) is not meant to apply to such behavior when conducted in private between consenting adults.

The Supreme Court position did not meet with popular acclaim and did not provoke a reaffirmation of the righteousness of heterosexual ideals. On the contrary, public opinion polls showed that a majority of the populace opposed the decision; the legal issues on which the Court ruled—namely, that regulation of sexual activity is a state and not a federal question, that antihomosexual legislation is not unconstitutional—probably escaped all but a few observers. In effect, if this single weatherbell of unanticipated liberal popular reaction is indicative (and there are many supporting expressions of public sentiment), large numbers of people with no homosexual interests of their own, perhaps including many who are repelled by the idea of themselves being involved in a homosexual relationship, support decriminalization.

Legislation against adult consensual homosexual relations appears in many forms and under several headings.[11] For the most part, laws are not worded in such a way as to be specifically directed against sex committed by two males (or, less frequently, two females). In most jurisdictions, the wording is broad enough to encompass heterosexual as well as homosexual acts in which there is any insertion other than coital and in which there is any mouth-genital contact. Hence, the same law that illegalizes homosexuality also makes it criminal for a man and a woman to have consensual sex in the form of fellatio, cunnilingus, anal intercourse, or any other type of insertion or contact usually included under the heading of "extracoital." Arrests of heterosexuals for violation of such laws are even more infrequent than arrests of homosexual violators. Whether people are of the same or different sexes, arrests on this charge are rare not because no one knows (this is true, but it is not the relevant reason) but because there is no complainant and no one seems to care. In the rare instances of heterosexual arrests, the persons had had photographs taken or had permitted children to watch them, and there was outrage more because of the impairment of the morals of the children than because of the so-called unnatural acts themselves. Cases have come to light in the course of annulment, divorce or child custody actions in which one party accuses the other of insisting on such "perverse" sex play.

One of the peculiarities of such laws is that they also govern relationships between a man and his wife. By the 1970s, in some states in which the laws against sodomy or unnatural sex acts had not been repealed altogether, legislation had been passed specifically exempting spouses from culpability under such laws.

Many of the antihomosexual laws are vague, and they use phrases like "crimes against nature," which themselves are not spelled out. Early in the history of such legislation, the vagueness was deliberate for it was considered that these acts were "unmentionable" and "unspeakable" and hence could be written about only in the most circumspect manner lest the law itself become lewd and salacious. The laws are found under a variety of headings including "lewd and lascivious conduct," "indecent behavior," "buggery," "sodomy," and "unnatural sexual acts." Some of the penal codes define the terms and others do not; some have definitions contained in annotations from decisions or commentaries by judges of state appellate courts.

By and large, laws of this type have been marked by little enforcement effort or public demand for arrest and prosecution. Even those who are opposed to their repeal on the ground that the law should be the expression of the moral sentiment of the community (the position taken by Patrick Devlin) [12] do not favor investigation and prosecution of all cases where there is "probable cause" to believe that a crime has been committed. Many prominent people, particularly in America, have made open and public announcement of their homosexual activities, and no one has seriously suggested that they be arrested for having confessed to violation of the law. For example, in 1975 a large open meeting of gay scholars was held without protest or hindrance on the campus of the John Jay College of Criminal Justice in New York, a college with a rather high proportion of students who are police officers, corrections officers, and in other law enforcement occupations. The law, then, it is apparent, fails to generate the respect that it must command if law-abidingness is to be instilled as a value among the people. In this regard, it appears that Devlin's argument fails because codified law as a symbol of the moral preferences of a society can only be self-defeating if the legal codes are ignored by law enforcement officers and courts as well as the general public.

The fact that an act is illegal, however, does have possible consequences other than arrest and prosecution of suspected participants. It gives legal argument to those who would exclude persons who apparently violate such laws from the armed services, certain government positions, and even private employment. The problem of blackmail is probably more acute, and its likelihood greater, where there is a violation of a law, although removal of the stigma appears to be a greater deterrent to blackmail than relief from the remote possibility of legal prosecution. Blackmail of persons engaged in homosexual behavior (a matter to which we shall return presently) has been a greater problem in England than in the United States. As late as the 1960s some prominent persons were prosecuted and served prison terms in England for adult homosexual acts. These activities usually crossed social class lines, and with stronger class cleavages in England than in the United States, this factor may have been conducive both to blackmail and to prosecution.

Solicitation in Semipublic Places

Solicitation for purposes of engaging in a "deviate" sexual act is almost always accomplished rather circumspectly and seldom occurs without some encouragement on the part of the solicited person. Acts of this sort are often denied, and there is no proof other than the word of the arresting officer, in which case the courts have generally ruled that there is insufficient evidence to convict in the face of a denial and a plea of not guilty. Even when the court so rules, a man arrested for solicitation often suffers great damage to his reputation and his family life. In Illinois, the framers of the revised penal code (modeled after the code suggested by the American Law Institute but in some respects more permissive) argue that when solicitation is made in an unobtrusive manner between adults and does not involve an exchange of money, the solicited individual can decline and walk away, even as a female can when she is approached, whistled at, or in some other way propositioned by a stranger on the street. Arrests in such cases seem to serve no purpose, do give rise to blackmail and shakedowns, and are not deterrents against the conduct itself. Occasionally it is argued that the police are protecting the homosexual against murder, assault, robbery, and other criminal acts of which he may be the victim by discouraging these types of casual stranger-to-stranger liaisons. The need for such protection is real, but it is doubtful whether this is a motivation of the police or a function of the antihomosexual law and whether this goal can be accomplished by arrests.

Most arrests for homosexual activities take place because of the apprehension of the participants in an adult consensual act in a parked automobile, public restroom, theater, public park, alleyway, or some similar place. In most cases, they are strangers to each other. What proportion of homosexual acts takes place in semipublic or public places no one can estimate, but it is not small. Such activities seem to cross social class lines with ease. During 1976, three very prominent Americans (a former federal appellate judge, a retired major general, and a national legislator) were all subjected to devastating publicity after solicitation arrests, and a well-known prosecutor managed to clear himself of a false accusation allegedly instigated by a police chief, although in the opinion of most observers the accusation itself ended the man's political career. Some years ago, the president of a California college and somewhat later the mayor of an upstate New York municipality were arrested and charged with soliciting vice squad plainclothesmen in New York. Although both were exonerated, their careers were ruined.

The American Law Institute suggests that the following be part of a penal code:

Section 251.3. Loitering to Solicit Deviate Sexual Relations. A person is guilty of a petty misdemeanor if he loiters in or near any public place for the purpose of soliciting or being solicited to engage in deviate sexual relations.[13]

Another paragraph, very general in its wording and hence likely to be attacked as unconstitutional if it were enacted into law, might also apply to homosexual cases.

> Section 251.1. Open Lewdness. A person commits a petty misdemeanor if he does any lewd act which he knows is likely to be observed by others who would be affronted or alarmed.[14]

In a commentary on section 251.3, it is noted that it is the intention of the framers of the proposed law not to illegalize "purely private conversations between persons having an established intimacy, even if the conversations occur in a public place" but to direct the law against those who indiscriminately seek or make themselves available "for deviate sexual relations." Solicitation "for hire" was not the concern in this section (in other words, the paragraph outlaws loitering without regard to the intentions of either party as to payments for sex).[15] Furthermore, it is made explicit that

> the main objective is to suppress the open flouting of prevailing moral standards as a sort of nuisance in public thoroughfares and parks. In the case of females, suppression of professionals is likely to accomplish that objective. In the case of males, there is a greater likelihood that nonprofessional homosexuals will congregate and behave in a manner grossly offensive to other users of public facilities.[16]

In short, the Model Penal Code, if enacted, would permit apprehension and arrest on the same charge and in the same manner as for the majority of actual arrests in homosexual cases, in states where old laws remain intact. However, it would decriminalize other forms of homosexual behavior, and while this would probably not affect arrests directly, it might have other beneficial social and personal effects.

An arrest under the public indecency law took place in Canada when two males were apprehended in an automobile. One pleaded guilty, the other not guilty. In many respects, the case itself is typical of events occurring in the United States, and the complete trial transcript is reprinted by Alex. Gigeroff.[17] A few highlights and excerpts from some courtroom speeches are reproduced here.

To provide some background, the encounter was voluntary, and both men were in their late twenties; thus, age of consent was not an issue in this case. One man was being watched as he loitered on a street corner. He got into an automobile after a short conversation with the driver, and the car was followed to a parking lot, where the men were apprehended in the act of fellatio.

Charged with gross indecency, the men were placed under arrest. On cross-examination, the arresting detective, twenty-one years on the force, said that he had charged many others with gross indecency but none of the cases had involved adultery, fornication, or masturbation. The detective was dismissed, with the clear indication that the law was being selectively enforced against participants in homosexual acts. It was brought out that there were no pedestrians in the parking lot; the defendant had no previous record; and he was gainfully employed as a choir director at a church. His attorney addressed the court:

> Your Honour, my motion is to the effect that the Crown has not proven its case. The obligation of the Crown is to bring in some evidence as to indecency and gross indecency. It would seem that indecency . . . or gross indecency is a matter of degree according to the very norm of our society. I would think, your Honour, that when the Crown was to prove its case it would have to show what decency means in our society by perhaps calling some scientific evidence or modern scientific evidence that would say according to the customs and morals of our time this is indecent or this is what the customs and morals of our time is and this is the behaviour and beyond that this is gross behaviour or behaviour beyond that.
>
> The only fact before your Honour is a physical act. There is nothing more. There is nothing to say it is indecent. There is nothing to give that physical act any colour whatsoever; in order to find that, your Honour must take some kind of judicial notice, in my submission, as to what the norms of our society are or what the customs of our society are, and I submit the Crown should have brought that evidence.
>
> In view of the recent findings in the Wolfenden Report I do not think evidence of this kind is indecent, that the Court can take judicial notice that it is indecent behaviour or homosexual behaviour is indecent. The Wolfenden Report indicates 37 per cent of all males have some form of homosexual behaviour and that Report says this kind of conduct the criminal law should not associate itself with.[18]

At this point there was an exchange between the judge and the attorney for the accused, in which the former asked whether the Wolfenden Report differentiated between such acts committed in

public and in private. The defense attorney argued that the act
ought not to be illegal and that the prosecution should be compelled
to show what is notorious in a community, what is normal, and what
is gross behavior.

The prosecutor argued that common sense itself determines what
gross indecency is; his line of distinction was not between the
public and the private but between the heterosexual and the homosexual.

> I think anything that happens between a male and female pro-
> viding they have consent, I suppose that is perfectly all right
> providing it is done in private, in my submission that is natural.
> But in my submission the unnatural part—and I do not think I
> need dwell upon this—is when it happens between two males.
> It is my respectful submission that is abnormal and unnatural and
> something that should not be condoned because it may be—I
> should not dwell on it too much, but it is done and I do not think
> [it] should be more or less sanctioned.[19]

The attorney for the defendant made an impassioned response.

> I have listened, gentlemen of the jury, to my learned friend;
> we stopped burning witches a long time ago. The onus is upon the
> Crown to prove beyond a reasonable doubt that this man com-
> mitted an act of gross indecency. You gentlemen of the jury have
> been chosen to pronounce upon that act. You are here to judge
> [the defendant], but in a very much larger sense you are here to
> judge this society and to judge every man who may be brought
> before the Court in a like or similar offence. You must at all times
> remember that this is a criminal act which you are judging, it is
> an offence under the Criminal Code, and before you judge [the
> defendant], a man whom you have heard has no previous con-
> viction, is not a convicted criminal and a man who has been asso-
> ciated with a church for a great number of years, you must
> consider that he is a criminal, that he has committed a criminal
> indecent act and an act that is criminally gross because if you
> convict him he will stand condemned as any murderer, arsonist,
> rapist, thief, or armed robber, and that is the kind of conduct you
> must associate [him] with. . . .
> I would have thought the Crown would have presented evi-
> dence before you to show the norms and morals and customs of
> our society and there is psychiatric evidence they might present
> in that regard but they chose not to call anyone. I wonder why.
> I wonder why there is no sociologist or psychiatrist on behalf of

the Crown to say this is what is decent in our society and the behaviour that you have heard about today is indecent. Perhaps they have not found it because they stopped burning witches, as I say, a long time ago. . . .

Fornication in some quarters may be considered indecent; masturbation may be considered indecent, and one of the most indecent acts of our society is adultery. It is one of the few acts for which you can get a divorce in this country. These gentlemen could not get a divorce for gross indecency but no one is ever arrested for adultery. What sort of value has that in our community? Are you prepared to prosecute people as criminals for adultery and, if not, surely gross indecency which the law and the legislature considers less offensive should not be considered as criminal.[20]

The defendant was found guilty, given a two-year suspended sentence, and placed on probation, with the proviso that he must attend a clinic for treatment.

The circumstances of this case are quite typical of homosexual incidents leading to arrest. Only the nature of the defense is here unusual. The defense argued that the act itself is not indecent, or at least no more so than adultery, and that heterosexual encounters in the same or similar surroundings would not be prosecuted. Many have contended that homosexual activity even when carried out in semipublic places is sufficiently removed from public view not to be a nuisance; that police could be better employed than in conducting surveillance of encounters considered essentially harmless even by those who deem them unfortunate; and that careers are needlessly ruined by such arrests. On the other hand, local communities have objected to the fact that certain parks, beaches or sections of cities have gained such a reputation as being off limits for anything other than homosexual activities that many people are reluctant to be seen in the vicinity; department store owners, YMCA managers, and others want their premises to be free for use without innocent males being accosted or ogled, much less propositioned; heterosexual acts, it is argued, are not so blatant an affront to community standards of morals, even if committed in an automobile in a parking lot, as are homosexual acts; and the analogy with adultery, it is stated, would not hold because it was not merely the fact that two males were involved in this and similar cases that led to prosecution but that the act occurred in a semipublic place.

Homosexual Prostitution *

Male prostitution was traditionally a little recognized and little studied aspect of life. Known to the police, it flourished in major metropolitan areas of the United States and abroad, often without the knowledge of the heterosexual citizenry. In the 1960s and 1970s, it became better known and began to be researched.[21]

By "male prostitution" is meant the conferring of sexual favors by one male on another for a monetary consideration—not occasionally but as a major or supplementary means of livelihood, regularly, and over a span of several months or years. It does not refer to homosexuals supported by their lovers in pseudomarital settings, payments made by prison inmates to others (usually younger prisoners) for sexual acts, or payments made by lonely females to males derisively known as "gigolos." On the margins of male prostitution are those juvenile delinquents who occasionally or frequently indulge in these practices either as incidental to their general delinquent orientation or as part of planned criminality, including extortion, "rolling," and sadistic assault.

It should scarcely come as a surprise that so widespread a method of earning a living as prostitution has at virtually all times and in all places attracted males as well as females. The male of the species in most societies is, after all, supposed to be the entrepreneur, and in prostitution he can fill this role as pimp or as homosexual prostitute. In the homosexual culture, prostitutes more often are part-timers; they tend to drift in and out of the occupation, which heterosexual prostitutes do not. The homosexual prostitute is almost never called a prostitute or a whore, sometimes a call boy, usually a hustler. The word "trade" (and the phrase "rough trade") generally refers to aggressively masculine persons in a homosexual encounter, not necessarily to a person who is being paid for engaging in sex.

From our studies, it would appear that there is a hierarchy in male prostitution from "rough trade" to "effeminate queen," and another continuum from the lone hustler to the highly structured male houses of prostitution or call boy enterprises, which receive protection from police, politicians, and/or minor figures in organized crime.

It is likely that male prostitution can be found in any major city

---

* The authors are indebted to the late Thomas Simpson, who turned over his own research findings to us and approved their use in this book.

in the United States and most other countries and that it may very well play a role in convention cities not unlike that of female prostitution. If this is so, it would require some degree of organization, as does any service industry. Because male prostitution is socially defined as an activity far more deviant than female prostitution (particularly for the customer), those involved in it tend to be vulnerable to extortion and blackmail and not infrequently involved with other criminal activities (for example, the distribution of narcotics or even espionage).

In research of this phenomenon, MacNamara employed a technique of surreptitious interrogation known as "roping." [22] In a typical roping, an investigator under an appropriate guise strikes up an acquaintance with the subject, inveigles his way into his confidence, throws out conversational leads that focus on the area of interest without asking direct questions, and uses the initial contact to introduce new subjects, as done by sociologists in the snowballing technique. A first study was conducted in this way with thirty-seven male prostitutes; additional data were available on 125 subjects in seven American cities.

The age of the persons under study ranged from fifteen through thirty-one, with the younger ones attempting to add on a few years to permit them to be taken to bars, and the older ones dropping as many as ten of their years to cater to their clients' demands for youths. However, the owners of gay bars were wary both of young patrons and of persons whom they knew were "hustling" or "cruising" for paying partners. Those in the sample were of a variety of ethnic and racial backgrounds and of a range of educational achievement. However, only three of the thirty-seven had completed high school; two others had qualified for the high school equivalency diploma. Three were attending or had attended trade schools; nine had been in the armed services, one of whom had been discharged for homosexuality. One was married (a claim that was verified), and another said that he was the father of an illegitimate child. Many presented themselves as having bisexual interests and activities.

Sixteen had penal institutional experience: seven in juvenile institutions, five in local jails, two in military detention facilities, one in a state prison on a burglary charge, on which he was out on parole. Only one, however, had been arrested specifically for prostitution, and it appears that the likelihood of an arrest on this charge is much greater for a female than for a male. Nearly all of the thirty-seven admitted repeated minor criminal acts (principally larcenies and assaults), and at least four hinted at the commission of much more serious crimes. Venereal disease was readily admitted to be quite common.

Contrary to the stereotype of the male hustler as "rough trade," thirty-one members of the group studied were mildly to extremely effeminate in dress, appearance, and/or manner; five were what might be described as "junior hoodlum" types in their self-presentation; and one was an all-American, prep school type. It would appear that the occasionally available sailor or soldier or young manual worker preempts the market for the ultramasculine sex object.

Some of the prostitutes claimed to service as many as five or six clients in one evening. (This is possible if they are insertees and not insertors in oral-genital or anal relations.) Their clients apparently were lonely, defeated, middle-aged men, largely lower to middle income, clerical and semiprofessional in occupation, often masochistic in their acceptance of the indignities heaped upon them by their paid bedmates.

Other than the effeminacy of most of the youths and the seemingly self-dramatizing truculence (modeled after favorite television or movie tough guys) of the "junior hoodlum" types, there were few gross external symptoms of psychopathology. Not one of these men attributed his prostitutional activity to an early history of seduction or rape; in fact, a majority indicated that their initial homosexual experience was not only voluntary but self-initiated.

In a study conducted by the late Thomas Simpson, the sample was drawn mainly from New York City although the individual backgrounds of the hustlers were quite varied. The religious and racial makeup of the thirteen hustlers studied was diverse; only one was Roman Catholic, in contrast to the MacNamara group, in which the percentage of Catholicism was high.

The individual hustlers occupied the expected points on the continuum from the rough-trade freelancer, to the medium-range independent known to an extensive clientele, to the "pro" organized in a call boy type of arrangement or employed by some sort of front such as a male modeling agency or a masseur. Specifically, two were described by Simpson as freelance "midnight cowboys," five fell somewhere in the middle category, and six were pros.

In MacNamara's study, a considerable number of the youths were living at home or in close relationships with their families; in the Simpson group, they tended for the most part to be out of touch with family and although still young were not living with relatives. In both groups, the family income appeared to be from low to lower-middle levels. Whereas MacNamara found that only a small percentage had completed high school, Simpson's group contained eight who had been graduated from high school or from trade school that was of the equivalent level; of these eight, three had attended college for a short while but had dropped out and a fourth was in college at the time of the study.

A piece by the English novelist Simon Raven, although based on a small sample, is instructive because of the detailed knowledge he gained from his respondents.[23] Raven discerned five categories on what appears to be a continuum: (1) the young military man of modest education initiated into the system by more experienced friends in order to obtain extra money for heterosexual dates; (2) persons employed at low salaried jobs who sought luxuries beyond their means; (3) those of low intelligence with poor jobs on a "drifter" basis; (4) the layabout who had a variety of illegal or semilegal occupations of which hustling was but one; and (5) the full-time pro who did well, was cultivated, and either was "organized" or had his own organization through referrals by important upper-class contacts. This last is the professional prostitute par excellence, who has the ability of a con artist. He is potentially the international hustler who is an important component in the contemporary jet set. The rewards apparently corresponded from less to more in Raven's cases.

Possibly one of the first modern observers of the homosexual prostitution scene was the noted Englishman Richard Burton,[24] who is paraphrased and quoted in the excellent study of homosexuality by Donald West. Burton's work covers male prostitution in ancient times (taking the form of both male brothels and specialized "patronage") in Mediterranean countries, the Far East, the Pacific, and the Second Empire in France. West also notes that male prostitution was often connected with religious practices—for example, the grand priestly castes from Mesopotamia to Mexico and Peru. He notes that "legislation provided for the removal of all civil rights from any Athenian citizen who prostituted his body for money." The hierarchical implication here is somewhat different from what we find today because Athens was a different type of society with different value systems from our own. Further historical information is offered by West who states that "in the eighteenth century convictions and executions were frequent, but that male brothels and homosexual clubs thrived in London.[25]

Historical and comparative evidence may be found in the general study by Wainwright Churchill. For example, in discussing the glorious American West in frontier times and later: "Homosexuality was also very common among the troops of both the North and the South during the Civil War, and there are accounts of male prostitutes who followed the armies."[26] Thus we seem to have a camp follower type who would surely fit our lowest echelon, midnight cowboy category. Churchill continues:

> That homosexual love was never abandoned by the Japanese in modern times may be seen in the fact that teahouses with male *geishas* still existed in Japan until the end of the Second World War, when they were suppressed by the American occupation forces. . . .
>
> Homosexual practices seem to have constituted a part of the sexual repertory of all classes in China during ancient and modern times. Male brothels were common in that country as recently as the beginning of this century. . . .
>
> In India . . . we hear of "peg boys," boy prostitutes trained to cater to the pederastic urges of older male clients.[27]

Churchill is instructive, but much of his material is undocumented, and what is presented as history is often at best speculation.

There have been some more specialized studies germane to this field. In *Tearoom Trade*, Laud Humphreys makes a passing observation on lower class participation: "Like others of his class . . . George may have learned this sexual game as a teen-age hustler."[28] This lower class aspect is discussed by Albert Reiss[29] and by John Gerassi.[30] Both Reiss and Gerassi note that rewards were closely commensurate with lower class expectations in a nonmetropolitan setting—sometimes consisting of only a bottle of beer or two for a casual act of fellatio.

Thus, homosexual prostitution, like heterosexual, would appear to be a socioeconomic phenomenon. Whether it also attracts youths with previous interests in homosexuality as such or whether those not previously so inclined drift into this occupation for kicks, money, and without emotional involvement, only to retain learned homosexual patterns, are important questions in the formulation of social policy.

That the phenomenon of homosexual prostitution was widely observed although little researched until rather recently seems clear.

Writing about the European scene in Germany before World War I, Abraham Flexner noted that

> prostitution in Europe as an organized business is by no means limited to the intercourse of persons of opposite sexes. A homosexual prostitution . . . has developed on a considerable scale. . . . It is estimated that between 1,000 and 2,000 male prostitutes live in Berlin.[31]

Even earlier, an American physician, William Sanger, fully supported Richard Burton's observations on Rome and Greece, adding that there were as many male as female prostitutes.[32] Then, strangely enough for a lengthy scholarly treatise on the subject, Sanger had nothing further to say about male prostitution.

For many reasons, sex slavery of males is highly unlikely. There are two types of male prostitutes in demand, the extremely young and the very strong, the latter the muscle-flexing stereotype of the sailor, soldier, or truckdriver. The strong type psychologically, if not physically, subdues and dominates his "trick," and it is difficult to envisage this occurring in a situation in which the hustler is held captive. Such young men may be among the residents or employees of male houses of prostitution, but it appears that they are not being forcibly held.[33]

It has been said that there is a clientele seeking very young boys, and perhaps there may be a market for very young girls as well. Whatever the size of this clientele (which is an embarrassment to gay liberation groups and whose needs and activities are denounced by such movements), rumor has it that there is some traffic in very young boys, no more than eight or nine years, who do not understand what they are doing and are compelled to commit the acts in question. Without denying this rumor, it is apparent that such activities would be extremely precarious for the adults involved. The children would have to be kept locked up lest people became suspicious of their failure to be in school, and they would have to be disposed of in some manner after the pedophile had tired of them. It is true that persons are missing in large numbers without great outcry, as witness the many boys in their teens who disappeared in Texas before it was discovered that they had been killed in a homosexual slaughter, some of them as much as eighteen months earlier. But any considerable commerce in unwilling young boys is even more improbable than that in young girls.

MEDICAL AND PSYCHOLOGICAL STUDIES

Psychologists, psychiatrists, and pediatricians, among others, have begun to turn their attention to male prostitutes. A seventeen-month study of thirty-three young men was conducted by Sivan Caukins and Neil Coombs; in addition, they were able to interview twenty customers. They found male prostitution to be rampant, possibly as extensive as female prostitution, with a great deal of exploitation taking place. "Hustlers are expected to perform any sex act with any customer," they write, in apparent contradiction to the findings of Albert Reiss.[34] Caukins and Coombs continue:

> The price is crassly adjusted to the law of supply and demand. Deep psychological problems arise and the relationship between the score and the prostitute is tenuous, symbiotic, and fraught with pathology.[35]

A study of sixty-three hustlers in San Francisco and Seattle was conducted by medically trained and oriented personnel and was reported by Robert Deisher and his colleagues. The youths ranged in age from fifteen to twenty-three, mainly between nineteen and twenty-two. Most were high school graduates, and a considerable number had some junior college or university education. A remarkable feature of the sample was the transience of the group; more than half the sample had been in the city of current residence for less than one year. Military background, religion, drug use, interest in legitimate employment, claimed earnings, amount of money in their possession at the time of the interview, and other data are presented. The researchers found that of the sixty-three boys and young men in the study, twenty-nine were good candidates for rehabilitation, eleven fair, thirteen poor, and ten unknown. They concluded that the real tragedy "is the effect that this life style has on the young man engaged in it." [36] In an editorial in *Pediatrics,* the medical journal in which the study appeared, the work was commended for demonstrating "the pediatrician's scientific and humanitarian concern about a group of homosexual boys." [37]

THE OUTLOOK FOR THE HUSTLER

Before attempting to place this behavior in some theoretical perspective, let us look at some sociological implications of these patterns. The life-style of the hustlers is highly provisional, tentative, tenuous, and flexible in degree and direction of mobility. It is a kind of stabilized instability. Constant conflict in values and behavior patterns become entirely normalized, to the point that the Weltanschauung is a nonview of either the world or the self. Regardless of the ultimate destinies of individuals—entrance into the gay subculture, drift out of the hustling subculture, or upward mobility within hustling—these elements are present while participation in this life-style continues although their importance changes within the hierarchy.

The central fact of the hustler's life is found in the total loss of community in the classic sense in which sociologists use this term. Though hustlers may meet in the wee hours of the morning and compare notes, there is a sense of defensive estrangement within the group. There is no reinforcement of values although there is often protection and not infrequently a sort of philanthropy, with those who have "scored" providing meals and sometimes overnight lodging for those who failed to "turn a trick." Homosexual relations between hustlers, denied vehemently in interviews, are apparently not uncommon. Not only is there evidence of such activity in the (perhaps malicious) statements elicited from the interviewees about relationships among their peers, but an interview by Simpson with three retired male prostitutes disclosed a pattern of short-term sexual liaisons.

One need not insist on a dogmatic answer to the question of whether male prostitution is a pathological phenomenon; certainly it is socioeconomic circumstance that plays no small role in making prostitution an acceptable way of life for certain young males, granting of course previous homosexual experience or interests, or some polymorphous undifferentiated capacity. The case against pathology (other than the controversial question of homosexual psychoneurosis itself) is strengthened by MacNamara's and Simpson's studies, which pointed to limited consumption of alcohol by this group, and by the fact that very few of the youths studied were hard narcotic users (although at least half had experimented with marijuana, barbiturates, amphetamines, and/or mescaline).

Like their female counterparts, male prostitutes for the most part are the flotsam and jetsam cast up on an unfriendly shore (except for the occasional college youth). They sell their bodies for their supper largely because they have nothing else salable, or at least they so believe, and if they are acting in accordance with a false belief—if in fact they do have more to offer to themselves and to society—their patterns of behavior may be all the more tragic.

Homosexual Rape

Rape, it has been emphasized, is almost invariably defined in penal codes as sexual assault upon a female. While such a statutory definition would constitute a perfect defense if a charge of rape were to be brought against a man by a male victim, it would seem that criminology could here depart from the legal definition and speak meaningfully of homosexual rape. In the legal codes, this act generally is included under such headings as assault, sexual assault, gross sexual assault, or sodomy.

Sexual assault of a male is probably rare outside prison but is said to be quite common in prison, particularly in local jails. A vivid description of such activity, in a Philadelphia jail, is given by Alan Davis.

> He laid there for about 20 minutes and Cheyenne came over to the kid's bed and pulled his pants down and got on top of him and raped him again. When he got done Horse did it again and then about four or five others got on him. While one of the guys was on him, raping him, Horse came over and said, "Open your mouth and suck on this and don't bite it." He then put his penis in his mouth and made him suck on it. The kid was hollering that he was gagging and Horse stated, "You better not bite it or I will kick your teeth out."[38]

There have been various estimates of the extent of prison homosexuality, but these include both voluntary, or consensual, acts and forcible rapes, as well as many instances that fall somewhere between the two. A review of this literature was made by Peter Buffum, who estimated that 30–45 percent of jail and prison inmates have homosexual experiences while incarcerated, whereas John Irwin has offered a lower figure.[39] Buffum then goes on to state:

> Working on the assumption that 40 to 50 percent of a penal institution will have homosexual experience in prison, Gagnon has estimated that 5 to 10 percent will have had casual or intermittent prior experience, and 5 to 10 percent will have had extensive or nearly exclusive homosexual commitment in the free community.[40]

It is difficult to translate these percentages into absolute numbers, and even more difficult to separate homosexual rapists and their victims from those who enter a relationship voluntarily. While there are approximately 280,000 inmates in federal and state prisons at any one time in the United States (mostly males), the figure becomes much larger when the inmates of local lockups and city and county jails (and the many thousands in institutions for juvenile delinquents) are included. On the one hand, the incidence of homosexuality may be larger in these local jails, with their inferior security, poor recreational facilities, and diverse difficulties; on the other hand, some of the local lockup residents are confined for such a short time, perhaps overnight while making bail, that they may not have the opportunity to become a victimizer or a victim. Nevertheless, using John Gagnon's numbers, one could estimate that there are probably 25,000 males (a very rough estimate indeed) presently in jails or prisons whose initial homosexual experience took place during incarceration. Furthermore, it is the contention of Ronald Akers and his colleagues that there is considerably more homosexuality (as well as use of drugs) in custodial-type than in treatment-type institutions.[41] The custodial institutions are more deprivational, punitive, and repressive, and they are more likely to have a higher proportion of violent offenders; the treatment institutions are more open, nonpunitive, imbued with some humanitarian concerns for inmates, and utilize the rhetoric, if not the means, for correction. The implication from the work of Akers, then, would appear to be that prison homosexuality is indeed related to violence. It is not only the amount of homosexuality that would differ with the two kinds of institution but also the content, with brutality, rape, and gang sodomy more likely in custodial institutions. It is generally accepted among corrections professionals that the incidence of homosexual relations, voluntary and coerced, is highest in juvenile institutions.

Working in the California prison system, George Kirkham found that there were three categories that prisoners themselves used to describe inmates involved in homosexual relations.[42] In the vernacular of the prison, these are "fairies," "punks," and "jocks" (or "jockers"), with numerous synonyms available for each word. Sagarin has suggested a less pejorative description: effeminates, involuntary recruits, and voluntary aggressors.[43]

The effeminates are males with obviously recognizable feminine traits and mannerisms, all of whom have had a considerable history of homosexuality before incarceration, who make a homosexual identification, and who usually seek to utilize their availability for sexual purposes to their advantage while in prison. Although there is a prison population of males who have been convicted of homosexual offenses against adults, minors, or children, as described by Gebhard and his colleagues,[44] it is probably the case that most effeminate prisoners are not incarcerated for sex-related crimes except in jails, which usually have a considerable population of male prostitutes, men arrested for solicitation, and general disorderly conduct cases.

The involuntary recruits have come into prison with a heterosexual self-image and are raped, cajoled, threatened, or in some other way made into the passive partner (or insertee). One manner in which such a new inmate was recruited was described by Robert Kelly.[45] Once raped or seduced, these persons become known as "jailhouse turnouts," or JTOs, a term that is used even when the event takes place in a prison rather than a jail.

The voluntary participants here described as aggressors utilize the effeminates or the involuntary recruits for homosexual acts (anal intercourse or fellatio) and are (or claim to be) the insertors.

These do not exhaust the possibilities for types of prisoners involved in homosexual conduct. According to a considerable amount of popular and even scientific literature, the majority of men following an exclusive or nearly-exclusive homosexual pattern are not effeminate. If such men find their way into prison, they would not fit into any of the three categories. Their relationships would be voluntary and nonaggressive, but once it became known, or even suspected, in the inmate community that they participated in such acts, they would become classified with and treated like the effeminates and the JTOs.

Finally, there is the question of whether inmates in a sex-segregated institution might make sexual alliances of a more voluntary and affectional nature regardless of previous homosexual history or lack of it. Instead of rape and threat, or the promiscuity so often associated with homosexuality, might there not be stable homosexual couples similar to those described by David Ward and Gene Kassebaum in female prisons?[46] There is little indication that such couples are to be found in male institutions. This may be merely a reflection of the generally lesser stability of all-male as compared with all-female couples in maritallike situations. But toughness itself is a male prison value and affection is its reverse, having an implication of softness. The male prison atmosphere is not only not conducive to affectional homosexuality but also may be so hostile as to make it almost impossible.

For an inmate to escape stigmatization for his homosexual behavior, George Kirkham suggests that he must fulfill two criteria.

> (1) the homosexual act or acts must represent only a situational reaction to the deprivation of heterosexual intercourse, and (2) such behavior must involve a complete absence of emotionality and effeminacy—both of which are regarded as signs of "weakness" and "queerness." An inmate who engages in homosexual activity must present a convincing facade of toughness and stereotypical "manliness" in order to escape being defined as a homosexual.[47]

These conditions are not compatible with affectional homosexual coupling.

Kirkham notes that if the involuntary recruit has been in prison before and has been "turned out" there, his reputation will follow him and any effort he might make to rebuff homosexual advances is doomed from the start. He is usually among the youngest prison inmates and after being subdued is highly stigmatized; like the female who is a victim of rape, he has what Goffman calls a "spoiled identity."[48]

The voluntary aggressors, on the other hand, are usually older. Sometimes they commit forcible rape and even gang rapes on others, as vividly described by Davis. They are physically bigger and stronger, are frequently part of the inmate power group, show no signs of effeminacy, and make a heterosexual identification not only for their preprison but also for their incarcerated life. In biracial institutions, they are often black, and it is said that they sometimes work with the tacit consent or approval of corrections officers, a statement that is difficult to validate.

Working with the data developed by Alan Davis and based on studies of local lockups, not state or federal prisons, and where 81 percent of the inmates were black, Anthony Scacco notes that 85 percent of the aggressors were black.[49] The difference between the two figures is negligible. However, 71 percent of the victims were white. To explain, 56 percent of the offenders were blacks who victimized whites; whereas the 15 percent of the offenders who were white chose only white victims. That white aggressors victimized only whites may be accounted for by their fear of reprisal by a tough and powerful black inmate population. That blacks so often victimized whites underlines the meaning of the act, as John Gagnon and William Simon have pointed out; for these black prisoners, forcible rape is an expression of dominance needs rather than of sexual needs.[50] It is clear, as Scacco discusses in detail, that the atmosphere of racial oppression in America, particularly as seen by an inmate, would bring forth an urge to lash out at whites and express mastery at a moment of utter powerlessness. Nevertheless, Buffum suggests that some of the instances of interracial sex may not be rape, but may reflect "the desire of some overt white male homosexuals for Negro 'jockers.' "[51]

A study of persons who had had (or claimed to have had) their first homosexual experience while in prison was conducted by Sagarin. He found that the aggressors made a heterosexual reorientation and abandoned homosexuality when released, but the victims were often less likely to do so.[52] This is an irony, in that the aggressors had entered the relationship voluntarily, the victims involuntarily, yet those who came to it because they sought homosexual activity were more likely to be able to walk away from it when no longer imprisoned. The aggressors were reluctant to admit the degree of aggression, their culpability as rapists, and they generally insisted that the victims were not so reluctant as they claimed to be.

The aggressors all said that at times they had had a single inmate as sex partner, using the same person over and over and not permitting him to be touched by any other inmate. But these exclusive arrangements were short-lived. In one instance, an aggressor insisted that he was taking care of three younger inmates over the same period of time, that he did not allow any of them other experiences, but he appeared to be exaggerating, perhaps fantasizing with regard to power and sexual prowess. When there were new arrivals in prison, or someone tired of an old "lover," partners were frequently exchanged (sometimes without the prior consent or knowledge of the weaker partner) and new bedmates acquired. One aggressor claimed to have had a homosexual pimping operation going in the prison for a time, in which he "rented out" to others a group that he called "my boys." Not only are claims of this sort unverifiable; they also tend to be braggadocio. Despite the damaging nature of the admissions (made to someone pledged to secrecy), they may indeed be false.

One may ask why there is no complaint from the victim, if indeed he is the unwilling recruit. Buffum writes:

Today, if one who is the victim of a prison sexual attack has the temerity to complain, the likely result will be (1) retaliation by other prisoners, (2) segregation and attendant loss of privileges within the prison, (3) ridicule and embarrassment, and (4) possible prosecution of the offender, which in fact provides the prisoners with no tangible relief.[53]

Scacco emphasizes that the correction officer rarely aids the victim either because of a desire to keep the peace by not antagonizing the most powerful groups in the inmate society or because of corruption.[54] Don Gibbons puts the issue of staff involvement very strongly.

This kind of violence has usually been covertly encouraged by the institutional staff. It is not the work of disturbed youths or mess-ups; instead, it must be seen as a basic feature of the social organization of correctional institutions.[55]

The prison rape victim often finds that he has no alternative but to submit, that submission is the only path to survival, very much like the method of survival in concentration camps described by Bruno Bettelheim.[56] The rape victim discovers that almost immediately after the first event, which becomes known throughout the prison with great rapidity, he is labeled, not as victim or scapegoat, but in the pejorative terms applied to one who has sought and enjoyed the experience. Everyone looks upon him as homosexual, and he is regarded as open territory unless the consent of a specific aggressor is required.

Gagnon and Simon, who contend that a great deal of nonsexual motivation lies behind sexual activity, cite prison rape as a particularly compelling example of their point of view.

The sources of this homosexual activity for the predominantly heterosexual and aggressive male seems to be twofold. One element is certainly a search for meaningful emotional relationships that have some durability and serve as a minimal substitute for affective relationships that they normally have on the outside. . . .

A second motivation underlying many of these relationships transcends the level of affectional need and essentially becomes a source for the continued validation of masculinity needs and a symbol of resistance to the prison environment. The male whose primary source of masculine validation in the outside community has been his sexual success . . . and who has conceived of himself as aggressive, competent, and dominant in his responses to his world (commonly expressed in sex with women), finds that in prison he is deprived of these central supports for his own masculinity. In reaction to this, he enters into homosexual relationships in which he can be conceived as the masculine, controlling partner and which for him and for other males in the system validate continued claims to masculine status.[57]

Rape is a severe problem in the jails and prisons of America and perhaps of other parts of the world as well. Judicial notice was taken of the problem in March 1976, when a federal judge denounced the U.S. Bureau of Prisons for failing to protect youthful offenders in a federal reformatory from sexual assault. A nineteen-year-old youth who had served less than two months of a sentence up to six years was ordered freed after he testified that three older inmates had raped him in his cell.

As a result of this and other cases, more protection may be given to potential victims in the future.

Homosexuality and Concomitant Crime

Illegal, stigmatized, and concealed behavior lends itself to concomitant crime. This is true of homosexuality at least as much as it is of prostitution; homosexuals emerge sometimes as victimizers, more often as victims, and occasionally as both.[58] Crimes in which homosexuality appears to be an important factor include murder, assault (both sexual and other), robbery, extortion, shakedown, and blackmail.

According to Milton Helpern, New York City's former chief medical examiner, murders arising from sexual assault are not infrequent. "They occur before, during, and after sexual encounters—heterosexual and homosexual. Children, young adults, and elderly women and men are the victims. Prostitutes are included." [59]

The President's Commission on Law Enforcement and Administration of Justice set out to study (as part of its determination of the extent and impact of crime) all crimes reported for one week in one police precinct in Chicago (a precinct with a heterogeneous social and ethnic makeup). It may be only coincidence but the one homicide reported was of a homosexual nature. A twenty-five-year-old male was murdered by a twenty-year-old youth after they became acquainted at a bar. The survivor, whose story cannot be confirmed, claimed that his planned participation in a sexual encounter was exclusively to obtain money. The two went to the younger man's apartment, undressed, argued about what acts each would perform, and then the twenty-five-year-old said that he had no money, a statement that led to his immediate death.[60]

Assaults on an older male who has promised financial compensation to a youth and then reneges (either before the sex act or after) do not seem to be rare. In our own interviews with hustlers, we were told of several such incidents. The respondents often claimed to have made felonious assaults or to have threatened the customer until money was produced; respondents also reported being told of such incidents by friends. Although such assaults may be not uncommon, they probably are linked to only a small fraction of all male homosexual activity of a prostitutional nature.

In a study of fifty theft-related homicides that occurred in Austria, Ezzat Fattah found that two of them were the result of homosexual encounters. Again, one must rely on the survivors for details that they may well have embellished. "In these two cases," writes Fattah, "just as in those where the relationship between the criminal and the victim was heterosexual, it was the younger person who committed the crime against the older one." Fattah concludes that there is no doubt as to the special predisposition of the homosexual to become a victim of a theft-related murder. Yet, in one of his cases, as in the Chicago homicide, it is not at all clear whether there would have been murder or even petty assault had there not been default on a promise to make payment.[61]

In New York City during the winter of 1972–1973, three murders of homosexuals took place within a short period; the homicides exhibited curious similarities and to a large extent all followed a script spelled out in Gerald Walker's novel *Cruising*, published some years earlier.[62] While the motivation of robbery is not to be excluded, what seems uppermost in these homicides was a hatred of homosexuality that led the perpetrators (or perpetrator) to make a contact for the purpose of killing the victim before a sexual encounter took place. An analogy can be drawn to the murders of prostitutes by Jack the Ripper in London, unsolved but attributed by many to a man who was acting out his hatred of (and perhaps his erotic attraction to) such women.

Homosexuals are probably victimized by blackmailers much more than are prostitutes. In fact, while prostitutes are almost invulnerable to this type of criminal predator, other transgressors against the sex norms (including heterosexual "johns") are not. Spokesmen for the gay liberation movement have asserted that a man who openly proclaims his homosexual activity is almost immune to blackmail, but the adulterous husband is certainly very much subject to this type of pressure.

Despite the greater problem of homosexual blackmail in England than in the United States, several American cases have received wide publicity. For the most part the press (which is not as easily controlled by the courts as it is in England) has been cooperative in refusing to divulge the names of victims. In what was probably the most widely publicized case, it was said that the victims included a congressman, a high ranking Pentagon official, and others whose descriptions attested to their importance. The courts in blackmail cases generally refused to display any leniency toward the offenders, even before the diminution of hostility toward homosexuality.

Blackmail of homosexuals, when it does occur, is an "organized ring" type of crime that may reach into the peripheries of "organized crime." Like bribery, it is an offense that can take place only if it is not reported, and hence one cannot conjecture with any confidence of accuracy as to its frequency.

Extortion or "shakedown" by police plainclothesmen is another crime against homosexuals that is difficult to research. Many persons have reported to us that they have been shaken down for all the money that they had on them, anywhere from $10 to $50, when apprehended loitering or engaging in solicitation in public parks, restrooms, and elsewhere. In some instances of shakedown, the alleged officer accompanies the man to his house in order to obtain more money; in other cases, he makes an appointment to meet the victim subsequently. Several officers have been apprehended in the course of this last type of shakedown: the victim or his lawyer contacts a district attorney and arrangements are made for the passing of marked money.

What makes these crimes particularly difficult to study is that the "shakedown artist" in plain clothes may simply be using forged police identification. In his anxiety, the victim either does not consider this possibility or is powerless to pursue his suspicions. Police organizations and their defenders would like the public to believe that almost all such shakedowns are committed by impersonators, and this claim may well be true.

Robbery in which a homosexual is victim, often but not necessarily victimizer as well, is facilitated when an intimate but anonymous relationship develops. The victim is reluctant to report the matter to the police, which the offender realizes. There is a frequent inequality of strength, particularly with age differences, and robbery is justified in the mind of the offender by defining the victim as "queer"; whereas often, the offender does not define himself as homosexual, thus neutralizing normative restraints.

We have noted that homosexuals have been victimized by forcible sexual assaults, but the major group of victims of such assaults would appear to be young males who have strong heterosexual definitions of self at least at the time of the assault.

Finally, there is the important question of legal and extralegal discrimination against persons with known, suspected, or openly avowed homosexual life-styles. In the United States, such discrimination has been the focus of lobbying, protest movements, pressure groups, legislative action, civil libertarian studies, court suits, and the like. While the discrimination is sometimes illegal, it does not constitute what might be called "ordinary crime." However, as part of the pattern of stigmatization, it facilitates blackmail, extortion, and even robbery and homicide because of the fears of victims and the identification of offenders with the antihomosexual attitudes of large sectors of the populace.

Homosexuality and concomitant crime have some features quite distinct from those of prostitution and concomitant crime, as well as some similarities. Secrecy and the danger of disclosure lead not only to blackmail but also to robbery, assault, and even homicide, and this is true of organized crime groups and those engaged in cloak-and-dagger activities for political or monetary motivations. A low regard for the victim leads to crimes against homosexuals, as well as to offenses against alcoholics, prostitutes, and blacks, among others. A belief that the victim has little influence with courts and police officers neutralizes normal deterrents, as is true with persons of low socioeconomic status. A fear of arrest leads to shakedowns whether by the police or by police impersonators, as is true with prostitutes. Close relationships with strangers lead to robbery and assault, as is exemplified by hitchhikers and those giving them rides, bar girls, and many others. Casualness of acquaintance gives many offenders a feeling that they are beyond apprehension for there is no clue to their identity, which is true, again, for hitchhikers as well as others who initiate relationships under circumstances of anonymity. Rootlessness and instability seem to be factors that foster criminal activity: the supermobile become more easily drawn into committing offenses and more easily victimized by others who commit them.

The outlook for the homosexual as victim is mixed: there are some indications that victimization will diminish; some, that it will increase. For one thing, victimization of homosexuals will probably follow the general pattern of crime in America, where violence is at a high level, morality at a low, and tensions between people so strong that they create both criminal acts and severe protective measures. Any increase in violent acts against the person or in larcenous offenses is likely to find its analogue in homosexual victim statistics.

At the same time, there are several new features that confuse the outlook. Major among these is the greater visibility of homosexuals, with large numbers proclaiming their predilections and lifestyles and becoming known to their families, colleagues, co-workers, and neighbors. While this trend may contribute to reducing casual and promiscuous relationships, it could also result in the greater social acceptance creating more open areas for casual encounters (because of decreased fear on the part of the potential victim of social opprobrium or police apprehension) without producing greater security against victimization.

Public indignation against the victimizer and increased vigilance by the police in pursuing him can likewise serve as a double-edged weapon: on the one hand, to deter a would-be offender through fear of apprehension or to lessen the motivation to commit a crime by not offering ready-made definitions of certain victims as evil; on the other, to cause people to let down their guard.

Problems and Outlook

The legal debate over homosexuality has been beclouded by essentially irrelevant considerations. Whatever position one takes on the controversy over whether homosexuality is usually or infrequently accompanied by mental disturbance, and whether an exclusive or near exclusive pattern of homosexuality should be classified as mental illness, should in no way influence support for (or opposition to) the decriminalization movement. A society can find better ways to transmit its values to the young than by declaring criminal all forms of behavior that it wishes to discourage, regardless of the degree of harm they are alleged to inflict; it can build greater respect for the law if it does not pass legislation that it fails to enforce.

One of the difficulties in establishing a legal age of consent for an adult-adolescent homosexual encounter is in determining the effect of such an event on the later sex pattern of the younger person.* Certainly, research in this area is negligible; yet, without it, intelligent social policy is difficult to formulate. The Wolfenden proposal for a higher age of consent for homosexual than for hetero-sexual relationships could be studied now that there are several years of British experience with this policy.[63] An age of consent of eighteen appears reasonable and, taking into account the proposal of the American Law Institute on age differences between the younger and the older partner, this figure could be lowered to six-teen in those instances in which the age difference were no more than four years. In cases in which both boys (or both girls) are adolescent or preadolescent, it might be better to ignore noncoerced sex play.

Homosexual prostitution could well be handled legally in the same manner as heterosexual, although if the British pattern is emulated, it might be more difficult for an all-male encounter to be effected without resort to street solicitation. The British, it will be recalled, have banned streetwalking but not prostitution in which the solicitation takes place in other ways (including handbill advertising, telephoning, and the like). A permissive attitude to-ward such activities, except for the recruitment of very young males and the vigorous enforcement of a reasonable age of consent, is probably something that would do little or no harm to the society. As for open invitations for sex made to strangers on the streets, they are usually not frighteningly blatant but consist of cues and sug-gestions that the innocent may not respond to because they do not understand them, and the more sophisticated accept or reject at will. There are few civilian complaints about such acts, and were it not for police decoys there would be few arrests.

The problem of sex in public and semipublic places is a more difficult one. It seems unreasonable that people who intend no harm be followed into dark alleyways and unused parking lots; if exposure requires a trailing plainclothesman with flashlight to find transgressors, the transgression hardly seems a public affront to the moral standards of the community. Where the act does occur in places that the general public regularly uses, it does not appear proper that either heterosexual or homosexual activity be permitted. The definition of public place, or public accommodations, is not easy to give. There are health clubs that give massages and there

---

* This matter is discussed in Chapter 3 in the context of adult-child sexuality and age of consent (pp. 84–88).

are massage parlors that are rather obvious fronts for prostitution; little confusion of the two is made. In the same way, there are sporting or health clubs whose steam rooms are sought for salutary effects and others in which the phrase "Turkish bath" signifies a meeting place for impersonal homosexual activity. Occasional mistakes, embarrassment, perhaps even outrage may be a small price to pay for giving an outlet for such activities under relatively safe conditions to people who have urgent needs or desires in this direction. Public restrooms, on the other hand, should be off limits for sex solicitation so that people who wish to utilize them for the purpose for which they were constructed will be protected. The problem becomes more complex when one asks whether expensive police surveillance of public facilities is worth the effort and whether more harm than good is worked by apprehending such offenders who live otherwise useful and law-abiding lives.

Decriminalization will not solve the problem of homosexuality in society. On the one hand, it will be solved at least partially by destigmatization, and there is considerable progress in this direction. These two forces, change in law and change in public attitude, are dynamically interrelated. On the other hand, the National Task Force on Homosexuality, headed by Evelyn Hooker, as notable a champion of gay rights as America has produced, has suggested a number of steps, including not only changes in law, campaigns for public acceptance, and struggle against discriminatory practices but also research into methods for the prevention of the development of homosexuality and the combating of pessimism with regard to the possibility of successful change in sexual preference and orientation through therapy.[64]

Since publication of the original edition, the Florida Supreme Court has ruled that an otherwise qualified candidate for admission to the bar cannot be refused admission on the grounds of admitted homosexuality; and the San Francisco City Council, with only one dissenting vote, has passed the strongest homosexual civil rights ordinance in the nation. In New York City, Mayor Edward Koch has by executive order prohibited employment/promotion discrimination based on sexual orientation in any city agency; Cleveland has appointed Richard Hongisto, a champion of homosexual rights, as its new Chief of Police; and the United States Supreme Court has ordered the University of Missouri to grant full recognition and facilities to an on-campus homosexual student organization.

6 Offenses Against Public Order and Consensual Morality

In Chapters 2 and 3 we dealt with the two major areas of offenses that are generally conceded to be beyond the level of tolerance of a society: sex with an unwilling partner and sex with a child. Chapters 4 and 5 dealt with adult consensual acts that are not met with either the outrage aroused by forcible rape and child molestation or the near acceptance of, for example, fornication or open cohabitation. A large and significant section of American society seems to hold that prostitution and homosexuality are patterns that should be neither encouraged nor suppressed and that they could best be handled in a manner that is outside the legal and police procedures. Here one could perhaps draw an analogy with public intoxication, and some people would make an analogy with narcotics use as well. In Chapter 7 we will describe some rather common activities that are against the law in most jurisdictions, at least until recently, but that bring forth only mild outrage at most, and sometimes even approval, and the perpetrators of which would hardly be considered criminals.

These acts, however, do not exhaust illegal sexual behavior. The major areas remaining, as we see it, are actions that not only are infrequent but also involve peculiar patterns; furthermore, they are sometimes harmless or have relatively little potential for harm except to the perpetrator; and finally, in all likelihood the perpetrator exhibits gross signs of psychopathology. Yet not all of these factors are present in each instance. It is not certain that voyeurism is as harmless as many have claimed, nor is it likely that adolescents indulging in obscene telephone calls are manifesting pathology although adults who do so, particularly as a pattern, are probably not emotionally untroubled.

To put these actions together under a single heading is difficult; perhaps Krafft-Ebing had the best such heading when he used the Latin phrase *psychopathia sexualis*.[1] Clifford Allen, a British psychiatrist, uses the term "the paraphilia" to describe all the orientations in which sexual energy is diverted away from an adult partner of the other sex,[2] but such a broad spectrum (whatever value it may have) comes to include homosexuality and other rather common trends, as John Money and Anke Ehrhardt show when they define the term.[3] The six types of activities described in this chapter (seven, if one wishes to separate necrophilia from bestiality) are in our view offenses against public order and what can be called consensual morality: the moral order that is just that—a moral order by agreement of almost all sectors of the populace. Some of the acts are nuisances; others are victimless crimes; many are manifestations of pathology. It is our belief that all of them are rather rare. It is a combination of several or all of these features—infrequency, affront to a morality on which there is general agreement in the society, nuisance rather than endangerment, and possible presence of psychopathology—that brings these offenses together as a single unit. Perhaps the word "nuisance" is too mild for some of the acts described in this chapter; one might call them offensive to large sections of the populace who nonetheless do not see them as dangerous.

Exhibitionism

Exhibitionism can be defined as the display of one's genitalia or erotically arousing parts of the body to an audience that did not invite or encourage the display and is probably unwilling to view it; it is committed for the purpose of obtaining sexual gratification through the exhibition itself (and the reaction of the audience). It is almost always committed by males, from adolescents to mature adults to elderly men, and it is often done in front of, or in the view of, female children.

There is a borderline area between what constitutes normal exposure and what would be described as illegal and often pathological exhibitionism. For several reasons a woman wearing a see-through or no bra cannot be classified as an exhibitionist: she is following a fashion that makes the act permissible for some women; her audience is not unwilling or captive; the act is not one that outrages people in the context of the time and place in which it occurs; she is not actually displaying a part of the body generally covered; and there is no reason to believe that she obtains explicit sexual gratification from what she is or is not wearing and the way in which parts of her body are being viewed. Even complete nudity in the form of streaking is not quite exhibitionistic although it may have some features in common with exhibitionism; the streaker is not making a specifically sexual statement, overture, or threat to possible victims. In this respect, arrests of males for urinating in public (usually prosecuted as indecent exposure), offensive as such acts are to those who observe them, are a perversion of the intent of the law forbidding exposure of the genitals because although the act involves exposure, it does not meet the criteria for exhibitionism, which the law is intended to deter, punish, and control. Even more in conflict with the intent of the law is arrest of nude swimmers under laws forbidding exhibitionism. This behavior is usually engaged in collectively, with co-participants or a willing audience, is not frightening to others, and in other respects is not exhibitionistic. That public nudity might well constitute a nuisance is not here under dispute for certainly people are entitled to use beaches not frequented by nude bathers. However, that the latter should be prosecuted under statutes that make exhibitionism illegal only serves to confuse two types of behavior that have important differences despite their common elements.

Exhibitionists have generally been thought of as passive, frightened individuals who cannot make overtures to females in the normative manner for fear of being rejected. Whatever danger resides in their activities is the matter of engendering fright in the audience, particularly a young girl alone, who may fear rape or sexual assault, and the possibility that the act may be the prelude to child molestation if the exhibitionist is not rebuffed. However, Gebhard and associates would exclude these last persons from the category of exhibitionists, declaring: "Our concept of the exhibitionist is a male for whom the exhibition is a desired end in itself." [4] If the male does hope that the display will lead to further sexual activity, "this is only a subsidiary motivation." [5] The problem here is that from a viewpoint of the criminal law and of definition, arrest, and conviction one cannot make a separate category out of those who exhibit as an end in itself and those who do so in the hope that it will be the first step toward successful solicitation.

In the study by Gebhard's group of incarcerated exhibitionists, the average age at the time of offense was thirty-five years, and 64 percent of the men were married. Many of them had other sex offense convictions, most of which were for exhibitionism. This would seem to indicate not only recidivism but also compulsivity, a difficulty on the part of the person even after conviction to control behavior for which he knows that he is going to be punished more severely because of prior convictions. Some were also voyeurs, some, rapists. These data would indicate that whatever truth there may be in the stereotype of the frightened and passive male who indulges in exhibitionism, it cannot be used to guide social policy. Finally, about a third of the exhibitionists in this sample claimed they were intoxicated at the time of the crime—an allegation common among sex offenders. (Alcohol consumption aside, most of the cases seemed to involve advance planning).[6]

There were 288 cases in the Gebhard study, and the age of the victim (if that word is appropriate, or perhaps the complainant) was not always available. However, it was known that there were thirty offenses with girls under the age of twelve; another nineteen in front of girls between twelve and fifteen. It is difficult to know whether adult females are more likely to complain than are children and whether the offenses against adults were more seriously meant as a first step toward sexual solicitation.

Some persons have emphasized that the exhibitionist is seeking to affirm his masculinity by displaying proof of it in front of others; others, that he deliberately seeks to frighten his audience, thus showing hostility, even sadistic tendencies. In either case, the possibility of rape or assault—to prove one's potency or masculinity, to show hostility—is real indeed. Nevertheless, the closing remarks of Gebhard, that the exhibitionists on the whole "are to be pitied rather than feared," would seem to be a generally acceptable formulation.[7]

A study of a considerable number of sex offenders was conducted by Albert Ellis and Ralph Brancale.[8] Of all sex offenders confined at the New Jersey State Prison at the time of this study, 10 percent had been convicted of exhibitionistic sex acts; however, of 300 offenders examined at the New Jersey State Diagnostic Center, 29 percent were exhibitionists (eighty-nine men, the largest single group of offenders). Of these eighty-nine men, thirty-six had exhibited their genitals to adult females, twenty-five to minor females, twenty had been arrested for masturbating in public, and the remaining eight for "indecent exposure." Offenders with previous sex offenses, with or without arrest, made up 67 percent of the exhibitionist sample, exceeded only by those arrested for homosexuality, and 34 percent had had previous arrests for sex offenses, again higher than the average for all offenders yet exceeded not only by the homosexual sample but also by adult males who had had noncoital sex with a minor.

While few offenders at the diagnostic center were found to be psychologically normal (the major exception was for those convicted of statutory rape), the exhibitionists included rather sizable proportions of abnormal men. Among them were eighteen classified as mildly neurotic, forty-six as severely neurotic, seven as borderline psychotic, two as psychotic, and three as psychopathic. Compulsivity was found to be widespread, and yet at the same time harmless rather than dangerous.

On the question of dangerousness, one returns to the problem of defining exhibitionism. It sometimes appears that there is a tautology here: the element of danger is excluded because if it were present the act would not be classified as exhibitionism. Thus, Johan Mohr and his colleagues in Canada define the term as "the expressed impulse to expose the male organ to an unsuspecting female as a final sexual gratification." [9] Aside from the arbitrary exclusion of both female perpetrators and, even more important, male homosexual perpetrators from the definition, the expression "final sexual gratification" may compel diagnostician, court, or others to see the exhibitionist as harmless. However, if one regards a severely neurotic or a borderline psychotic person as often being unstable in behavior over a period of time, not readily controllable, then one may well perceive that someone who engages in exhibitionism for final sexual gratification may on a later occasion or even during the course of one exhibitionistic encounter become potentially dangerous.

There is furthermore the question of the psychological danger to children and others who have been subjected to exhibitionistic exposure, often under frightening conditions. Little is known of what occurs to such persons over a long period of time, whether the one event has long-term traumatic consequences.

We do not deny that the danger of exhibitionism has often been exaggerated; nevertheless, it ought not be minimized out of well-meaning sympathy for the psychologically disturbed individual who has committed exhibitionistic acts. Despite the putative and probably real harmlessness of most such activities, few would argue with the need to retain some legal restraints against exhibitionism. Only in a society of complete nudity, an unlikely prospect in our urban and industrialized world, would there be no need for a law against those who inappropriately displayed their genitals because there would be no display that would be inappropriate.

Voyeurs and Peepers

The word "voyeur" originally meant one who sees or observes. Men stand on street corners and stare at the women who walk by, they ogle, admire, and whistle, and then they continue what they had been doing: work, conversation, drinking, or gambling. Although many women have taken exception to this type of activity, these men are not voyeurs, or, to use a distinction made by some, they are not peepers.

The peeper, or the Peeping Tom, is distinguished from the ordinary person who has something of the voyeur in him, according to Gebhard and his co-authors, by his compulsivity.[10] He peeps regularly and takes great risks in doing so. More than that, his satisfaction is often (but not always) in the act of peeping, which is usually not a stepping-stone to a further act. Following Gebhard's definition, we would classify as peepers only those persons for whom the act of uninvited looking is sexually gratifying as an end in itself. There are certain problems with such a definition, however, for it ignores the gradation between lookers and peepers, the possibility that the former may develop into the latter, and the likelihood that the peeper himself may develop interests in which looking is not the sole gratifying end product. The distinction between "normal voyeurs," as one might call many men, and compulsive peepers may well revolve around the intrusion on the privacy of someone (usually a female but sometimes two persons in embrace); the "normal voyeur" has what Birenbaum and Sagarin have referred to as "a right to be present," although a passing girl might wish that he did not stare.[11]

If all males are a little exhibitionistic and a little voyeuristic, few have a strong inner demand to display themselves under inappropriate conditions or to watch surreptitiously what they have not been given the right to see. Many people, probably most, demand privacy for their sexual acts and in the same way that they would find the presence of another person (even concealed behind a peephole) disturbing and repugnant, they would not want to cause that disturbance to others. In fact, Ford and Beach were able to name only a few primitive societies in which sex was not conducted under the most carefully controlled private conditions.[12]

As a sexual offender, the peeper has been considered a nuisance, more pathological than criminal, although for want of an effective alternative, he has been treated as a criminal. A generally held belief, which seems logical but has not been clearly validated, holds that most peepers are frightened persons (they are almost invariably males) who would not attack or in any other way harm the object of their view. As a result of extreme timidity, it is claimed, many have substituted seeing for doing. They cannot approach a woman because of overwhelming fear of rejection and defeat, characteristics that Albert Ellis contends are present in humans generally but to a far greater extent in the emotionally distressed.[13] Some people, Ellis maintains, have a pathological inability to face such a rebuff and hence create mechanisms (neurotic and self-defeating) to avoid situations in which such an outcome may be possible. The peeper plays it safe by never making the approach, thus deflecting sexual energies into the kicks of looking and watching. However, categories based on shared behavioral patterns do not generally have members who are homogeneous in other respects, and many peepers fail to fit this description.

Of the early writers on sexual anomalies and disturbances, Krafft-Ebing literally ignored voyeurism and in fact showed neither interest in, nor knowledge of, its existence.[14] Most of his patients either came to a physician for aid (as neither exhibitionists nor peepers generally do) or had gotten into trouble with the law (which is more likely to happen to exhibitionists than to peepers). Those who exhibit must do so before an unwilling audience, and to be successful they must be seen; therefore, it is not unusual that they are apprehended. Those who peep must do so by looking at an unknowing person or persons, and to be successful they must not themselves be seen; therefore, apprehension is less frequent. The exhibitionist takes his victim by surprise, and unless the victim sees him and is outraged, he has failed; the peeper comes to the victim by stealth, and this victim would be outraged only if he knew of the peeper's presence, but usually he does not. The normal voyeur, who is far from being a pathological peeper, has his counterpart in the normal "advertiser" or "showoff" who is not an exhibitionist.

Havelock Ellis, in whose classic work an entire chapter is devoted to exhibitionism, has only a few words on this side of the coin, on what might today be called the "normal deviant," [15] the person (in the instances noted by Ellis usually a child) who stops to watch the copulation of animals and finds it to be "mysteriously fascinating."

> It is inevitable that this should be so, for the spectacle is more or less clearly felt to be the revelation of a secret which has been concealed from [the children]. It is, moreover, a secret of which they feel intimate reverberations within themselves, and even in perfectly innocent and ignorant children the sight may produce an obscure sexual excitement. It would seem that this occurs more frequently in girls than in boys. Even in adult age, it may be added, women are liable to experience the same kind of emotion in the presence of such spectacles.[16]

That humans of all ages and both sexes would be attracted to the sight of animal copulation seems easy to accept although one must express considerable doubt, for want of validating evidence, that this occurs more frequently in females than in males. That watching animals copulating has become a legal issue is seen from an examination of statutes that are described by Robert Sherwin as

> making it a crime if animals such as horses, donkeys, cattle, and goats are permitted to mate within a certain number of feet of or in view of a school, public street, church, private home, or tavern. In some jurisdictions the penalty for permitting such an offense can go as high as a fine of $1,000 or one year in prison, or both.[17]

More important, there is some question as to whether the attraction to the spectacle constitutes an arousal. To use Gebhard's distinction between voyeurs and peepers, the boys and girls described by Havelock Ellis were the former, not the latter. They did not seek out such activity but also did not turn the other way when coming across it. The peeper wants to see what he has no right to see, nudity or sexual intercourse, and this is what gives him his gratification. As distinct from the voyeur, the peeper thus becomes a nuisance, and perhaps his behavior is pathological.

This kind of peeping, broadly defined as voyeurism, was given considerable attention by the Freudian analysts of psychosexual development. Benjamin Karpman,[18] for one, has pointed out that prohibition is "an indispensable proviso" for the peeper's pleasure although there is a gray area that must be considered: "He must be able to look without being seen. The excitement ranges from no genital response to compulsive exhibitionistic masturbation. . . . Frequently voyeurs [peepers] are fixated on experiences that aroused their castration anxiety by either primal scenes or the sight of adult genitals." [19]

One of the problems with the voyeur, Karpman states, is that when he is detected, his motives may be misunderstood—he is likely to be mistaken for a potential burglar. So long as he remains undetected, it is claimed, he disturbs no one.

But this widely held stereotype may be most misleading, and the peeper should not be dismissed as universally harmless. It is difficult to know, as he prowls and peeps, whether he *is* a potential burglar; in fact, even when arrested, if he is a burglar he may be pleased to find that he can cop a plea by causing it to be believed that he is only a somewhat disturbed man who was there to see, not to take. Furthermore, he may be *both* a peeper and a thief.

A study of clinical cases of peepers was made by Irvin Yalom. For this purpose, Yalom preferred the term "offensive voyeur" to distinguish the habitual peeper from the ordinary curious gazer, starer, or looker. He defined as characteristic of the offensive voyeur "an exaggerated desire to see, by stealth, a member of the opposite sex in some stage of undress, in the sexual act, or in the act of excretion, which [desire] is so intense that it surpasses in importance the normal sexual act." Yalom further explained that even the expression "exaggerated desire" is an understatement, too moderate "for the drive most voyeurs experience—a drive which has many of the qualities of a compulsion except that it is ego-syntonic, i.e., something the person wants and likes to do." [20]

Some of the peepers studied by Yalom were sadists, and among the crimes they committed were arson and rape. All were aggressive persons, but this may be because the nonaggressive peeper, genuinely timid, less frequently comes to the attention of clinicians. Of one patient it was reported: "About one-fourth of the evenings he went out he only peeped; one-half of the evenings he burglarized; and one-fourth of the time he did both." Forbiddenness was absolutely essential, and pleasure seemed to increase when the voyeur could observe without detection.

One of Yalom's patients stated:

> Looking at a nude girlfriend wouldn't be as exciting as seeing
> her the sneaky way. It's not just the nude body but the sneaking
> out and seeing what you're not supposed to see. The risk of get-
> ting caught makes it exciting. I don't want to get caught, but
> every time I go out I'm putting myself on the line.[21]

Of Yalom's subjects, some were on the road to more serious
crimes, and some of the people committing more serious crimes are
former voyeurs. A short time before committing rape, assault, arson,
and burglary, many of them would have been diagnosed as voyeurs
and, according to Yalom, would have been declared nuisances, offenders of good taste but not dangerous to society.

How does one account for such seemingly passive lookers becoming so actively aggressive? They have not undergone a sudden
conversion, Yalom contends.

> Long before the serious criminal offense, aggressive impulses
> were present, being expressed symbolically and temporarily sati-
> ated in the not so passive act of peeping. It is entirely possible
> that voyeurism may be used as a defense against aggression in
> that it is safer to look and destroy unconsciously than to act and
> destroy literally—a defense which in these cases has ultimately
> failed.[22]

Like Yalom, Gebhard and his co-workers found that the stereotype of the peeper as an almost always harmless individual is
belied by reality. Some of the peepers had committed rape, and
this was more common among the habitual peepers than the occasional ones. To differentiate the harmless man from the one who
will go from peeping to rape is difficult, "but we do have the impression that peepers who enter homes or other buildings in order
to peep, and peepers who deliberately attract the female's attention
(tapping on windows, leaving notes, etc.) are more likely to become rapists than the others."[23] Furthermore, Gebhard found
that a large number of individual peepers, possibly a majority,

> generally have inadequate heterosexual lives, and the remaining
> peepers are a miscellany of persons whose peeping is not so
> habitual and who generally have adequate sex lives. At this point
> it should be reiterated that peepers rarely spy on relatives and
> friends, but seek strangers.[24]

There is, however, a high incidence of sibling voyeurism, especially in early adolescence, and it appears to be a form of sex education for many young people; and perhaps a somewhat lesser but still significant incidence of children viewing or attempting to view their parents' sexual activities, with what effects on the children one does not know.

Quite obviously, a nudist colony—mentioned by Hartman and his colleagues as a possible therapeutic milieu for potential voyeurs or exhibitionists[25]—goes contrary to the need of the voyeur for forbiddenness and to his aggressive and hostile attitude toward the victim. Certainly, it fails to offer the excitement produced by the use of stealth and risk. At best, however, one might explore the possibility of using social nudism as a therapeutic measure for those who feel that they are becoming voyeurs; satiation may nip it before it has developed. On the other hand, voyeurs are frequent customers of burlesque houses, topless bars, and similar sex exhibitions; if one interprets letters to Playboy and similar publications correctly, voyeurs number significantly among their readers. They are also quite heavy purchasers of hard-core pornography. It might be interesting to speculate that police activity directed against these vicarious satisfactions might well prove counterproductive, actually increasing the incidence of peeping.

Robert Sherwin found that most states do not make a legal distinction concerning the sex of the person spied upon by the peeper, but Sherwin did find one state in which the peeping was criminal only if the person spied upon was female. Like many of the other sexual anomalies, peeping is almost exclusively, if not exclusively, a male trait.[26] Although homosexual peeping would be possible, and homosexual exhibition is not a small proportion of all exhibitionism, no cases of arrests and prosecutions for peeping on other males has come to our attention. Interviews have indicated, however, that many clients of homosexual baths seem contented to be "lookers" rather than participants, and men's room voyeurs are not unknown, including those who watch the participants and at the same time act as lookouts for them.

What is the social harm of voyeurism? Other than its use as a mask for, or a stepping-stone toward, more serious crimes, why is it objectionable? Primarily, voyeurism is an invasion of privacy. But what is privacy? Privacy is the circle we draw around ourselves and what we do, in which we, the participants, decide who shall be permitted to see, to hear, to know, or to be present. Barry Schwartz has described the universal need for regulations governing privacy.

> Guarantees of privacy, that is, rules as to who may and may not observe or reveal information about whom, must be established in any stable social system. If these assurances do not prevail—if there is normlessness with respect to privacy—every withdrawal from visibility may be accompanied by a measure of espionage, for without rules to the contrary persons are naturally given to intrude upon invisibility.[27]

Some have suggested that looking may take the place of doing and that under certain circumstances this substitution not only might *not* lead to antisocial acts but also could actually be a vicarious substitute for such acts. This problem will be discussed in our consideration of pornography. However, it does not seem that if voyeurism were turned into a great national pastime it would replace sexual activity itself. Whether it would replace it for a few who are the nuisances, and the potential or real criminals, is another issue.

Alan Westin notes the tendency to curiosity among individuals, the insatiable inquisitiveness, the interest in watching forbidden things, visiting forbidden places, eating forbidden fruit, uttering forbidden words.[28] To this individual curiosity there is now added the governmental process of surveillance. Every society wants to protect itself against those who are breaking its rules or whom it suspects of conspiring to break them, and in acting in behalf of this protection, authorities have gone to enormous lengths toward the invasion of privacy. That there is a great difference between a Peeping Tom peering through a window and a hidden camera watching one's every move (including those in a bedroom or bathroom) cannot be denied, but the similarities should not be overlooked. The victim in each case suffers from what Sagarin has called "the power of the peephole," [29] and if the former instance is for the satisfaction of an individual with a peculiar psychosexual development and the latter for the protection of an impersonal government, the latter may nonetheless be more dangerous, particularly because we live in an age of remarkable minitransistors, what Westin has termed the marvels of microminiaturization and circuitry, chemical synthesis and projective psychiatry.[30]

In 1964, a husband and wife in Gilford, New Hampshire, discovered that the landlord had installed an electronic ear in their bedroom. Carefully concealed wires carried every sound from the couple's room to the landlord's house. The couple sued, and the court, in deciding in favor of the tenants, stated:

> If the Peeping Tom, the big ear and the electronic eaves-dropper (whether ingenious or ingenuous) have a place in the hierarchy of social values, it ought not be at the expense of a married couple minding their own business in the seclusion of their bedroom who have never asked for or by their conduct deserved a potential projection of their private conversations and actions to their landlords or others.[31]

Thus, on two grounds we will be reluctant to look upon voyeurism as behavior that has little or no potential for social harm: first, the evidence that the pathological voyeur, or peeper, is already engaged in, or is likely to become involved in, more serious crimes that cannot be described as victimless; second, the very narrow and tenuous line that separates, when it does, the sexual voyeur from landlords, White House operatives, and others who illegally look and listen with instruments far more sensitive and delicate than the human eye and ear.

The sociosexual meaning of peeping, staring, and leering is a subject worthy of further investigation. There is a continuum that begins with the man who whistles and ogles to impress other men with his masculinity and includes the peeper, to whom voyeurism is an end in itself. There is no evidence that for the former, looking is the final gratification sought although the impression that he makes upon male comrades may well be as important to him as the remote possibility that the leer will lead to physical contact.

The objection of women generally, and of feminists specifically, to leering males, to catcalls and whistles, to offensive, uninvited solicitations by strangers, to treatment as sex objects rather than as persons is indubitably legitimate. Such activities by males may well be a reflection of the low esteem in which they hold women. It is true that the street is a public thoroughfare, the bedroom and its window are not, but this is all the more reason that persons should be able to walk on that thoroughfare without being verbally assaulted or otherwise offended. The distinction between those who normally stare and those who circumspectly peek, however, is a real one, and it hardly seems logical, practical, or worthy of serious consideration to criminalize the former any more than to lift all criminal sanctions against the latter.

Transvestism

Transvestism (sometimes called transvestitism) is a technical term for cross-dressing, but it is generally extended to impersonation of the opposite sex.[32] Like most sex crimes, anomalies, and peculiarities, transvestism is found far less among females; however, this may in part be because almost any type of clothing is acceptable for women in Western society under most conditions. Transvestism is often accompanied by extreme and exaggerated effeminacy, which can be turned off at will by some transvestites. The extent of homosexual interests and/or activities among people who cross-dress and who impersonate females is a matter of controversy. Some authorities have suggested that there are people who have desires, needs, or compulsions to cross-dress but who are aroused and gratified only heterosexually, while others are very effeminate homosexuals. Little is served, it appears, by a diagnosis of the heterosexual transvestite as a repressed or latent homosexual.

Homosexual transvestites are often known as "drag queens," and to dress as a woman is known in the vernacular as being "in drag." Although this description is pejorative, it is frequently used by transvestites or in their presence. To be capable of carrying out the impersonation without discovery is to "pass" (a word borrowed from the language of race relations), while someone who penetrates the mask of the transvestite is said to be "reading" that person.

Cross-dressing is sometimes confined only to the privacy of one's home or to parties, balls, masquerades, Halloween gatherings. In such instances, there is no violation of the law. However, it is against the law in most areas for a person to appear in public impersonating the sex of another.[33] In the United States some laws against cross-dressing originated to protect the colonists from raids by Indians, and the laws were worded so as to cover many types of outfits and masquerading activities in public. Only later, were the laws invoked against males impersonating females.

Transvestism, or TV, is probably rather uncommon. Why should it be illegal? It is argued that any form of masquerading makes identification more difficult and thus provides a cover under which a crime can be committed; and that the appearance in public of a male dressed as a female creates a public nuisance and a public disorder.

The first of these arguments would appear to be reasonable except that crimes committed by men dressed as women for the purpose of avoiding identification are probably rare. There are occasional reports of such incidents. Some men, later apprehended, apparently had no conscious interest in, or record of, cross-dressing but had donned feminine apparel for the first time with illegal activity in mind (a prime example from American history is found in the killings and dynamitings in the coal mining areas in the late 1860s and 1870s, when on some occasions the Molly Maguires used women's cloaks to conceal their identity). Prisoners have occasionally cross-dressed and escaped in the guise of female visitors. These instances aside, it is doubtful whether many males can carry through such an impersonation with finesse and grace; to be a successful transvestite requires a great deal of practice. If a crime is committed by an impersonator, there are likely to be clues that will help rather than hinder criminal investigation.

Cross-dressing is at worst a nuisance for the public and for the family of the individual who has a need to engage in this practice.[34] It is regarded by most authorities as a manifestation of pathology. Psychiatrists and other behavioral scientists, including those like Richard Green [35] who have taken a most compassionate attitude toward adult transvestites, nevertheless advocate measures to socialize children, whenever possible, into the sex role more congruent with their anatomy. The young boy who shows interest in wearing girls' clothes and acting in an effeminate manner should be discouraged from cross-dressing, and given male-oriented goals that are within reach of achievement and are not likely to prove discouraging or difficult. However, a totally different situation is that of the child who enjoys costume parties but who no more desires to be like a female, or to be a female, when in costume party dress than he would want to be like a wolf, or to be a wolf, when playing the villain in Little Red Riding Hood.

For teenagers and mature men who persist in such patterns, sympathy and compassion can be proffered. A legal question arises as to whether schoolchildren in elementary and high schools are harmed by exposure to teachers who cross-dress. While the civil rights of the teacher are important, the possible effect on the children cannot be ignored.

Daniel Brown is one of many authorities who stress that transvestism "often becomes fixated during childhood . . . [and] is highly resistant to modification or extinction." [36] Psychotherapy has not proved successful, Brown indicates, but he advocates psycho-sexual "immunization" through an educational program directed to parents.

There seems to be no demonstrable good that is accomplished by the laws against transvestism. They serve to persecute people with deep-going problems. Such persons often encounter difficulties in life that stem from their cross-dressing; for example, transvestites are not uncommonly beaten up by unsuspecting males who discover their gender during a sexual encounter. That transvestite behavior is illegal is little or no protection against such a victim-precipitated assault.

The transvestite who cannot easily pass invites ridicule on the streets and in other public places. He will not change because of arrest and imprisonment, and to add fear of the police to his burdens appears to be unnecessarily cruel.

Transsexualism

There are people who are deeply dissatisfied with those aspects of their anatomy that identify them as being male or female. They do not wish to masquerade, for longer or shorter periods of time, as members of the other sex but desire to *become* members of that sex. The word "transsexual" has been coined to describe such persons.[37] Although the anatomically male transsexual (or TS, as it is often abbreviated) may consciously harbor sexual desires for a male, he does not make a self-definition as homosexual because he refuses to accept the biological decision that he is male. While to many this might be seen merely as a flight from reality, the individual involved conceptualizes himself as "a female trapped in a man's body" (or vice versa).

So long as such an individual is engaged in cross-dressing, the process is one of impersonation regardless of the self-definition. Where there are laws against cross-dressing and impersonation, the transsexual would be violating such laws.[38] Nevertheless, psychiatrists and other professionals have often advised and encouraged persons who present themselves as transsexuals to assume the dress and identity of the other sex for a considerable period of time (usually two or three years) before attempting such drastic and irreversible surgery.

The surgery that a transsexual undergoes is often referred to as a "change of sex" operation, but John Money, who feels that such surgery is indicated as a matter of last resort in some instances and does not believe that the medical profession should oppose it, has categorically stated that it is not a change of sex that takes place but a reassignment of sex.[39] For the male, this involves removal of penis, testes, and scrotum, construction of an artificial vaginalike aperture, and hormone treatment to encourage the growth and development of breasts, together with depilation of facial hair and other measures. Surgery of this type was at one time illegal almost everywhere in the United States, and doctors performing it were liable for criminal prosecution under the mayhem and other laws. It is now being openly performed in many parts of the United States and elsewhere in the world, and prosecutions of physicians are almost entirely unknown (although there have been civil suits by a small number of persons who regretted the operation).

Violation of the statutes against cross-dressing aside, the transsexual has legal problems that involve administrative rather than criminal matters. These include but are not limited to discriminatory action on the job, difficulty in obtaining identifying papers in which the individual is recognized as female, and problems of obtaining visiting rights to children in cases of fathers who have undergone sex reassignment surgery.[40] A well-publicized case of transsexualism involved an expert tennis player who met militant opposition when attempting to compete in female tennis tournaments.

Necrophilia and Bestiality

In a volume on sex crime, only passing interest need be paid to such activities as necrophilia and bestiality (also called zoophilia).

Necrophilia (love of death or of the dead) refers to sexual contact with a dead person. While there are often rumors, and sometimes jokes, about people who work in hospital morgues, in funeral homes, and in other places where those recently dead are kept, it is unlikely that there is much "action" or that there are many people who have the need, desire, or even potential for responses in this direction.

Necrophilia is almost universally a violation of some statute whether it be under the heading of depravity, crime against nature, unnatural sex act, or even sodomy and whether the statute is merely a vague catchall for numerous types of sex conduct not enumerated or specifically mentions this act. Gerhard Mueller uses necrophilia as a prime example of the uselessness of a law not because the act is victimless (as is argued in instances of homosexuality and heterosexual extracoital activity, for example) but because it is rational to handle such matters solely as psychiatric and not legal problems.

> Our statute books contain some prohibitions which describe conduct so clearly indicative of the mental abnormality of the perpetrator as to draw the very purpose of the law in question. For example, the law threatens long terms of imprisonment for intercourse with a corpse. I simply cannot conceive of a psychiatrist who would succeed in this second half of the twentieth century in establishing that a person who engages in such conduct is perfectly mentally healthy. Indeed, no behavior can better illustrate a symptom of the loss of a meaningful conception of one's behavior or of a sense of right and wrong as such fantastically perverse conduct as that. There is absolutely no justification for continuing such offenses on the statute books. Such matters must be taken care of by the mental health laws, but not by criminal law.[41]

The rare instances of criminal prosecutions involving necrophilia tend to be based on a charge of rape that followed murder. Sometimes a prosecutor will attempt to show that this was the sequence of crimes, probably for the purpose of inflaming a jury and the public. Rape and murder, in whatever order, can hardly be surpassed for the enormity of the outrage, and to add necrophilia to the list of accusations against a defendant does little more than place the crime in a context of psychopathology.

Occasional or sporadic bestiality, particularly among adolescent rural males, is probably not uncommon; according to Kinsey and his co-workers, as many as 20 percent of all males have had one or more such experiences.[42] There are probably very few instances of continued patterns of behavior of this type, and those that occur would be pathological. Arrests and prosecutions are not unknown, usually occurring because the human was apprehended during the act.

Both males and females in Western society have engaged in ever more open erotic fondling of house pets, particularly dogs, and veterinarians and psychiatrists report cases of the masturbating of dogs by humans, of dog bites on penis and female genitalia, and of other injuries caused by efforts to effect a human-canine sex relationship.

Although Kinsey emphasized that there is a mammalian capacity for interspecies (or, to use the biological term, interspecific) sexuality, overwhelmingly arousal and gratification are directed toward one's own species. A cat in heat attracts other cats, not dogs. Most female animals will resist being mounted by males outside their own species, and most males prefer to be without sexual outlet or to rub the genitals against some object in a manner similar to human masturbation than to approach a female of another species. The capacity of which Kinsey wrote is just that and no more, and the direction toward one's own species, involving an overwhelming preference, is probably instinctual, and surviving in the animal libido because it is favorable to perpetuation of the species.

Although there are individual instances and studies of bestiality, the numbers of persons accused and convicted are probably too small to permit systematic research on this type of behavior. In the Ellis-Brancale study of 300 sex offenders examined at the New Jersey Diagnostic Center over a thirteen-month period, two had been charged with bestiality and convicted. Neither admitted a prior offense although both had been previously arrested for nonsexual crimes. One was classified as mildly neurotic, the other as mentally deficient; the former as dull-normal, the latter moronic.[43]

What Mueller has stated about necrophilia can be repeated about bestiality; namely, that it is a psychiatric and not a legal problem and ought to be handled accordingly. Sporadic playful contact between an adolescent and an animal, if ignored, in most instances (if one is to give credence to the Kinsey statistics) appears to have no significant effect on adult sex patterns. For adults who seek out or prefer animal contacts, the conduct falls outside the realm of normality but not necessarily outside the bounds of tolerance in a society. Little or nothing is served by laws against bestiality, and certainly nothing at all is served by the long prison sentences that have been meted out to a few unfortunate persons. However, animal lovers (not pathological zoophiliacs) might well view human-infrahuman sex, particularly with a small pet, as subsumed under laws criminalizing "cruelty to animals."

Adult Consensual Incest

The major criminological interest in incest is undoubtedly in the relationship between adult and child or minor, particularly in those between father or stepfather and daughter or stepdaughter (discussed in Chapter 3). However, the legal problem extends to adults as well. Kirson Weinberg cites what he terms as an extreme instance of incest the case of a Mormon who wed three women of direct descent: grandmother, mother, and daughter.[44] Once he was married to any one of these women, both of the others were related to him by marriage, and hence any union with the others fit the legal definition of incest. One writer, going back to 1577, cites a case in which a man was hanged for adultery with his stepmother,[45] a theme also developed in Eugene O'Neill's *Desire under the Elms,* in which an elderly man marries a young woman whose sexual and amorous interests are directed toward her stepson, not her spouse.

When marital relations are included under a definition of incest, the act is probably not at all rare. Certainly, adultery between a woman and her brother-in-law or father-in-law, or a man with the corresponding females, is probably not uncommon. In their meanings to the participants, however, these are extramarital rather than incestuous events. There are numerous instances of marriages of just such a nature following death or divorce, and there are societies in which such marriages are expected, approved, or made compulsory. It should be clear that one cannot define the attraction as incestuous, compel the members of a society to internalize the strongest of taboos, and then redefine the same attraction, following death, as permissible or socially desirable.[46]

It is our belief that a relationship involving two adults whose ties to one another are legal and not genetic should not be conceptualized as incestuous by the law or by social science. If, as would in all likelihood be the case, it is extramarital, it should be legally treated as any other type of adultery (or legally ignored).

More controversial, however, is the problem of a genetic or truly incestuous union between consenting adults. More so than controversy over homosexuality, the conflict over decriminalization of such activities would probably bring into sharp relief the entire question of whether private and sexual morality should be made a matter of criminal law concern. Unlike homosexuality, true incest has few defenders although it may well have participants. There is an unknown number of people, possibly rather few, driven in this direction, who choose it as a matter of preference, or who find that they cannot embark on another path.

A penal law could well ignore adult consensual incest without encouraging the activity, without causing it to increase, and probably without lessening the moral opposition of society to it. More than any other activity, incest is shunned because the mores are strong, not because of legal prohibitions. While it is unlikely that illegalization does great harm, decriminalization of adult incest would be a symbolic statement of the firm belief that law is not concerned with private morality but only with matters that affect public welfare and safety. The Model Penal Code of the American Law Institute recommends that incest be a felony of the third degree but limits the restrictions to blood, half-blood, and adoptive relationships, with no restrictions on "in-law incest." In 1976, Canadian and Swedish law reform commissions both recommended decriminalization of incest, and the same year Guam reduced incest to a misdemeanor.

Obscene Telephone Calling

Another annoyance: the obscene telephone call. The victims are almost always women, the callers men, and sometimes the calls arrive at very late hours. The calls can contain threats; the caller presumably knows the name and address of the person receiving the message, but the recipient knows nothing about the identity of the caller. These can be frightening and disturbing experiences.

Few callers are apprehended. Donald Russell tells of one such person who had made a call,

> a long-hospitalized psychotic patient of 32 who was on brief parole with his family. He had become fascinated by the "Weather-Girl" on television and had besieged her station telephone with calls expressive of his devotion to her and his sexual interest in her.[47]

Adult males making such calls are probably deeply disturbed individuals, but adolescents occasionally indulge in the same type of behavior just "for kicks" and without giving serious thought to the distress they are causing to others. In the landmark case *In re Gault,* which resulted in a decision of the Supreme Court entitling an accused juvenile to certain basic constitutional rights in a juvenile court proceeding, the youth was charged with having made obscene calls to an elderly lady.[48]

Probably only a small number of callers are apprehended, and these may be the most persistent, the chronic, and possibly the more disturbed. Gebhard and his associates found, among the incarcerated offenders, six males who derived sexual gratification from communicating with females by telephone, using taboo vocabulary, and who were in consequence arrested and convicted. The females were almost all total strangers, usually selected randomly from a telephone directory. Not infrequently the males would masturbate while telephoning.[49]

While protection of the innocent and laws against those who offend are necessary, there is general agreement that the chronic obscene telephone caller is in need of psychological or psychiatric counseling. According to the New York Telephone Company, approximately 50,000 complaints are received annually in New York City regarding "annoyance calls."[50] Of these, about one-fifth are classified as obscene. The frequency of obscene phone calls in smaller cities is not known, but there is reason to believe that most instances are not reported. It is difficult to trace local calls, and police may advise complainants to hold the caller on the line and make an appointment to meet; a trap to apprehend the caller can then be set. When the same individual makes repeated calls, tapes can be obtained, and the development of voice identification technology makes conviction more likely. In the meantime, many people prefer unlisted numbers, and some women identify themselves by last name and first initial in telephone directories so as not to reveal their gender.

Frotteurs and Touchers

A very annoying group, to which feminists have rightly directed indignation, are frotteurs, touchers, feelers, goosers, rubbers, and pinchers. They are almost invariably male, and they include heterosexual as well as homosexual touchers. They are men who seize every opportunity to explore with their hands, or who press their bodies insistently against the bodies of others in crowded trains, elevators, even stores, and derive sexual satisfaction therefrom. In our opinion, these are simple assaults, or perhaps disorders, and should be treated thus in law.

7 On the Periphery of Crime

There are many sexual acts that have been illegal and still are punishable in numerous jurisdictions but that are seldom viewed by even the most moralistic section of the public as criminal; often these behaviors are regarded as being either a private matter, at worst, or quite acceptable, at best. Under such a heading we would discuss a wide range of behaviors generally thought of as normal (that is, free from pathology) and not a public nuisance and often considered either normative or only a slight deviation from the normative, conduct that is widely practiced and condoned yet not given legal approval; together with a disapproved act (adultery) that is seldom regarded as a proper area for criminal prosecution. All of these types of behavior fall within the category of consenting adult heterosexual acts.

Although the term "consenting adults" has most frequently been used by partisans of homosexuality, the fact is that many types of adult consensual heterosexual acts fall into this domain, yet remain illegal in many jurisdictions of the United States and in most other nations. There are some adult consensual heterosexual acts that if not pathological border on pathology (such as sadomasochism); whether they can logically be seen as crimes without victims is debatable. Others are usually condemned or socially degraded even when tolerated (as prostitution). Still others outrage the morals, traditions, and concepts of the family held by many people (as incest). But these aside, there is an interesting grouping of offenses: fornication, seduction, lewd and open cohabitation, miscegenation, adultery, and extracoital behavior.

Fornication

Although the word "fornication" is often used by laymen as synonymous with heterosexual copulation, legally it refers to such activity between two unmarried persons and is limited to those instances in which a more serious affront to law and morality does not exist (for example, rape, incest, adult-child sexuality, or even adultery). Hence, by definition fornication is consensual heterosexual intercourse between two unmarried adults or juveniles. Fornication is sometimes confused with seduction (to be discussed presently), and in sex research it is often found under the heading of premarital sex. Because the label "premarital" can be applied only ex post facto and since at the time of the act neither party can be certain that marriage will take place (often it does not), the term "nonmarital" would appear to be more exact.[1] Furthermore, since nonmarital applies to the unwed of any age—including divorced and widowed persons—it brings under a single umbrella all those who would be affected if the law were to be indiscriminately applied.

Fornication was traditionally illegal in all jurisdictions of the United States but was only a misdemeanor, infraction, or offense in some states. In law, Gerhard Mueller points out, "fornication is commonly regarded as an ordinary and uncomplicated act of intercourse between unmarried persons of opposite sexes, though . . . some statutes require a living together, or an open and notorious act."[2] "Ordinary and uncomplicated" means that the act is private and consensual and that the partners are adults (if they are both under the age of consent, the act usually is considered fornication rather than statutory rape). While, as Mueller states, some laws require that the act be open and notorious, more commonly, otherwise acceptable sexual behavior between unmarried persons, when "open and notorious," comes under the heading of "lewd cohabitation" or "lewd and lascivious conduct" (discussed on pages 192–194).

Punishment for those found guilty of fornication, often the same as that for adultery, has ranged from small fines to several months' imprisonment; in Utah, a maximum sentence of six months in jail is prescribed. In addition to laws that have been applicable only in cases of open cohabitation, many state laws under fornication statutes specifically applied only in instances of miscegenation (such laws, discussed on pages 194–196, have been held unconstitutional and are no longer in effect in the United States); finally, some laws were held to apply only if the couple registered falsely in a hotel as man and wife. The Model Penal Code of the American Law Institute dropped all penalties for adult nonmarital sexual behavior, as was done by Illinois, New York, and several other states during the years following World War II.

There have seldom been prosecutions for fornication: the law has been invoked generally to express public indignation, real or feigned. Still, the law has not been without its ill effects. The continued illegality of nonmarital sex has not rarely been used as a weapon in court to show "bad character," to rebut a character witness, to harass a complainant in a rape case, to dig into the premarital background of a woman in a custody proceeding, to revoke parole, to expel a student from college, to discriminate in employment (particularly in government employment), to justify an arrest under the Mann Act, and in numerous other ways. Thus, the law becomes excuse and justification for private or police action that would probably otherwise not have occurred, but the illegality of fornication gives legitimacy to such discriminatory behavior both in court and out. Such action has been directed more against women than men, reflecting the double standard that traditionally has encouraged the single male "to sow his wild oats," the unwed female to be pure, virginal, and virtuous: a case in point—while disciplinary action was taken against a woman enrolled in the Naval Academy who became pregnant, no action was taken against the midshipman who was her lover (and fiancé). (The Naval Academy eventually did rescind its action against the woman.) On the rare occasions when the official norms against fornication have been invoked against males, those who took the initiative for punitive action were usually held up to public ridicule, as in the instance of an unmarried FBI employee who during the tenure of J. Edgar Hoover was discharged on the sole ground that he was known to have spent a night in the home of a girlfriend. This example points up the danger of laws that can be selectively and capriciously used against a few individuals and on rare occasions.

The law against fornication, when it has not been repealed, has fallen into decline, withering away under the impact of mass open defiance, lack of prosecution and enforcement, a complete absence of public support, and apathy toward the law (including ignorance of it) on the part of the violators. Occasional and rare invocations illustrate the danger of allowing an unenforced law to remain on the statute books, particularly when there is no public demand for it and when it does not reflect (and perhaps never reflected) the public morality. While the same arguments are germane to the laws against seduction (a special form of fornication), open cohabitation, adultery, and adult consensual homosexuality in private, insofar as the rare and occasional use of the law is highly discriminatory and dangerous to a system of justice, the laws against fornication are distinctive in that they lack any semblance of public support.

Not only are laws repealed or forgotten, they are sometimes "amended" by new court interpretations. Thus it has been with fornication. In many jurisdictions, statutes have been interpreted as referring only to open cohabitation (a matter that will be discussed separately), and in others the law has been invoked only against interracial couples. It is generally agreed, even by upholders of a traditional morality and a nonpermissive if not a repressive sexuality, that fornication is not the business of the law. Whether the law should even permit discrimination against fornicators on the part of employers, educational institutions, and others is a related matter. As late as 1976, it was reported that Brigham Young University demanded chastity and celibacy of all its unmarried students. Certainly, criminologists virtually unanimously include fornication among those consensual or victimless offenses which are prime candidates for decriminalization.[3]

Seduction

Slightly more complex, although related to fornication, is seduction. Not always defined in a clear-cut manner that distinguishes it from fornication, seduction nevertheless does have some special features of its own. Both terms refer to adult consensual nonmarital heterosexuality, but in seduction the woman is said to have been persuaded to enter the relationship by an unconditional promise of future marriage and otherwise would not have consented to have intercourse.

Thus, several interesting legal factors arise in a charge of seduction. Only the male can be indicted for this offense; the female is not an accomplice, as in fornication, but a victim. In many cases, her previous chastity becomes an issue, and some legal interpretations have been based on the premise that only a previously chaste girl can be seduced. This stipulation was on the one hand meant to protect the male from being forced into a marriage unwillingly because he had made promises or had even presented himself fraudulently: if the woman were not chaste, it is presumed that she would have (or at least might have) consented without the promise of marriage, a rather dubious presumption in many instances. On the other hand, this premise served to embarrass the females in these cases, opening them to vigorous cross-examination on intimate details of their sex lives and even offering the defendant an opportunity to bring to the stand other males who claimed to have had sexual relations with the complainant. While this tactic is analogous in some respects to the efforts made by some defendants in rape cases to make relevant, and hence public, details of the sex life of the complainants, the positions of the females in these two situations are in other ways dissimilar; that of the males, even more so.

A second issue in seduction cases is the willingness, under certain conditions, of the defendant to marry and hence to fulfill the obligation he allegedly undertook. Such marriages may have some advantages for the complainant: legitimacy of the child if the woman is pregnant or has given birth (there is a side issue here as to whether legitimacy is established if the child has already been born), improvement of the reputation and standing of the woman in the community, and child support and alimony if the marriage is dissolved.

An offer to remedy the situation by agreeing to marry the complainant has not always served to exculpate the accused. Gerhard Mueller writes, along this line: "In 1964, the New Jersey Supreme Court sustained a 4- to 6-year sentence upon a seducer of a girl who became pregnant" although he did offer marriage (the woman was in fact already married to another man).[4]

In the United States, although laws criminalizing seduction remain on the books in some states, and while in some the penalties are harsh, they are seldom invoked. Nevertheless, an examination of state statutes reveals maximum prison terms of up to ten years; only a few states specifically limit seduction prosecutions to cases in which the complaining witness is underage.

Today extralegal pressures are exerted on males accused of seduction less frequently than they once were and such instances seldom come to public attention. There is always a possibility that a woman (more likely a girl) having been discovered by her parents, or herself finding that she is pregnant, will attempt to redeem herself by claiming that she was previously "pure" and that there had been an unconditional promise and expectation of marriage. A vengeful parent is more likely to handle this situation by extralegal means, ranging from persuasion to violence, than by taking the matter to a prosecutor. Earlier in this century, numerous civil cases involving seduction were argued under the heading of what was known as breach of promise; it was claimed that a contract had been made and broken when the man refused to marry the woman. However, in a series of such cases the courts ruled against the plaintiffs, and the tactic of attempting to collect monetary damages in lieu of marriage seems to have disappeared from the American scene.

The laws against seduction, like those against fornication, simply no longer reflect a widely accepted moral or sexual code. The main concern of society seems to be with the care of a child emanating from nonmarital relations, for paternity is putatively less easy to determine when the child is born out of wedlock.

In America, the female is free to engage in nonmarital sex although from a social viewpoint no doubt she cannot with impunity be as indiscriminate as the male. The male, if he does not use force, is free to suggest, implore, beg, and persuade, even to the extent of making a false presentation of self with promises that he does not intend to fulfill. He will be regarded as at worst a cad but not as a criminal; she, as a fool but not as the victim of any crime.

In this connection, Mueller writes (although he is more sanguine about the equality and freedom women have attained than we are):

> The crime of seduction is an anachronism in an enlightened age in which men and women are equal and free to make whatever arrangement regarding their sexual affairs they please. Recent major international gatherings of experts in criminology and criminal justice clearly and almost unanimously went on record as calling for the repeal of all sex prohibitions which concern sexual arrangements among adults and not involving force or public menace.[5]

Adultery

A third form of adult consensual heterosexual activity is adultery, which differs from fornication and seduction in that one or both parties are married but not to each other. If they are both married, this situation has been called double or compound adultery; if only one partner is married, then it is single, or simple, adultery. In some jurisdictions, only the married partner is legally an adulterer or adulteress; the unmarried, a fornicator—still, the act itself is adultery.

Traditionally, laws penalizing adultery were considered to be desirable and necessary as a moral expression of the sanctity of the family and as a means of ensuring that a child would not be born illegitimately or of doubtful paternity. In the case of the married woman, adultery was an invasion of the husband's property rights, for his wife was legally his chattel. The laws were seldom invoked although social pressure against known adulterers (particularly women) is still brought to bear.

For many years, while divorce by mutual consent was difficult to obtain in most American jurisdictions and adultery remained the only legally acceptable basis for divorce in such states as New York, there were thousands of divorces on the ground of adultery, yet few resulted in the prosecution of the alleged offenders. This anomalous situation has three possible explanations: first, the laws were not taken seriously for purposes of criminal prosecution; second, it was generally understood by the litigants, their attorneys, and the court that the adultery charge was a collusion arranged so as to circumvent a legal system that would not grant divorce by mutual consent; and third, even if one took seriously both the penal code and the divorce procedure, in a criminal case one would have to prove the guilt of the defendant beyond a reasonable doubt, while in a civil divorce proceeding, the uncontested action provided a prima facie case sufficient to grant the divorce. Probably all three—but particularly the first two—explain the discrepancy between the divorce statistics and the lack of arrests, indictments, and criminal prosecutions of adulterers.

Unlike fornication, however, adultery does not meet with social approval although there is no longer any serious movement to maintain its criminal character. Probably most people disapprove, and few openly acknowledge their adulterous acts, unless while they are still wedded legally they are no longer maintaining a marital relationship with their spouse.[6]

Adultery is sometimes committed with fraud, in such manner that one of the partners, more frequently an unmarried female, does not know that the other is married. The law itself does not specifically condemn such action on the part of the deceiving partner. Much more common is the fraud committed upon the marital partner or partners not involved in the activity. Members of social groups have regarded the deceived husband as a fool, reflected in the aura surrounding the term "cuckold." No corresponding term describes the deceived wife perhaps because men, the dominant sex, were more tolerant of straying husbands. Furthermore, the adultery of the husband does not bring into question the biological fatherhood of the offspring of a faithful wife. In the view of some, promiscuity offers an outlet for the varietist and what might be called polygynous needs of the male without necessarily endangering the continuity of the family. Even an affectional adulterous relationship can survive side by side with a permanent family, as witness the mistress maintained by many European and Latin American married men, a situation that is frequently public and is virtually institutionalized.

Adultery is not always a secret act.[7] It is sometimes committed with full knowledge of the adulterer's spouse. In some cases both husband and wife are engaging in sex acts with other partners, with each other's approval, even assistance. During the countercultural movements of the 1960s, group sex and mate swapping received a good deal of publicity, giving the impression that such activities were widespread, and some social scientists estimated that a considerable minority of the population was participating in the swinging scene.[8] By the mid-1970s, it was said that swinging was on the decline. It is likely that there were fewer participants at the peak than either media or social investigators led the public to believe.

Legal sanctions against adulterers, including swappers, are rarely exercised, but discriminatory action is not unknown. Furthermore, swappers may be harassed from time to time for lewd and lascivious conduct or under some other catchall sex statute. In the Model Penal Code of the American Law Institute, adulterous relations as such are not illegal.

Lewd and Open Cohabitation

Nonmarital sex, at least until the 1950s or 1960s in the United States, was most frequently conducted between people not domiciling together. The rare prosecution of fornication and adultery usually involved an open flouting of community morality, most often in the form of open cohabitation, without pretense of marriage and without recourse to furtive and secret mechanisms. In fact, in some states the courts went so far as to interpret the laws against fornication as applicable only in such instances.[9]

Starting in the latter part of the 1960s, open cohabitation became common, and by the mid 1970s, it could be said to have become institutionalized.[10] On many college campuses, cohabitation is no longer discouraged. Parents are aware of, and often speak openly of, such arrangements. Some of these prove to be "trial marriages" (recommended by Judge Ben Lindsey half a century ago) [11] that result eventually in an agreement to part; others continue indefinitely very much like legally licensed unions and many eventuate in a legal marriage, particularly if pregnancy results or a family is planned. Such arrangements are not uncommon, too, among the middle-aged and the elderly, who find that social security, tax,* and other benefits are greater if they domicile together unmarried. In the event that one or both parties have children, a desire to protect their offspring's inheritance may discourage remarriage.

Unlike the laws on fornication and adultery, those prohibiting open and lewd cohabitation have been enforced with occasional vigor, although usually selectively, discriminatorily, and arbitrarily. Such legal actions have become rare and will probably disappear in years ahead or may even be declared unconstitutional; hence, decriminalization will have taken place by judicial fiat. It can be said that at one time the laws did reflect the moral attitudes of the populace: so long as fornication was private and furtive, it was not seriously condemned; communities did not wish to have this behavior openly flaunted, known, or tolerated. The moral climate has changed, a full circle has been navigated, and what was a short time ago strongly condemned is now condoned, tolerated, even encouraged and institutionalized.

Although there is no longer a serious problem of criminal prosecution with regard to open cohabitation, many difficult legal matters remain. At one time in New York and many other states, two persons who lived together for a period of years without benefit of state or clergy, acting as if they were married, and generally were considered married by those around them were said to have contracted a common law marriage, which gave some protection to the survivor (and to the couple's children) in case of death, separation, or desertion. Many years ago, New York and other states ceased to

---

* Under American income tax laws, two unmarried persons living together and filing separate tax returns may pay considerably less tax than a married couple having the same income, and the social security laws similarly discriminate against the legally married.

recognize such unions as legal marriages, and the concept of common law marriage fell from favor, although in the mid-1970s California's community property laws were held to apply to such "common law" unions.

With the resurgence of "unmarried marrieds," new problems have arisen that will require clarification. There has been an effort by some insurance companies to demand higher automobile insurance rates from an owner cohabiting with a member of the other sex than that owner would pay if alone or if married. Ex-husbands have sued to end alimony on the grounds that cohabitation involves de facto remarriage and that the failure legally to marry is purely an attempt to ensure continuation of alimony payments. Numerous other problems of a civil nature will be encountered, including community property rights, inheritance rights, and responsibility for debts incurred. There are indications that unmarried cohabitants are experiencing social discrimination; at the same time, some are using their ambiguous status to perpetrate frauds.

Nevertheless, criminal enforcement, where the laws remain, is almost unknown. From a legal point of view, a change in law may not be so necessary as the changing climate of morality would indicate. The penal codes can sometimes be allowed to remain intact, while activity formerly contained under the rubric of lewd and lascivious conduct is now nothing less than taken for granted and even normative behavior. However, as pointed out earlier, unenforced and unenforceable laws are undesirable and dangerous: undesirable in that they encourage disrespect for all law, dangerous in that they permit discriminatory enforcement or private blackmail.

Miscegenation

Miscegenation refers to a sexual relationship, with or without marriage and almost always heterosexual, between persons of different racial groups whose sexual mingling, in a given society, is discouraged if not forbidden by reason of their group memberships.

Although antimiscegenation laws were declared unconstitutional or repealed in the United States by the mid-1960s, social pressure against interracial sexuality continues. Previously, the laws in most southern and several other states forbade sexual relations between black and white persons and, in some jurisdictions, relations between whites and Amerindians, whites and Orientals, and other combinations. In many countries of the world, there are restrictions on sexual relations, marriage, or both between people of different groups. The strongest such law is in the Union of South Africa, where severe penalties (legal as well as social sanctions) face whites who are guilty of sexual cohabitation with Africans, the theme of Alan Paton's powerful novel *Too Late the Phalarope*.[12]

In the United States, until the Supreme Court declared the still remaining statutes against interracial marriages unconstitutional, there had been sporadic enforcement of a highly selective nature. White males were in no way inhibited from exploiting black females so long as the relationship was without affection, permanence, or nonsexual meanings; such alliances were used by black women for economic and other gains (described in *Caste and Class in a Southern Town*, the brilliant though no doubt dated classic by John Dollard).[13]

A dictionary definition of miscegenation limits the activity to relationships in which one of the couple is white. In law, miscegenation has usually meant white-nonwhite sexual relations. Although interfaith and interethnic sexuality is usually not classified as miscegenation, and often there is not the same fear, mythology, and fantasy surrounding such relationships as there is in interracial ones, great similarity of attitudes and reactions is apparent in descriptions of intermarriage and the related area of sex between persons of different faiths, ethnic origins, or race.[14]

In Israel, two persons must be of the same religion to marry, but there is no law against interfaith nonmarital sexual relations or against foreign marriage and Israeli domiciling. In Northern Ireland, there is tremendous social pressure against sexual congress between Catholic and Protestant but no legal bar to such marriages. The social pressure against the sexual or marital union of Catholic and Protestant does not seem to prevail strongly among the Irish in England, Eire, or the United States. Despite the frequency of the occurrence, there is often vehement opposition in the United States from both sides to a Christian-Jewish marriage.

Miscegenation is no longer illegal in the United States. Still, in many parts of the country, particularly smaller communities, interracial couples—both dating and married—face considerable social pressure. Black prostitutes with white customers constitute a prevailing pattern in many American cities, and this has resulted in hotel and police harassment of interracial dating and married couples. Strong condemnation of black-white sexuality is increasingly voiced by leaders of the black community.

Extracoital Heterosexual Acts

The final category of heterosexual acts between consenting adults in private, for which the phrases "crimes without victims" and "not the business of the law" are used, includes acts that have been described under such rubrics as "crimes against nature" and "the abominable, unspeakable and unmentionable crimes." In scientific terminology, these are called extracoital or noncoital sex, and the laws are usually worded in such a manner that they can be invoked against two persons of the same sex or of different sexes. The emotional and colorful language was sometimes used in the law to avoid the unpleasantness of having to detail the physical nature of the acts themselves.

A wide variety of types of physical congress between a consenting adult man and woman are covered by the law, including contact of penis with mouth (fellatio), of vagina with mouth (cunnilingus), and/or insertion of penis into anus (sodomy or buggery). But these do not exhaust the possibilities.

The penalties traditionally prescribed in the laws against sodomy and other extracoital acts have been severe, although not uniformly so. State penal codes have called for prison terms as high as twenty years, but most arrests and convictions under such laws have been on charges of homosexual behavior (semipublic activities or solicitation of strangers) or sex with underage partners, or assault. In the last instance, assault with intent to commit sodomy aggravates the charge and raises the maximum allowable sentence. In all such instances, one is not dealing with private consensual acts between adults. Nevertheless, the laws as originally written, and as they appeared on the books in a majority of the states in 1977, covered and illegalized the private extracoital sex between two adults consenting to participate and occurring in privacy, although New York and some other states specifically exclude prosecution of married couples for such conduct.

It was often a matter held up for ridicule, especially when marriage manuals began to encourage such acts, that extracoital sex was still labeled "unnatural" by the law and forbidden even between husband and wife. That the laws could not be enforced and almost never led to prosecution only made the illegality of extra-coital sex more pernicious in the eyes of many, who saw this situation as fostering erosion of respect for law. Nevertheless, in divorce and annulment cases, one party (usually the wife) at times alleged "unnatural practices" as grounds for seeking termination of the marriage.

It has been argued by those who oppose extracoital sex (and their numbers apparently diminished in the years following the second world war) that the law is a symbolic expression of the moral stance of a community. Perhaps it can be said more pragmatically that those engaging in private consensual extracoital relations, unlike miscegenists, were not aware of, frightened by, or concerned with the law.

Changing Mores and Obsolescent Laws

The social scientist seeks to determine what the mores are. In the area of sexuality there are many difficulties: persons are not always willing to reveal their attitudes, and the attitudes themselves may be incongruent with behavior.[15] The mores are dynamic, in a state of flux in a rapidly changing society, and some sections of the society (different age groups, income groups, ethnic and racial collectivities, persons of varying educational levels) may differ in both attitudes and behavior.

Whether the laws against fornication and seduction, for example, ever reflected the moral sentiments of large sectors of the American society is debatable. Certainly, in the 1970s fornication and open cohabitation are accepted, not merely tolerated, by numerous people in the society (particularly in the lower and upper classes). Hostility to miscegenation may continue to be widespread but it takes the form of social pressure rather than legal pressure or violence.

Commonplace as adultery evidently is, and has been in the past (with little evidence that it is on the increase), it is probably true that a considerable portion of the American population regards it as a threat to the family. When consensual (i.e., approved of or engaged in by both husband and wife), adultery is often seen as evidence of a problem-laden marriage; when it is nonconsensual, it is regarded as infidelity and cheating. Nonetheless, there appears to be little support for criminal sanctions against such behavior.

Laws against consensual adult sex, such as those described here, are unenforceable, victimize some persons by selective or discriminatory enforcement, are used for harassment in judicial and other proceedings, do not discourage the activities (even when, as in the case of those who regard adultery as a threat to the survival of the family, there is reason to want to discourage a given behavior), may lead to blackmail and police corruption, and have other ill effects. To the extent that the public is aware that extracoital sex is illegal and that statutes are if anything enforced arbitrarily, the law is deemed an inappropriate expression of the moral values of the society.

In the title of this chapter we use the phrase "on the periphery of crime." This is an ambiguous expression and is not meant to imply that the activities themselves occur on the margins of serious and important crimes. Rather, these are acts on the periphery in the sense that they are crimes only so long as they remain proscribed by the penal codes (as most were at one time in all American penal codes, and as some continue to be in most such codes) but that they do not fit into the sociological concept of crime as an event that is illegal because it outrages the members of a society. Like traffic offenses, which H. Laurence Ross refers to as "folk crime," [16] they are not looked upon as criminal by the people who commit the acts, by those who do not do so but are tolerant or indifferent, or even by those who disapprove. But accepted and tolerated sex acts, when illegal, are fraught with consequences far beyond those of traffic offenses. They are not only crimes without victims but they are truly acts in which the perpetrators become the victims of bureaucrats, legislators, and punitive and vengeful prosecutors. Although the acts are frequent and the retaliation rare, the potential for such victimization is always present and for this reason alone the obsolescent laws require repeal.

The victimologist, too, would see in a life-style characterized by frequent participation in such socially disvalued behaviors the potential for differential victimization; thus, for example, the fornicator or adulterer (male or female) is perhaps more likely to be assaulted or even murdered than the less sexually promiscuous and those who engage in a miscegenated relationship of a secret nature might be especially susceptible to blackmail.

8   Pornography and Its Relationship to Crime

The first problem confronting anyone examining obscenity and pornography and its relationship to law, crime, morality, and society is that of defining the concept. There is little agreement on a definition of obscenity or pornography and even less on the criteria that can be logically established to determine whether or not a specific work—be it cartoon, novel, painting, movie, magazine, dramatic performance, or any other form of expression—falls within the purview of such a definition. Yet it is only after there is agreement on what is obscene or pornographic that one can proceed to the public issues of the desirability of permitting or forbidding such representations and the related question of the effect they may have on the prevention or commission of crime.

Most legal restrictions on pornography, in fact, use the term "obscene" in the statute. This is a word derived from roots that mean "off the scene," referring to expression that is prohibited. Thus, the definition is merely circular, stating nothing about the nature of the material that is labeled obscene but merely indicating that there are taboos on verbal and graphic expressions. While such taboos can exist against antireligious and blasphemous writings, paintings, and other forms of communication and can encompass political dissidence, the terms "obscene" and "pornographic" have come to refer to explicit representations of sexual and excretory functions that some segments of a society find offensive. How inadequate efforts legally to define the key terms are, particularly when there are severe punishments for violation of obscenity laws, can be seen from the report of the Commission on Obscenity and Pornography.[1] The commission, pointing out that there are five federal laws that prohibit distribution of obscene material in the United States, forty-eight states with statutes generally prohibiting the distribution of such material, and forty-one states having laws containing special prohibitions against the distribution of obscene material to minors, took note of the problem of definition.

> None of the federal statutes generally prohibiting the distri-
> bution of "obscene" material defines that term. State statutes
> generally prohibiting the distribution of "obscene" material either
> do not define the term or verbally incorporate the constitutional
> standard established by the Supreme Court . . . [in a series of
> cases]. State juvenile statutes frequently incorporate relatively
> specific descriptive definitions of material prohibited for minors,
> qualified by subjective standards adapted from the constitutional
> standard for adults.[2]

Since 1957, after the decision in *Roth*, definitions of obscenity have tended to follow the opinion of the Court.

> Obscene material is material which deals with sex in a prurient
> manner appealing to prurient interests. The test is whether to the
> average person, applying contemporary community standards, the
> dominant theme of the material taken as a whole appeals to pruri-
> ent interests.[3]

New York State, for example, relied on the *Roth* decision in amend-
ing its penal code to read:

> Any material or performance is "obscene" if (a) considered as
> a whole, its predominant appeal is to prurient, shameful or morbid
> interest in nudity, sex, excretion, sadism or masochism and (b) it
> goes substantially beyond customary limits of candor in describing
> or representing such matters, and (c) it is utterly without re-
> deeming social value. Predominant appeal shall be judged with
> reference to ordinary adults unless it appears from the character
> of the material or the circumstances of its dissemination to be
> designed for children or other susceptible audience.[4]

The phrase "without redeeming social value" also comes from the
Supreme Court decision in *Roth*.

With definitions vague and often absent, if not merely subjective, and with important legal decisions involving the freedom or
imprisonment of individuals, the desirability of suppression or the

right to express, to observe, and to read hinging upon such decisions, American law has relied largely on ad hoc Supreme Court interpretations of what constitutes obscenity and pornography. Inasmuch as many such interpretations are unpredictable, and the guidelines change over time because the social climate and membership on the Court change, there is uncertainty on the part of individuals and groups who perform particular acts as to whether they are violating criminal codes; victimization, including imprisonment, of some persons for publication and dissemination of material similar to, not more offensive than, and sometimes less explicit than that disseminated by others who continue their activities with impunity; and reluctance among serious film producers, publishers, and the like to invest large sums in explicit artistic works for fear that they will be banned in many communities, while at the same time more explicit but less artistic material is being created and distributed by small-scale producers. Additionally, vagaries in the law encourage organized crime to enter the pornography market.

Pornography changes with time and place. There have been many crusaders for the purification of the language, for example. One of these, Thomas Bowdler, lent his name to the act of expurgation, to "bowdlerize." Noah Webster, the great lexicographer, purged the Bible of its "dirty words," preferring *breast* to *teat* and *smell* to *stink*. More than a century later, the editors of Webster's *Third New International Dictionary* apologized because for commercial reasons the dictionary omitted one obscenity, thus making the list of words under the letter *f* incomplete.

Some definitions of pornography are limited to sexual depiction and arousal. Thus Paul Gebhard writes: "Pornography is material deliberately designed to produce strong sexual arousal rather than titillation and which usually achieves its primary goal." He then proceeds to point out that "the Hindu sculptor who with some religious symbolism in mind depicts coitus has not produced pornography, even though his work may inflame the imagination of most Occidental viewers." [5] Another way of approaching this question would be to state that the motivation or design of the sculptor or any other creator is irrelevant and that the sculpture that was not pornographic in India might be so before an American audience. Or that the depiction that is religiously symbolic in one culture outrages the standards of morality in another. For legal and social purposes, it appears to us preferable to avoid a definition of pornography as the graphic presentation of sexuality (or of any other biological process) whether deliberately designed for arousal, titillation, or amusement. At issue, rather, is the presentation of such material in a manner outrageous and offensive to large sectors of society. Whether a powerful sector of the population should have the right to deny access to certain material to persons who find it satisfying, sometimes but not always artistic or literary, is debatable. Related questions involve the social harm, or potential for such harm, of legal suppression and censorship; and the relation between obscenity and pornography and violence and crime, particularly so far as rape and other admittedly antisocial acts are concerned.

These issues are not always separated, and those espousing the permissive view of freedom from censorship will often conclude on the basis of flimsy evidence that obscenity and pornography do little or nothing to stimulate crime and, if anything, deflect the potential criminal from such behavior by vicariously satisfying his needs; while those who take the conservative (often religious) view on censorship and social control of explicit material likewise conclude on equally flimsy evidence that pornography is a major cause of sex crime, general violence, and juvenile delinquency in society.

The third quarter of the twentieth century was an era of pornographic revolution, if not of sexual revolution. Large quantities of material defined by the official culture as immoral and outrageous were legally rather than surreptitiously published and distributed in the United States. Most other countries are in less conflict over this issue; some are more permissive, many less so. The Scandinavian nations were among the first to relax censorship, and in the case of Denmark, to permit live sex shows and allow sexually explicit printed and graphic material to be distributed. By 1976, some Danish authorities were rethinking this policy and were urging at least mild restrictions, while others were attributing small but significant declines in sex crimes to the more permissive climate. Communist, Islamic, and many African nations are quite nonpermissive; on the other hand, and by contrast, a less stringent code is enforced in many countries with strong influence of the Catholic Church, particularly Italy, France, and, in very recent years, in what once was the citadel of Catholic antisexuality, Eire (where it is nevertheless a crime to sell contraceptives even to married couples).

In the United States, the situation is extremely confused as a result of numerous decisions of the Supreme Court and of local courts. The sometimes successful prosecution of defendants charged with showing or distributing material that others were showing or distributing elsewhere with complete impunity, a situation that occurs in few other countries, is profoundly disturbing.* The report of the Commission on Obscenity and Pornography, for example, published by the Government Printing Office, was reprinted as "a New York Times Book" by a major publisher and as a paperback by another important house. A small, somewhat marginal company reprinted the same work with illustrations that had not been part of the other editions; the publisher, William L. Hamling, was indicted, prosecuted, convicted, and sent to prison.[6] The selective prosecution, always a danger in criminal law, was excused on the basis of the illustrations and an alleged pandering to titillate readers rather than to educate them on the subject of pornography, but one suspects that establishment houses can do what shoestring publishers cannot.

In New York and many other cities, hard-core pornographic movies are shown and advertised openly and are even available on cable television. (Parents are provided with a key to lock the television set so that children cannot watch without parental consent.) Nevertheless, prosecutions and even jailings (but more frequently harassment or closing of bookshops and theaters) on questionable charges of obscenity take place, and one produces and distributes with apprehension because there is no nationwide prepublication or prerelease clearance.

In an effort to reconcile freedom of expression with the desire of some persons not to be exposed to materials they consider obscene, the Supreme Court promulgated a community standards test. In other words, a work would be considered acceptable if it met the moral standards of the community in which it was to be displayed or sold. On the surface, there is a modicum of logic in this approach, but it actually means that those living in smaller cities and in some regions of the country who are interested in erotic materials will be denied access allowed elsewhere; and that producers and publishers, applying the least common denominator principle which has resulted, for example, in bowdlerized textbooks, would precensor materials to insure litigation-free nationwide distribution.

---

* The situation in the United States is complicated by our federal structure (with little criminal jurisdiction allocated to the national government), state sovereignty (which, although severely limited, allows for significant variations in penal codes), and the shibboleth of home rule and local autonomy for large cities, and with "community standards" converted into ordinances by tiny towns.

Some question whether the erotic should be required to have redeeming social value when political, social, and other commentaries do not have to meet such a test. The problem leads to the second part of the pornography controversy; namely, the effect of the material (particularly hard-core) on impressionable readers and viewers. Research on this subject, as summarized for the Commission on Obscenity and Pornography, indicates clearly that pornography is at worst harmless and is sometimes beneficial. A criminologist so sensitive to the problems of violence in our society as Marvin Wolfgang [7]—who has for years been insisting that crime in America can at least partially be attributed to the subculture of violence in which some persons are socialized and in which they live—was one of two minority dissidents on the commission, contending that even children should not be prevented from buying pornographic material. In fact, given the militant opposition to and the inadequacy of sex education, some commentators have viewed pornography as a perhaps unfortunate but necessary substitute.

Many observers think that limits should be drawn, that not all pictorial and written presentations can be shown without possible damage, but this view opens the door to censorship and to a judgment of each movie, book, or other material as an individual item, on its own merits. Historically, it has been amply demonstrated that such censorship has led to subjective discrimination based on political, religious, and social biases.

There is an oft repeated gender differentiation in the erotic impact of pornographic materials. It is frequently claimed that they affect the male far more significantly than the female (there was almost no favorable response to the male nudes in *Playgirl*, except among male homosexual purchasers). It is fashionable to attribute such differential responses only to culture, but the possibility should not be excluded that the male has a greater innate capacity for arousal by pictures, words, and other symbolic representations than has the female.

Among those who assert that little or no harm can come of pornography, and perhaps some good, are John Gagnon and William Simon. For them, pornography is more a "paper tiger" than a "raging menace," and it is far from being a strong determinant of sexual behavior.

> Pornography is only a minor symptom of sexuality and of very little prominence in people's minds most of the time. Even among

those who might think about it most, it results either in masturbation or in the "collector" instinct.[8]

A major problem that must be faced by those who oppose pornography is whether in a hierarchy of social dangers it rates higher or lower than the continued presentation of nonsexual violence by the media, of the reality of wars and terrorism, and indeed of the daily betrayals of trust by public officials, corporate executives, and members of the medical, legal, and other professions. If indeed pornography is making a contribution to moral corruption and decay—itself a debatable question—then surely it is doing so to a lesser extent than many of the other social evils that surround Americans and presumably most other peoples of the world.

A number of questions are involved in the study of pornography and crime, and they may lead to contradictory and mutually exclusive conclusions so far as public policy is concerned. What harm is done, if any, to given young or impressionable individuals by the dissemination of material that not only is erotically arousing but also may pique their curiosity about such types of behavior as sadomasochism and homosexuality? What are the dangers to free interchange of expression when measures are taken to suppress the dissemination of such literature? What of the rights of the public or of such members of the public as do not wish to view or to be confronted with pictorial and other graphic presentations offensive to them, who wish to be protected from the display of such material in places where they have a right to be present? Are there people who are assisted in meeting the problems of daily living in a socially acceptable way by finding a fantasy outlet in pornography? And are there others who by exposure to such material are driven to acts of an antisocial nature and who there is good reason to suspect would otherwise not have committed these acts? What is the role of obscenity as part of the arsenal of oral violence against one's enemies?

Both the harmfulness and the harmlessness of obscenity have been asserted with little substantiating evidence, although research scientists lean in the direction of its being harmless or even beneficial and politicians and theologians the reverse. To say that pornography cannot influence a person is to contend that books and the printed word, graphics, art, and slogans cannot move people and cause changes in their thoughts and hence their actions. But the evidence is contradictory and often based on vulnerable assumptions. In the terrible murders that resulted in the Moors trial in England, a story of sadism almost unbelievable in the depths of degradation and degeneracy manifest in the accused, the latter had in their room, at the time of arrest, some explicit sexual literature.[9] Some of this literature would not be found seriously objectionable by anyone, such as a volume of Krafft-Ebing. Little was what even a conservative would suppress as hard-core pornography. But one could as easily conclude that sadists would seek out erotica as that otherwise law-abiding persons would be turned into murderers when the books fell into their hands.

Gebhard and his co-workers reported that of those sex offenders guilty of violence or force "between one-eighth and one-fifth reported arousal from sadomasochistic noncontact stimuli" or from reading and graphic material.

> While it is probable that in a few cases such stimuli triggered an offense, it seems reasonable to believe that they do not play an important role in the precipitation of sex offenses in general, and at most only a minor role in sex offenses involving violence.[10]

Among those most responsive to pornography were the aggressors against nature.

> They seem in general a group of uninhibited young men who respond unthinkingly and violently to various stimuli. Their reaction to pornography is merely a part of their exaggerated reaction to almost everything.[11]

It is difficult to interpret statements of this sort for purposes of formulating social policy. Should an effort be made to keep pornographic material out of the hands of such persons? Could this goal be achieved without censorship and other social harms to the rest of society? Or did this group have so strong a potential for sexual (or nonsexual) violence that to ban pornography would not be to eliminate possible triggers of antisocial behavior.

What complicates this matter is not only the probability that for some youths pornography serves as a safety valve, and indeed as a form of sex education in an overly puritanical society, but also that the most innocuous biological tracts may implant false or harmful ideas in the heads of the young and impressionable. Thus, a boy may be led in an unpredictable direction by material harmless to a more mature man.

What could happen to a young man exposed to explicit material about sex? The general opinion (elaborated upon by Ned

Polsky) [12] is that most likely he would masturbate; he may have done so anyway, but if aroused he might masturbate a little sooner or a little more often. No harm done. Or perhaps he might be sufficiently excited to use more persuasion on his teenage girlfriend than he had employed hitherto, resulting in nonmarital petting to the point of orgasm or to intercourse by mutual agreement. If both partners are above the age of consent, few now would find this an objectionable course on which to have embarked. If both are children, there will be little real harm although perhaps much adult perturbation.

But what if frustrated, aroused, searching, pressed by what he has seen, read, and heard, seeking to handle this material within the framework of a moral order to which he wishes to adhere but increasingly cannot, beset by conflict, the youth has a violent outburst? He attacks a girl. No one can dismiss the event as harmless to either party; it is an evil that should have been avoided. That the behavior could have been triggered by innocent literature as well as pornographic would not lead anyone to advocate a return to mass. illiteracy; indeed, the human sexual response being quite complex, such sexual violence may be triggered by stimuli wholly unrelated to pornography or to obscene performances.

There is a further question of frequency, of the chances that are taken when this youth is given Shakespeare or a biology book, as against when he finds himself with outright pornography. The latter may serve as a safety valve, a vicarious outlet without which a more violent outburst might occur.

If it is true that for some pornography serves as a catalyst for crime and for others as a protection against crime, then the problems of handling such material seem best left to family, schools, and counselors, not government agencies. Criminologists seeking in pornography an etiological explanation for violent sexual attacks must content themselves, at best, with the Scottish verdict: not proved.

Research on the Effects of Pornography *

What antisocial effects result from exposure to sexually explicit materials? The answers to this question have been debated ex-

---

* The authors are indebted to Charles Winick, who wrote the section of this chapter from this point to the middle of page 211.

tensively since it was posed directly to the Commission on Obscenity and Pornography in 1970.

The commission found a paucity of existing empirical studies addressed to this question when it began its work in 1968. The major such study was the examination of sex offenders by the Institute for Sex Research, in the course of which various kinds of background information were obtained from incarcerated offenders. They were asked about their previous exposure to sexually explicit materials. After analyzing the relationships between such exposure and the later offenses, the institute team concluded that responsiveness to pornography cannot be a consequential factor in their sex offenses.[13]

The institute researchers, comparing offenders with two control groups (nonoffenders and offenders for nonsexual crimes), felt that the inferior intelligence and education of the average sex offender precluded his deriving enough sexual arousal from pornography to trigger overt antisocial activity.

A study specifically done for the commission was directed by K. E. Davis and G. N. Braucht,[14] who made a retrospective survey of 365 male subjects from seven types of social groups (jail inmates, college students of three ethnic backgrounds, and members of Catholic and Protestant religious organizations). The subjects were between eighteen and thirty years old, with a mean age of twenty-two. The jail sample had the greatest family pathology, highest exposure to pornography, peer and neighborhood deviance, and lowest scores on an index of character. At the opposite extremes on all these variables stood the three religiously oriented subsamples. The authors concluded that there is a possibility that early exposure to pornography plays some causal role in the development of a sexually deviant life-style. There is also a possibility that exposure is part of, or a product of, adopting a sexually deviant life-style.

In another commission-sponsored study, reported by Michael Goldstein and his colleagues,[15] a sample of rapists and pedophiles who were incarcerated after conviction was compared with three different groups in California: homosexuals, male pornography consumers, and ordinary heterosexual males. The sex deviate groups reported less than average exposure to erotica than the controls. This finding reflects either avoidance of heterosexual stimuli or development in an extremely restrictive atmosphere, either of which pattern may lead to later deviant sexual development. The authors concluded that extent of exposure to erotic materials during adolescence is not positively associated with the later emergence of sexual pathology.

A unique opportunity for testing hypotheses about the relationship between pornography and sex offenses was provided by changes in the Danish law between 1965 and 1969, when hard-core sex materials became widely available to adults. Concurrently with the increasing availability of pornography, there was a significant decrease in the number of sex offenses registered by the police. In at least one type of offense (child molestation), reduction was significant, and the availability of pornography was believed to have been the cause of the decrease. Bert Kutschinsky, director of the Institute of Criminal Science at the University of Copenhagen, which conducted several studies of the Danish experience for the American Commission on Obscenity and Pornography, suggests that the newly available pornography served as a substitute for several kinds of sex offenses.[16] However, he found that pornography for exhibitionists and rapists cannot easily be substituted for the criminal act.

On the basis of these and other studies, the commission made several recommendations.* Furthermore, its report concluded that empirical research has found no evidence to date that exposure to explicit sexual materials plays a significant role in the causation of delinquent or criminal behavior among youths or adults or causes social or individual harms.[17] The Effects Panel of the Commission on Obscenity and Pornography, which evaluated the research, included three sociologists with distinguished research backgrounds (Joseph Klapper, Otto Larson, and Marvin Wolfgang) who felt so keenly about the "no harm" finding that they wrote separate statements denying not only causal linkages between exposure to pornography and harm but also any significant correlations or relationships between the two.[18]

V. B. Cline cites the literature on modeling and laboratory-created sexual deviations, selective reinforcement of aberrant sexual fantasies by masturbating to them, a study of reformatory inmates, and other sources in support of his view that the commission recommendations are erroneous.[19] Cline also notes that the commission conducted no longitudinal studies, did not explore sadomasochism, used only volunteers, and inaccurately represented the extent to

---

* Major recommendations of the commission are summarized at the end of this chapter.

which satiation occurred as a result of exposure to erotica. Many of Cline's strictures are valid and reflect the limited time within which the commission was in existence as well as the uncertainty of its financing. Created by President Johnson in 1968, it did most of its work in the next two years, during the presidency of Richard Nixon, who was not enthusiastic about its mission.

Other sources of information are interview studies by Charles Winick, who interviewed 100 erotica consumers for the commission and has since interviewed an additional 300.[20] He found that for most such consumers the interaction with the sexually stimulating material is itself fulfilling on informational, fantasy, connoisseurship, and other levels. There appeared to be relatively few action consequences of exposure to hard-core erotica.

There is one additional possible consequence of exposure to such materials. Since 1971, there has been a quantum leap forward in the movies, books, and magazines available in the erotic marketplace as a result of liberal court decisions and increasing unwillingness of juries to convict in obscenity trials. It is therefore possible that the great increase in sexual explicitness in American media, attested to by the fact that hard-core films like *Deep Throat* and *The Devil in Miss Jones* were, respectively, the sixth and the twelfth highest grossing movies released during 1973, could raise the erotic expectations of various publics and could lead to the acting out of antisocial behavior. The consequences of any revolution of rising expectations, erotic or otherwise, may be serious if the expectations are not met. Another possibility, of course, is that the ready availability of sexually explicit materials will have a cathartic effect on potential sex offenders, by channeling potentially offensive sexual behavior into various kinds of self-relief. Only careful studies of potential populations at risk will enable us to make predictions about which subgroups will be affected in what way by which kinds of materials.

It is interesting to take note of the opinion of psychiatrists and clinical psychologists. A study conducted by M. Lipkin and D. Carns covered 7,484 psychiatrists and 3,078 clinical psychologists. There was a 35 percent response rate. The following are the questions asked and the answers received:

> Question: "In your professional experience, have you encountered any cases where it appeared that pornography was a causal factor in antisocial behavior?"

Yes, convinced	7.4%
Yes, suspected	9.4
No such cases	80.0
Not ascertained	3.2

Question: "Persons exposed to pornography are more likely to engage in antisocial acts than persons not exposed."

Strongly agree	1.1
Agree	12.9
Disagree	56.4
Strongly disagree	27.3[21]

Outlook and Policy

Not many decades ago, two important literary achievements, *Ulysses* and *Lady Chatterly's Lover*, were banned. Americans have since learned that the open dissemination of such works is in many ways desirable and certainly has little or no potential for harm. In the changing attitude toward depiction of sexuality, it became possible to disseminate material whose literary, artistic, and redeeming social pretensions were minimal. Such works seem to have provided vicarious pleasure for some, stimulation to autoeroticism or to consensual heterosexuality for others; the contention that they are responsible for an increase in sex crimes remains unproved. Indeed, the evidence seems to be to the contrary.

Selective prosecution is dangerous to society. Ralph Ginzburg, publisher of the magazine *Eros* (which many consider a landmark in the serious and artistic treatment of the subject of sexuality), was sent to prison although the material he published could hardly be considered outrageous when compared to many publications displayed on newsstands throughout this country.[22] That his advertising sought to titillate one can hardly deny, yet far more titillating were many books, films, and other explicit material presented to the public with impunity. Was Ginzburg singled out in a campaign against pornography because he had shown an erotic interracial scene in a very appealing manner? If one even suspects that the answer to this question is in the affirmative, then one must confront serious problems of the abuse of censorship, suppression, and prosecution inherent in antipornography legislation.

The question of the effect of erotica on behavior is an open one, and thus far the most carefully thought out recommendations available are those made by the Commission on Obscenity and Pornography. The commission favored a broad sex education program aimed at people of all ages, conducted jointly by families, schools, and churches, to contribute to "healthy attitudes and orientations to sexual relationships." [23] It called for further discussion, and the development of further factual information, on obscenity and pornography, and on a legislative level the commission recommended "that federal, state, and local legislation prohibiting the sale, exhibition, or distribution of sexual materials to consenting adults should be repealed." [24]

This last recommendation was based upon nine considerations, summarized below:

1. There was no evidence that exposure plays a significant role in crime, deviance, delinquency, or severe emotional disturbance.
2. Explicit sexual material is a source of entertainment and information for many Americans.
3. Attempts to legislate in this area have been unsuccessful and unsatisfactory.
4. Prohibition of pornography is not supported by American public opinion.
5. There are many problems in enforcement, including vagueness and subjectivity of the law, lack of support by the public for legislation, and questions of resources and their utilization.
6. The tradition of free speech and free press is threatened by such legislation.
7. Adults ought not and need not be restricted in order to protect youth from pornography.
8. Repeal of legislation would have no adverse effect on the business of those who produce, publish, and disseminate material other than pornography.
9. There is no reason to believe that repeal of such legislation would have "a deleterious effect upon the individual morality of American citizens and upon the moral climate in America as a whole" nor "that exposure to explicit sexual materials adversely affects character or moral attitudes regarding sex and sexual conduct." [25]

In addition to published material, there is the related issue of burlesque, strip-teasers, topless and/or bottomless waitresses, male go-go dancers, nudity on stage, risqué or even obscene night club comics or satirists, drag shows (whether for homosexual or mixed audiences), and other presentations. There is a tendency on the part of many to apply the findings and recommendations of the commission as to pictorial and verbal pornography to these related aspects, and it would appear to us that this is a reasonable policy, at least until demonstrable proof of their harmfulness is developed. Since publication of the original edition, the United States Supreme Court has approved pre-publication censorship of sex-related materials in high-school newspapers and Larry Flynt, publisher of HUSTLER, has been shot and critically wounded during a recess in his trial for the dissemination of obscene-pornographic materials.

9 Legal Reactions and Legal Reform

In this book, we have sought to distinguish sharply among sex acts that are so patently harmful to the victim that they are beyond the level of tolerance of a society; those that would be better tolerated, handled through educational measures, discouraged without being suppressed, or conceptualized either as nuisances or as psychological disturbances; and those that not only are victimless but also are probably accepted as normative by large parts of society.

Two major problems remain in the formulation of social and legal policy.

1. There is a need for systematic examination of the evidence with regard to rehabilitation of sex offenders, rates of recidivism, successes and failures of therapeutic methods, particularly for those acts (forcible rape, sexual assault, and child molestation) on which there is consensus that there is need to prevent the activity, protect the victim, apprehend the offender, and mete out the most fitting and legally prescribed punishment. While a high degree of certainty that one will be apprehended and punished can serve as a deterrent (how effective a deterrent is the center of debate in criminological circles), one must face the question of restoration of the offender to society with the smallest possible risk that there will be further victimization.

2. At the same time, and related thereto, one must examine the sex psychopath laws that prevail in some parts of the United States. Over the past decades, a good deal of attention has been paid by

both public and pressure groups to the need for legislation decriminalizing adult consensual sex acts. However, at issue in regard to rape, child molestation, and certain other proscribed sexual behaviors is not decriminalization: rather, it is the nature of the legal and social reaction to these acts. How effective these laws may be, how humane or inhumane, what problems they solve and create are questions that should not be overlooked in the agitation over decriminalization.

These two problem areas are related. Both involve the reduction of sex crimes not by making acts legal and thus obviating official reporting but by preventing the behaviors from occurring. In both instances, the aim is prevention through rehabilitation. While such prevention may occur before there is an initial criminal act, through therapy given to someone who seeks aid because of temptation and fantasy, more likely it takes place after apprehension, if at all, and then only in an intensive, structured rehabilitation program.

Sex Offenders, Recidivism, and Treatment

Are sex offenders chronic and untreatable? Are they unlikely prospects for normal and safe interpersonal relationships in a free society? Confining oneself only to the most dangerous offenders (rapists and pedophiles), there is evidence that some are chronic and repetitive offenders but that many are not. Paul Tappan contended that many types of sex offenders are mild and submissive (this might well include pedophiles but is hardly likely to include rapists) and that of the various types of criminals they are among the least likely to be recidivists.[1] Albert Ellis is optimistic about the treatment of sex offenders, pointing out that successful treatment has been reported by a number of clinicians using a variety of psychotherapeutic techniques. It should be obvious from an increasing number of reports, he states, "that while the treatment of sex offenders is still difficult, it is by no means doomed to failure."[2] Both Tappan and Ellis, however, are writing generally of sex offenders, and not specifically of a category like violent sex offenders.

Much of the attention paid to recidivism of sex offenders involves the question of child molestation. It would appear that there are men whose major sex drive is centered around an interest in children—girls, boys, or both. These are chronic pedophiles in the sense that most men interested in sex with persons of the other or the same gender would be chronic heterosexuals or homosexuals, respectively. By contrast, it appears that while rapists are aggressive and are violence prone, as would be the case almost by definition, few are driven to seek sexual gratification primarily through violence or through overpowering unwilling and resisting victims.[3] Punishment and deterrence, together with persuasion and some treatment, would be more likely to lead to success because the very nature of the libido is not compelling a person toward proscribed behavior. The issue of recidivism among aggressive pedophiles was underscored by Donal MacNamara in his study of sex offenses and sex offenders.

> The aggressive pedophile who uses or threatens force to secure the child's compliance with his sexual approaches is considered to be the most heinous of all sex offenders. These men are less likely [than other offenders] to be senile or sociosexually underdeveloped. Many of them are alcoholics or at least heavy drinkers, usually of low socioeconomic status, from broken homes, and manifesting mental pathology or mental defect. Their adult sexual activity, not overly frequent, is largely confined to prostitutes. They are as a group, asocial, with a high recidivistic potential.[4]

Two studies of pedophiles on probation were conducted by Alex. Gigeroff and his colleagues. In the first, the offenders were diagnosed as heterosexual pedophiles. Most of the offenses of such persons, these researchers found, were situationally determined. The recidivist rate for first offenders was found to be low, and the probation risk was described as good. However, probation was not indicated for the chronic cases, in which there had been a fixation on prepubertal girls over a long period of time. "These cases," the authors concluded, "require more specialized treatment than probation officers can provide."[5]

In a second study, homosexual pedophilia was placed in the context of both homosexuality and pedophilia and was described as a "definite double deviance in terms of sex as well as age of object."[6] The condition was more persistent than heterosexual pedophilia, and recidivism rates were about twice as high. Nevertheless, the authors concluded that there is a good outlook for the first offender, while the repeater tends rather rapidly toward a chronic state.

At this stage of research, there is only incomplete information on therapeutic success and failure with offenders—renunciation of former activities versus recidivism. The public receives a distorted picture because it is the recidivist who makes news, not the person who after a prison term or even a suspended sentence never repeats the forbidden act. Counterbalancing this, at least to some degree, one must face the fact that only apprehended recidivists can be counted. The probation officer, heavily overburdened as all too many are, is not told of further crimes, and though he may believe that old patterns are being continued, he can hardly be expected to report suspicions based on little more than unsubstantiated impressions.

Some methods of treatment of sex offenders (and on occasion other offenders as well) are drastic, and ethical questions have been raised as to the propriety of offering such "therapy" to people not in a strong position to reject it. Controversy has developed over behavior modification techniques in which electric shocks (severe enough to be unpleasant but not to inflict permanent damage) are administered to the subject while he is looking at a picture of a child, for example; the shock, or rather unpleasant stimulus, is designed to be associated in the offender's mind with his fantasies of the child as sex object and thus to create an aversion to this type of sexuality. This modification of behavior, it is contended, is successful when accompanied by more traditional types of therapy.[7]

Even more drastic is surgery for the purpose of effecting change in behavior. In addition to brain surgery, which has been used and studied for several years, there has been at least one program of castration of violent sex offenders.[8] Georg Stürup has reported that castration has been successful in reducing violence, both sexual and nonsexual, and in many cases the offenders were able to return to society. Opposition to such severe, irreversible measures revolves around the possibility that they will be used punitively and even politically, the difficulty of overseeing judges and surgeons, and the ease with which surgery will be embraced and traditional therapy abandoned when surgery gives instant "cures."

Many have argued that positive alterations in both sexual and nonsexual spheres of life become much more likely if therapist and client plus significant others in the life of an offender share an optimistic belief in the prospects for change. E. Fuller Torrey has presented this point of view most persuasively with regard to mental illness;[9] Lawrence Hatterer,[10] among others, with regard to homosexuality. The sex offender is not doomed to life in an institution; he can be redirected in his sexual interests or at the least taught self-control, deflection, repression, and self-denial. On the other hand, the therapeutic model, however humane and optimistic, gives little surcease to a society plagued with violent sex crimes and less protection to individual child and female victims.*

The Sex Psychopath Laws

From the late 1930s through the 1950s, there was a proliferation of what came to be known as sex psychopath laws (of which the California statute was probably the best known). Although differing from state to state in wording and in persons covered, by and large they specified indeterminate sentencing for persons certified to be (sometimes with, sometimes without, trial or conviction) "sex psychopaths." The indeterminate sentence terminated only after a board, on the recommendation of psychiatrists, certified that the offender was "cured." Even then, upon release the individual had to register as a sex offender in any community in which he took up residence (although he could circumvent this provision by moving to another state, as was often done). The sex psychopath laws were invoked against the poor and not the rich although the latter are perhaps as well represented as the former in sex offenses, and they were used to incarcerate not only child molesters but also people committing harmless and at worst nuisance offenses. Samuel Brakel and Ronald Rock write of

> those persons whose antisocial and criminal conduct is motivated
> by sexual deviation and who as a consequence are subject to in-
> voluntary hospitalization. Such treatment results from special leg-
> islation broad enough to permit the involuntary hospitalization of
> mentally disabled persons who have a propensity toward the com-
> mission of antisocial and criminal acts. Not all such persons, how-
> ever, are motivated by sexual deviation.[11]

However, the authors continue, the statutes are seldom invoked except in matters involving sexual deviation.

Some of the definitions of psychopathic or mentally disordered or mentally abnormal sex offenders are extremely broad in wording. A few examples:

> Any person who is suffering from a mental disorder but is not
> mentally ill or feebleminded to an extent making him criminally

---

* We find paradoxical the opposition to behavior modification and incapacitative preventive surgery by those who do not cavil at the death penalty or long-term penal confinement.

irresponsible for his acts, such mental disorder being coupled with criminal propensities to the commission of sex offenses, is hereby declared to be a criminal sexual psychopathic person [Alabama].

[A sexually dangerous person is] any person whose misconduct in sexual matters indicates a general lack of power to control his sexual impulses, as evidenced by repetitive compulsive behavior and either violence, or aggression by an adult against a victim under the age of sixteen years, and who as a result is likely to attack or otherwise inflict injury on the objects of his uncontrolled or uncontrollable desires [Massachusetts].

Psychopathic offender is any person who is adjudged to have a psychopathic personality, who exhibits criminal tendencies and who by reason thereof is a menace to the public. Psychopathic personality is evidenced by such traits or characteristics inconsistent with the age of such person, as emotional immaturity and instability, impulsive, irresponsible, reckless, and unruly acts, excessively self-centered activities, deficient power of self-discipline, lack of normal capacity to learn from experience, marked deficiency of moral sense or control [Ohio].[12]

What many of these definitions stipulate is that the person is not judged to be insane and cannot claim an insanity defense. There have been numerous definitions offered as to what constitutes insanity in a legal sense; according to the *Durham* rule, for example, an individual who cannot control his behavior might be included as not being criminally responsible. However, short of insanity, the sex offender at the same time is judged to be in such a poor emotional and mental state that he is nonetheless a menace, and in some states his incarceration can take place without a trial and without a conviction. The law provides in some states that he be hospitalized, although the involuntary hospitalization in most respects resembles imprisonment and in some respects may be worse. The offender is thus left without recourse to defend himself against the charge. The indeterminate sentence leaves him at the mercy of psychiatrists and others who are agents of the state and who can play it safe by denying requests for release rather than granting the requests and making themselves vulnerable to the public and journalistic outcry should another offense be committed. "The release procedures of jurisdictions which stipulate that the patient must be cured or fully recovered from his psychopathy," write Brakel and Rock, "have been criticized as too stringent or unrealistic."[13]

The constitutionality of the sex psychopath laws has been challenged on the grounds of double jeopardy, vagueness of wording, and right to trial by jury, as well as on procedural grounds. The major charge has been that these civil commitments are made against alleged sex offenders only as a sham and smokescreen; that in effect they are criminal commitments, sometimes without benefit of trial; and that confinement is punishment whether or not it is also therapy. If indeed they are criminal commitments (and there is an interesting analogy here with the *Gault* case,[14] in which the Supreme Court ruled that a boy being sent to an industrial school was indeed being sent to a prison no matter what the institution was called), then they are commitments without the benefit of trial, the adjudication of guilt beyond a reasonable doubt, and the rights to counsel, to remain silent, to confront one's accusers, and to be presumed innocent until proven guilty. Nevertheless, as this is being written, the constitutionality of the sex psychopath laws has been upheld except for individual clauses and provisions in certain state statutes.

The sex psychopath laws have been criticized by many sociologists, criminal law professors, psychiatrists, and others, including Edwin Sutherland,[15] Paul Tappan,[16] Seymour Halleck,[17] and Nicholas Kittrie.[18] The laws, it is said, are not needed because other statutory provisions apply to dangerous criminals, sexual and other; if there is such a being as a sex psychopath, it is difficult if not impossible to identify him, and identification is fraught with possible error; treatment is seldom available, there is a pretense of treatment, and few are aided even when they desire to be; and there is a lack of protection of the constitutional rights and liberties of the accused in the process of commitment.

If the law were to be applied only to dangerous sex criminals, and if such persons could be identified and their potential danger (as well as past activities) evaluated with accuracy, the laws would not be subject to such severe criticism. Actually, one might say that to pass special legislation against sex offenders, on the ground that they are especially dangerous, is to misplace the emphasis; the special legislation ought to be against dangerous offenders whether or not the danger is of a sexual nature. The argument is sometimes made that the dangerous offender who commits armed robbery is more rational, less compulsive, more in need of punishment rather than treatment than the rapist or child molester. This is merely popular feeling on the question, no doubt fed by the mass media; while it is not supported by consensus in the scientific community, there is a considerable criminological and scientific literature favoring such a distinction.

It does not appear that the harshness inherent in the indeterminate sentence and in mental hospitalization, which can in some respects be literally worse than prison, is justified. Imprisonment of persons who are convicted of sex crimes in a crime-ridden society is best considered as a mechanism for isolating such convicted offenders (and thus incapacitating them or insuring their availability for treatment, coerced or voluntary) that is neither better nor worse than the mechanisms for handling persons convicted of other types of criminal offenses.

There is, however, still the question of treatment: its availability, its location—hospital, prison, or street (that is, treatment of the offender on probation), its efficacy, its voluntary versus involuntary application. There is the reality of an increasingly alarmed public, including highly vocal feminists, pressing for more immediate and effective measures to reduce significantly the number of rapes, attempted rapes, and sexual advances to very young children.

Decriminalization and the Changing Mores

Throughout this work, we have made frequent reference to two forces: decriminalization, on the one hand, and the modernization of penal codes through the voluntary adoption by states of provisions of the Model Penal Code promulgated by the American Law Institute.

Decriminalization is not seriously suggested by anyone for forcible rape, and by very few for adult-child sexuality. Against decriminalizing fornication, there is hardly an argument: even those who consider nonmarital sex a sin are no longer saying that it should be a matter of concern to the law. One comes into several gray areas, where decriminalization has enticing features: it clears the books of unenforced law, frees police and court personnel for more pressing areas of activity, expands freedom of sexual expression, reduces the possibility of official corruption. At the same time, there are some who feel that such a change will encourage and bring about patterns of behavior that are inimical to the smooth process of social living, that interfere with or go against traditional moral education and socialization, that challenge the family or at least meaningful affectional relationships of a quasi-family nature, that adversely affect the quality of life, particularly in small communities, and that there are victims although they are not affected to the extent that rape and child molestation victims are affected and often traumatized. Primarily, these gray areas involve prostitution, consensual homosexuality, and some of the "nuisance offenses," as well as adult-minor or jailbait cases in which the age differential is minimal.

To the extent that nonlegal means can minimize the ill effects of these activities, certainly such means are preferable. The answers are not clear-cut, but we would urge that major attention be given to alternatives to the legal process, particularly in light of the sexual revolution, the feminist revolution, and, of an entirely different nature, the rise in personal, political, property, white-collar, and corporate crimes that threaten the existence of the society and that demand a higher priority of attention.

These are the provisions that have generally been approved by the American Law Institute in the Model Penal Code, which was drawn up, after many years of study and travail, by criminal lawyers, judges, sociologists, psychologists, and others. It is not the aim of the authors of this code to impose a federal penal code upon the states. However, regionalism has declined in the United States. Technology has brought with it enormous geographic mobility, and there is no longer a compelling need, or even a strong justification, for penal codes that outlaw a practice in one state but legalize it in a neighboring one or that specify significantly different punishments for identical offenses. There has been a movement, starting as early as the 1930s, for the nationalization of the Bill of Rights—that is, the application of the constitutional rights of the accused, as put forth in the first ten amendments, to persons charged with state penal code violations. This is part of a larger social trend toward national homogenization: not one culture in the sense of the effacement of racial, age, social class, educational, occupational, and other differences—if anything, we have moved in the opposite direction; but one in the sense that these differences and similarities are very much alike in Maine, Alabama, Illinois, and Wyoming. This should logically call for greater congruence of laws and procedures governing sexual conduct.

To impose such a code nationally not only would require a constitutional amendment (unlikely of success and doubtful of merit) but also would move us toward further centralization of power. Yet to give each state discretion on such matters makes for inequities and injustices, on the one hand, and in some areas gives tremendous power to rural communities (although the one-man, one-vote decision of the Warren Court went a long way to remedy this situation). In some instances, judicial interpretation on a federal level, as in abortion, pornography, homosexual entrapment, and such matters, becomes the mechanism for erasing the differences across state boundaries. This, too, is not the ideal method: it is legislation by the judiciary. The American Law Institute thus has a strong recommendation for uniform state penal codes, a recommendation that falls far short of being an imposition; the recommended code has been hammered out with great care, with the aid of scholars from many disciplines, substantially free of the unnecessary and undesirable pressures that state legislators must face.

The Model Penal Code can be termed liberal, even permissive. It moves in the direction of decriminalization. It may have faults, inconsistencies, and injustices, and one may quarrel with some of its provisions; these can be corrected with experience. The code applies to much more than sex offenses—to all crimes, in fact. But its most important departures from both previous and current state penal codes are in the area of sex offenses because it is in this area that the greatest change in the mores seems to have occurred. Furthermore, sex is one of the areas in which legislators are not only prisoners of their early socialization and perhaps of sexual hangups but also are most vulnerable to special-interest lobbying and public pressures. The 1976 campaign to recriminalize abortion is an excellent demonstration of an attempt by a small but determined minority to impose under the threat of criminal sanctions its moral views on the whole population.

The basic philosophy of the Model Penal Code is, with some exceptions, the legality of sexual activities between consenting adults. The child is distinguished from the minor, and the difference in age between the older and the younger participant is a factor in determining the legality of sexual acts. The major provisions of the code have been enacted into law in Illinois first and later in several other states, in full or in part. While there is danger of backlash, decriminalization seems to be the wave of the future at least in the United States (many other countries have of course led the way in this area). Perhaps repeal of obsolete laws will foster the growth of religious, educational, familial, and other influences to channel the sexual energies of the populace, particularly the youth, into the most socially acceptable and potentially fulfilling directions.

In a majority of states the penal laws have not been thoroughly revised for decades. They have been changed piecemeal through amendments, repeals, and enactment of new legislation and have been subject to constant reinterpretation by the courts. Law can symbolize and codify the mores, thus giving leadership to a society in rallying the people around a set of values, and it can reflect the values and attitudes that the people hold. On matters relating to sexual behavior American laws have probably done neither. The laws have been largely hypocritical, equivocal, and pruriently pietistic. To the extent that they ever reflected widely held views they have become anachronistic as social mores and folkways have undergone change.

A transformation has taken place in American society with regard to sex. It is a pluralistic society; there is little cultural or moral consensus, with large numbers of people holding permissive and others retaining restrictive outlooks. Many have their prejudices, ideologies, and vested interests, and some exert pressure for legislation that may not be acceptable to other sectors of the populace. Nevertheless, given feminism and other protest movements, and the open espousal of a sexual morality that accepts sex for pleasure as a desirable end in itself, it is possible for American law in the last quarter of the twentieth century both to reflect and to mold attitudes that are rational, that do not challenge the central place of the family as a desirable institution but will allow it to develop in a flexible manner without legal restriction, and that are tolerant and nonpunitive in regard to harmless sexual conduct while freeing police and courts to pursue serious criminals. It is a difficult task but not one beyond possibilities of fulfillment.

Notes

Chapter 1.

1. Kingsley Davis, "Sexual Behavior," in *Contemporary Social Problems*, eds. Robert K. Merton and Robert Nisbet, 4th ed. (New York: Harcourt, Brace, 1976), p. 224.

2. John H. Gagnon and William Simon, *Sexual Conduct: The Social Sources of Human Sexuality* (Chicago: Aldine, 1973).

3. Sigmund Freud, *Civilization and Its Discontents* (New York: Norton, 1962), p. 44.

4. Max Weber, *Max Weber on Law in Economy and Society.* (New York: Simon & Schuster, 1967).

5. Clellan S. Ford and Frank A. Beach, *Patterns of Sexual Behavior* (New York: Harper, 1951).

6. Edwin M. Schur, *Crimes without Victims: Deviant Behavior and Public Policy: Abortion, Homosexuality, Drug Addiction* (Englewood Cliffs: Prentice-Hall, 1965).

7. Nebraska Revised Statutes, 1965, 828–919.

8. Gilbert Geis, *Not the Law's Business: An Examination of Homosexuality, Abortion, Prostitution, Narcotics, and Gambling in the United States,* NIMH Pub. No. 72–9132 (Rockville: National Institute of Mental Health, 1972).

9. Patrick Devlin, *The Enforcement of Morals* (New York: Oxford University Press, 1965).

10. H. L. A. Hart, *Law, Liberty, and Morality* (Stanford: Stanford University Press, 1963).

11. Menachem Amir, *Patterns in Forcible Rape* (Chicago: University of Chicago Press, 1971).

12. Gagnon and Simon, op. cit.

13. Nolan D. C. Lewis and Helen Yarnell, *Pathological Firesetting (Pyromania)*, Nervous and Mental Disease Monographs (New York, 1951); see also Brendan P. Battle and Paul B. Weston, *Arson* (New York: Greenberg, 1954).

14. Albert K. Cohen, *Delinquent Boys: The Culture of the Gang* (New York: Free Press, 1955).

15. Marvin E. Wolfgang, *Patterns in Criminal Homicide* (Philadelphia: University of Pennsylvania Press, 1958).

16. Benjamin Karpman, *The Sexual Offender and His Offenses: Etiology, Pathology, Psychodynamics, and Treatment* (New York: Julian, 1954), p. 133.

17. Ibid.

18. Ibid., p. 131.

19. Donal E. J. MacNamara, "The Criminal Signature Concept in *Modus Operandi*," *Journal of Offender Therapy*, 5 (1): 3–4 (1961).

20. Freud, op. cit., pp. 39–40.

21. Among important works on this subject see Kingsley Davis, "Illegitimacy and the Social Structure," *American Journal of Sociology*, 45:215–233 (1939); Clark E. Vincent, *Unmarried Mothers* (New York: Free Press, 1961); Frank F. Furstenberg, Jr., *Unplanned Parenthood: The Social Consequences of Teenage Childbearing* (New York: Free Press, 1976).

22. Davis, "Illegitimacy."

23. For statistics on the rise in illegitimacy during the 1970s see the *New York Times*, 12 November 1976, p. 1. For earlier statistics see National Office of Vital Statistics, "Illegitimate Births: United States, 1938–47."

24. On abortion see Paul H. Gebhard, Wardell B. Pomeroy, Clyde E. Martin, and Cornelia V. Christenson, *Pregnancy, Birth, and Abortion* (New York: Harper, 1958); for a pro-abortion viewpoint see Group for the Advancement of Psychiatry, Committee on Psychiatry and Law, *The Right to Abortion: A Psychiatric View* (New York: Scribner's, 1970).

25. References on venereal disease, particularly in relationship to prostitution, are given in Chapter 4, note 49 (p. 235).

26. The position against sexual permissiveness is put forth by J. D. Unwin, *Sex and Culture* (London: Oxford University Press, 1934); Pitirim Sorokin, *The American Sex Revolution* (Boston: Porter Sargent, 1956); and idem, "Love, Altruistic," in *The Encyclopedia of Sexual Behavior*, ed. Albert Ellis and Albert Abarbanel (New York: Hawthorn, 1961), pp. 641–645.

27. The most eloquent spokesman for this point of view was René Guyon,

The Ethics of Sexual Acts (New York: Knopf, 1934), and *Sexual Freedom* (New York: Knopf, 1950).

28. Albert Ellis, *The American Sexual Tragedy* (New York: Twayne, 1954); idem, *Sex Without Guilt* (New York: Lyle Stuart, 1958).

29. Hart, op. cit.

30. Commission on Obscenity and Pornography, *Report* (New York: Random House; New York: Bantam, 1970).

Chapter 2.

1. Kingsley Davis, "Sexual Behavior," in *Contemporary Social Problems,* ed. Robert K. Merton and Robert Nisbet, 3d ed. (New York: Harcourt, Brace, 1971). In the fourth edition, published in 1976, Davis slightly modified his position and no longer used such a phrase as "instinctively anarchic."

2. Clellan S. Ford and Frank A. Beach, *Patterns of Sexual Behavior* (New York: Harper, 1951), p. 59.

3. Alfred C. Kinsey, Wardell B. Pomeroy, and Clyde E. Martin, *Sexual Behavior in the Human Male* (Philadelphia: Saunders, 1948); Alfred C. Kinsey, Wardell B. Pomeroy, Clyde E. Martin, and Paul H. Gebhard, *Sexual Behavior in the Human Female* (Philadelphia: Saunders, 1953).

4. Ford and Beach, op. cit., p. 59.

5. Federal Bureau of Investigation, *Uniform Crime Reports: Crime in the United States, 1975* (Washington, D.C.: Government Printing Office, 1976).

6. American Law Institute: Model Penal Code. (Philadelphia: American Law Institute, 1962).

7. Ibid.

8. Ford and Beach, op. cit.

9. Ibid., p. 63.

10. Samuel Glasner, "Judaism and Sex," in *The Encyclopedia of Sexual Behavior,* ed. Albert Ellis and Albert Abarbanel (New York: Hawthorn, 1961), p. 511.

11. Calvin C. Hernton, *Sex and Racism in America* (New York: Grove, 1966).

12. Fred W. Voget, "American Indians, Sex Life of the," in Ellis and Abarbanel, op. cit., pp. 90–109.

13. R. A. LeVine, "Gusii Sex Offenses: A Study in Social Control," *American Anthropologist,* 61:965–990 (1959); see also discussion of Le-

Vine's report by Duncan Chappell, "Cross-Cultural Research on Forcible Rape," *International Journal of Criminology and Penology,* 4:295–304 (1976).

14. Morris Ploscowe, *Sex and the Law* (New York: Prentice-Hall, 1951), p. 170. The quote within the quote is from R. R. Beck, *Elements of Medical Jurisprudence,* 12th ed. (Philadelphia: Lippincott, 1863).

15. Ploscowe, op. cit., p. 172.

16. However, the defendant was sentenced for trespassing (unauthorized use of a friend's apartment).

17. Ploscowe, op. cit., pp. 173–174; ellipses in material as quoted by Ploscowe.

18. Federal Bureau of Investigation, op. cit.

19. For a report on this case see John M. McDonald, *Rape: Offenders and Their Victims* (Springfield: Charles C Thomas, 1971).

20. *Law Enforcement Assistance Administration, Criminal Victimization Surveys in Thirteen American Cities* (Washington, D.C.: Law Enforcement Assistance Administration, 1975).

21. Federal Bureau of Investigation, op. cit.

22. Menachem Amir, *Patterns in Forcible Rape* (Chicago: University of Chicago Press, 1971).

23. Paul H. Gebhard, John H. Gagnon, Wardell B. Pomeroy, and Cornelia V. Christenson, *Sex Offenders: An Analysis of Types* (New York: Harper & Row, 1965).

24. Amir, op. cit., chap. 13.

25. Marvin E. Wolfgang, *Patterns in Criminal Homicide* (Philadelphia: University of Pennsylvania Press, 1958).

26. Amir, op. cit., chap. 15.

27. Gebhard et al., op. cit., p. 177.

28. Kinsey et al., *Human Male.*

29. Gebhard et al., op. cit., p. 178.

30. Ibid., p. 178.

31. Ibid., p. 178.

32. Ibid., p. 199.

33. Ibid., p. 205.

34. Ibid., p. 206.

35. Eldridge Cleaver, *Soul on Ice* (New York: McGraw-Hill, 1968), p. 14.

36. Lillian Smith, *Killers of the Dream* (New York: Norton, 1949), pp. 116–117.

37. Ibid., p. 117.

38. Haywood Burns, "Can a Black Man Get a Fair Trial in This Country?" *New York Times Magazine*, 12 July 1970, pp. 5 ff.

39. Frank E. Hartung, "Trends in the Use of Capital Punishment," *Annals of American Academy of Political and Social Science*, 284: 8–19 (1952).

40. Marvin E. Wolfgang and Franco Ferracuti, *The Subculture of Violence: Towards an Integrated Theory in Criminology* (New York: Barnes & Noble, 1967).

41. Walter B. Miller, "Lower Class Culture as a Generating Milieu of Gang Delinquency," *Journal of Social Issues*, 14(3):5–19 (1958).

42. Robert M. Frumkin, "English and American Sex Customs, Early," in Ellis and Abarbanel, op. cit., p. 361.

43. Donald H. Partington, "The Incidence of the Death Penalty for Rape in Virginia," *Washington and Lee Law Review*, 22(1):43–75 (1965).

44. Jerome Kroll, "Racial Patterns of Military Crimes in Vietnam," *Psychiatry*, 39:51–64 (1976).

45. Ibid., pp. 57–58.

46. Albert J. Reiss, Jr., "The Marginal Status of the Adolescent," *Law and Contemporary Problems*, 25:309–333 (1960).

47. Bernard Rosenberg and Harry Silverstein, *The Varieties of Delinquent Experience* (Waltham: Blaisdell, 1969), p. 65.

48. W. H. Blanchard, "The Group Process in Gang Rape," *Journal of Social Psychology*, 49:259–266 (1959).

49. Ibid.

50. Gilbert Geis, "Group Sexual Assaults," *Medical Aspects of Human Sexuality*, May 1971, p. 101; see also Gilbert Geis and Duncan Chappell, "Forcible Rape by Multiple Offenders," *Abstracts on Criminology & Penology*, 11:431–436 (1971).

51. Cited in Geis, op. cit., pp. 109–110.

52. Ibid., p. 113.

53. Ibid., p. 113.

54. Ibid., p. 113.

55. This theme runs through a great deal of the literature of the 1970s; see particularly Susan Brownmiller, *Against Our Will: Men, Women, and Rape* (New York: Simon & Schuster, 1975).

56. Federal Bureau of Investigation, op. cit.

57. Robert Buckhout, "Eyewitness Testimony," *Scientific American*, 231: 23–31 (1974).

58. *New York Times*, especially 11 November 1972 and 18 March 1973.

59. American Civil Liberties Union, Board of Directors, "Policy on Prior Sexual History" (New York, February 1976).

60. The point is alluded to by Chappell, op. cit., and deserves further research.

Chapter 3.

1. Charles H. McCaghy, "Child Molesters: A Study of Their Careers as Deviants" (Ph.D. diss., University of Wisconsin, 1966).

2. Clellan S. Ford and Frank A. Beach, *Patterns of Sexual Behavior* (New York: Harper, 1951), p. 188.

3. Ibid., p. 191.

4. René Guyon, *The Ethics of Sexual Acts* (New York: Knopf, 1934); idem, *Sexual Freedom* (New York: Knopf, 1950).

5. Discussed by Laud Humphreys, *Out of the Closets: The Sociology of Homosexual Liberation* (Englewood Cliffs: Prentice-Hall, 1972).

6. Frederic Bernard, "An Enquiry among a Group of Pedophiles," *Journal of Sex Research*, 11:142–155 (1975).

7. Paul H. Gebhard, John H. Gagnon, Wardell B. Pomeroy, and Cornelia V. Christenson, *Sex Offenders: An Analysis of Types* (New York: Harper & Row, 1965).

8. Ford and Beach, op. cit., p. 181.

9. American Law Institute: Model Penal Code (Philadelphia: American Law Institute, 1962).

10. Gebhard et al., op. cit., p. 54.

11. McCaghy, op. cit; this work is excerpted in *Criminal Behavior Systems: A Typology*, ed. Marshall B. Clinard and Richard Quinney (New York: Holt, Rinehart & Winston, 1967), pp. 75–88; see also Charles H. McCaghy, "Child Molesting," *Sexual Behavior*, August 1971, pp. 16–24.

12. Gebhard et al., op. cit., p. 74.

13. Alex. K. Gigeroff, *Sexual Deviations in the Criminal Law: Homosexual, Exhibitionistic, and Pedophilic Offences in Canada* (Toronto: University of Toronto Press, 1968).

14. Alan P. Bell and Calvin S. Hall, *The Personality of a Child Molester: An Analysis of Dreams* (Chicago: Aldine-Atherton, 1971).

15. Ibid., p. 116.

16. Don C. Gibbons, *Changing the Lawbreaker: The Treatment of Delinquents and Criminals* (Englewood Cliffs: Prentice-Hall, 1965), pp. 277–280; note, however, that Gibbons points out that some offenders do commit these acts violently.

17. Clinard and Quinney, op. cit.

18. Gebhard et al., op. cit., p. 72.

19. Ibid., p. 73.

20. Donal E. J. MacNamara, "Convicting the Innocent," *Crime and Delinquency*, January 1969, pp. 57–61.

21. McCaghy, excerpted in Clinard and Quinney, op. cit., p. 88.

22. Ralph Slovenko, "Statutory Rape," *Medical Aspects of Human Sexuality*, March 1971, pp. 155–167.

23. Ibid., p. 158.

24. The case cited by Slovenko is State v. Snow 252 S.W. 629 (Missouri, 1923).

25. Gebhard et al., op. cit.

26. Ibid., pp. 102–103.

27. Ford and Beach, op. cit., p. 172.

28. Gebhard et al., op. cit., chaps. 13, 14.

29. Robin Lloyd, *For Money or Love: Boy Prostitution in America* (New York: Vanguard, 1976).

30. McCaghy, excerpted in Clinard and Quinney, op. cit.; also idem, "Drinking and Deviance Disavowal: The Case of Child Molesters," *Social Problems*, 16:43–49 (1968).

31. McCaghy, excerpted in Clinard and Quinney, op. cit.

32. Edward Sagarin, "Sex Raises Its Revolutionary Head," in *Deviance, Conflict, and Criminality*, ed. R. Serge Denisoff and Charles H. McCaghy (Chicago: Rand McNally, 1973), pp. 174–190; see also Humphreys, op. cit.

33. Richard C. Donnelly, Joseph Goldstein, and Richard D. Schwartz, *Criminal Law* (New York: Free Press, 1974).

34. Livingston Hall, Yale Kamisar, Wayne R. LaFave, and Jerold H. Israel, *Modern Criminal Procedure*, 3d ed. (St. Paul: West, 1969).

35. One of the few works devoted to this subject unfortunately ·sheds very little light on it; namely, Robert H. V. Ollendorff, *The Juvenile Homosexual Experience and Its Effect on Adult Sexuality* (New York: Julian, 1966).

36. On homosexuality as a learned pattern of behavior see Ronald L. Akers, *Deviant Behavior: A Social Learning Approach* (Belmont: Wadsworth, 1973). Also, although it deals with initiation into homosexuality at a much later age, Edward Sagarin, "Prison Homosexuality and Its Effect on Post-Prison Sexual Behavior," *Psychiatry*, 39:245–257 (1976).

37. *Report of the Departmental Committee on Homosexual Offences and*

Prostitution (London: Her Majesty's Stationery Office, 1956). This is generally referred to as the Wolfenden Report, as the Committee was headed by John Wolfenden.

38. Herbert Maisch, *Incest* (New York: Stein & Day, 1972).

39. Hector Cavallin, "Incest," *Sexual Behavior,* February 1973, p. 22.

40. Gebhard et al., op. cit., pp. 207, 230.

41. Ibid., p. 249.

42. Maisch, op. cit.

43. Hedwig Wallis, Foreword to Maisch, op. cit.

44. Franco Ferracuti, "Incest between Father and Daughter," in *Sexual Behaviors: Social, Clinical, and Legal Aspects,* ed. H. L. P. Resnik and Marvin E. Wolfgang (Boston: Little, Brown, 1972), p. 179; see also Clifford Allen, *A Textbook of Psychosexual Disorders* (London: Oxford University Press, 1962); and I. B. Weiner, "Father-Daughter Incest: A Clinical Report," *Psychiatric Quarterly,* 36:607–632 (1962).

45. Paul Sloane and Eva Karpinski, "Effects of Incest on the Participants," *American Journal of Orthopsychiatry,* 12:666–673 (1942).

46. Ferracuti, op. cit., p. 179; see also Leroy G. Schultz, "Interviewing the Sex Offender's Victim," *Journal of Criminal Law, Criminology and Police Science,* 50:448–452 (1960); and David Reifen, "Protection of Children Involved in Sexual Offenses: A New Method of Investigation in Israel," ibid., 49:222–229 (1958).

47. McCaghy, "Child Molesting."

48. Stuart M. Finch, "Adult Seduction of the Child: Effects on the Child," *Medical Aspects of Human Sexuality,* March 1973, p. 185.

49. Alfred C. Kinsey, Wardell B. Pomeroy, Clyde E. Martin, and Paul H. Gebhard, *Sexual Behavior in the Human Female* (Philadelphia: Saunders, 1953), p. 117.

50. Ibid.

51. Ibid., p. 116.

52. Lauretta Bender and Abram Blau, "The Reaction of Children to Sexual Relations with Adults," *American Journal of Orthopsychiatry,* 7:500–518 (1937); Lauretta Bender and Samuel Paster, "Homosexual Trends in Children," ibid., 11:730–743 (1941); Lauretta Bender and Alvin E. Grugett, Jr., "A Follow-Up Report on Children Who Had Atypical Sexual Experience," ibid., 22:825–837 (1952); Lauretta Bender, untitled comment in McCaghy, "Child Molesting," p. 21.

53. William R. Reevy, "Child Sexuality," in *The Encyclopedia of Sexual Behavior,* ed. Albert Ellis and Albert Abarbanel (New York: Hawthorn, 1961), pp. 258–267.

Chapter 4.

1. Morris Ploscowe, *Sex and the Law* (New York: Prentice-Hall, 1951), p. 242.
2. Samuel G. Kling, *Sexual Behavior and the Law* (New York: Bernard Geis, 1965), p. 181.
3. Isabel Drummond, *The Sex Paradox* (New York: Putnam, 1953), pp. 208–209.
4. NY PENAL LAW §230.00 (McKinney).
5. Kingsley Davis, "Sexual Behavior," in *Contemporary Social Problems,* ed. Robert K. Merton and Robert Nisbet, 4th ed. (New York: Harcourt, Brace, 1976), p. 245.
6. Ned Polsky, *Hustlers, Beats, and Others* (Chicago: Aldine, 1967), p. 193.
7. Edwin M. Lemert, *Social Pathology: A Systematic Approach to the Theory of Sociopathic Behavior* (New York: McGraw-Hill, 1951).
8. For historical material on this subject see Charles Winick and Paul Kinsie, *The Lively Commerce: Prostitution in the United States* (Chicago: Quadrangle, 1971).
9. Ibid.
10. Edward Sagarin, "Say, Cabbie, Where's the Action in this Town?" in *Sexual Behavior—Current Issues: An Interdisciplinary Perspective,* ed. Leonard Gross (Flushing: Spectrum, 1974), pp. 215–233.
11. Robin Lloyd, *For Money or Love: Boy Prostitution in America* (New York: Vanguard, 1976).
12. Winick and Kinsie, op. cit.
13. Jennifer James, "Prostitutes and Prostitution," in *Deviants: Voluntary Actors in a Hostile World,* ed. Edward Sagarin and Fred Montanino (Morristown: General Learning Press, 1977), pp. 368–428.
14. Ibid.
15. Harold Greenwald, *The Call Girl* (New York: Ballantine, 1958).
16. Winick and Kinsie, op. cit.
17. An early and rather thorough study of the pimp is by B. Reitman, *The Second Oldest Profession* (New York: Vanguard, 1936); on the racial aspects and other more recent features see Christina Milner and Richard Milner, *Black Players: The Secret World of Black Pimps* (Boston: Little, Brown, 1972).
18. NY PENAL LAW §230.05 (McKinney).
19. Kingsley Davis, "The Sociology of Prostitution," *American Sociological Review,* 2:744–755 (1937).

20. For example, Xaviera Hollander, *The Happy Hooker* (New York: Dell, 1972); and Polly Adler, *A House Is Not a Home* (New York: Rinehart, 1955).

21. NY PENAL LAW §240.37 (McKinney).

22. New York City Police Department. Legal Division Supplement No. 2 (1976). "Guidelines for Arrests for Loitering for the Purposes of Prostitution, Promoting Prostitution and Patronizing a Prostitute."

23. Federal Bureau of Investigation, *Uniform Crime Reports: Crime in the United States, 1975* (Washington, D.C.: Government Printing Office, 1976).

24. President's Commission on Law Enforcement and Administration of Justice, Task Force on Assessment, *Task Force Report: Crime and Its Impact: An Assessment* (Washington, D.C.: Government Printing Office, 1967), p. 53.

25. Winick and Kinsie, op. cit.; see also Harry Benjamin and R. E. L. Masters, *Prostitution and Morality* (New York: Julian, 1964).

26. Menachem Amir, *Patterns in Forcible Rape* (Chicago: University of Chicago Press, 1971).

27. James, op. cit.

28. For historical information see Winick and Kinsie, op. cit.; and Benjamin and Masters, op. cit.

29. Michael Pearson, *The £5 Virgins* (New York: Saturday Review Press, 1972).

30. Abraham Flexner, *Prostitution in Europe* (1914; reprint ed., Montclair: Patterson Smith, 1969), pp. 92–93.

31. International Agreement for the Suppression of the White Slave Traffic (Paris, May 1904), amended by United Nations, May 1949 (U.N. Pub., Sales No. 1950.IV.1).

32. International Convention for the Suppression of the White Slave Traffic (Paris, May 1910), amended by United Nations, May 1949 (U.N. Pub., Sales No. 1950.IV.2).

33. United Nations, Department of Economic and Social Affairs, *Study of Traffic in Persons and Prostitution* (New York: United Nations, 1959), p. 7.

34. United Nations, "Traffic in Persons, Prostitution, and Anti-Venereal Disease Measures in Selected Countries and Territories," *International Review of Criminal Policy*, (October 1960), pp. 69–86.

35. *New York Times*, 27 June 1975.

36. Edgar Morin, *Rumour in Orleans* (New York: Pantheon, 1971).

37. Sean O'Callaghan, *Damaged Baggage: The White Slave Trade and Narcotics Trafficking in the Americas* (New York: Roy, 1969);

Stephen Barlay, *Bondage: The Slave Traffic in Women Today* (New York: Funk & Wagnalls, 1968).

38. Barlay, op. cit.

39. International Criminal Police Organization, (Report submitted in the General Secretariat, XXXIVth Session of the General Assembly, Rio de Janeiro, 16–23 June 1965). "International Traffic in Women under the Cover of Exposing Them to Prostitution."

40. T. C. Esselstyn, "Prostitution in the United States," *Annals of American Academy of Political and Social Science,* 376:123–135 (1968).

41. Ibid., p. 125.

42. Benjamin and Masters, op. cit.

43. Charles Winick, personal communications.

44. Charles Winick, "Prostitutes' Clients' Perception of the Prostitutes and of Themselves," *International Journal of Social Psychiatry,* 8:289–297 (1962); see also T. C. N. Gibbens and M. Silberman, "The Clients of Prostitutes," *British Journal of Venereal Disease,* 36:113–117 (1960).

45. Alfred C. Kinsey, Wardell B. Pomeroy, and Clyde E. Martin, *Sexual Behavior in the Human Male* (Philadelphia: Saunders, 1948), p. 597.

46. See R. K. Bell and J. B. Chaskes, "Premarital Sexual Experience among Coeds, 1958 and 1968," *Journal of Marriage and Family,* 32:81–84 (1970), K. L. Cannon and R. Long, "Premarital Sexual Behavior in the Sixties," ibid., 33:36–49 (1971); Frank W. Finger, "Changes of Sex Practices and Beliefs of Male College Students: Over 30 Years," *Journal of Sex Research,* 11:304–317 (1975); J. J. Teevan, Jr., "Reference Group and Premarital Sexual Behavior," *Journal of Marriage and Family,* 34:283–291 (1972).

47. Polsky, op. cit.

48. Davis, "Sociology of Prostitution."

49. G. Idsoe and T. Guthe, "The Rise and Fall of Treponematoses," *British Journal of Venereal Disease,* 43:227–241 (1967); James, op. cit.; Edward Sagarin, "Swinging through the VD Tree," *Physician's World,* April 1974, pp. 70–74; Winick and Kinsie, op. cit., pp. 63–67; Department of Health, Education, and Welfare, *VD Fact Sheet: Basic Statistics on the Venereal Disease Problem in the United States* (Washington, D.C.: Department of Health, Education, and Welfare, 1971); and R. R. Willcox, "Prostitution and Venereal Disease," *British Journal of Venereal Disease,* 38:37–41 (1962).

50. American Law Institute, Model Penal Code (Philadelphia: American Law Institute, 1962).

51. Ibid.

52. Wayne R. LaFave, *Arrest: The Decision to Take a Suspect into Custody* (Boston: Little, Brown, 1965), p. 463.

53. Ibid., p. 464.

54. Winick and Kinsie, op. cit., pp. 287–288.

Chapter 5.

1. Edward Sagarin, "Homosexuality and the Homosexual: An Overview of the Former and a Denial of the Reality of the Latter" (Paper presented to the American Sociological Association and the Society for the Study of Social Problems, Montreal, 1974); also idem, "The High Personal Cost of Wearing a Label," *Psychology Today*, March 1976, pp. 25 ff.

2. Alfred C. Kinsey, Wardell B. Pomeroy, and Clyde E. Martin, *Sexual Behavior in the Human Male* (Philadelphia: Saunders, 1948); Alfred C. Kinsey, Wardell B. Pomeroy, Clyde E. Martin, and Paul H. Gebhard, *Sexual Behavior in the Human Female* (Philadelphia: Saunders, 1953).

3. Paul H. Gebhard, "Incidence of Overt Homosexuality in the United States and Western Europe," in National Institute of Mental Health Task Force on Homosexuality, *Homosexuality: Final Report and Background Papers*, John M. Livingood, ed. (Washington, D.C.: Government Printing Office, 1972), pp. 22–29.

4. Kinsey et al., *Sexual Behavior in the Human Male*.

5. *Report of the Departmental Committee on Homosexual Offences and Prostitution* (London: Her Majesty's Stationery Office, 1956), commonly known as the Wolfenden Report.

6. According to the *Sexual Law Reporter*, on August 6, 1975, New Hampshire became the eighteenth state to have repealed its laws against consensual sex in private.

7. Rittenour v. District of Columbia, 163 A.2d 560 (D.C. 1960).

8. These cases are discussed by Edward Sagarin and Donal E. J. Mac-Namara, "The Problem of Entrapment," *Crime and Delinquency*, October 1970, pp. 363–378.

9. The raid in question, and the homophile movement as it developed thereafter, are discussed by several authors. See particularly Dennis Altman, *Homosexual Oppression and Liberation* (New York: Outerbridge & Dienstfrey, 1971); Peter Fisher, *The Gay Mystique: The Myth and Reality of Male Homosexuality* (New York: Stein & Day, 1972); and Donn Teal, *The Gay Militants* (New York: Stein & Day, 1971).

10. Laud Humphreys, *Tearoom Trade: Impersonal Sex in Public Places* (Chicago: Aldine, 1970), p. 109. Ellipses in the original.
11. Gerhard O. W. Mueller, *Legal Regulation of Sexual Conduct* (New York: Oceana, 1961).
12. Patrick Devlin, *The Enforcement of Morals* (New York: Oxford University Press, 1965).
13. American Law Institute, Model Penal Code (Philadelphia: American Law Institute, 1962).
14. Ibid.
15. Ibid.
16. Ibid.
17. Alex. K. Gigeroff, *Sexual Deviations in the Criminal Law: Homosexual, Exhibitionistic, and Pedophilic Offences in Canada* (Toronto: University of Toronto Press, 1968).
18. Ibid., pp. 195–196.
19. Ibid., p. 197.
20. Ibid., pp. 198–201.
21. A small part of the work of Winick and Kinsie is devoted to male prostitution: Charles Winick and Paul Kinsie, *The Lively Commerce: Prostitution in the United States* (Chicago: Quadrangle, 1971). Researchers should start with the excellent bibliography by Martin S. Weinberg and Alan P. Bell, eds., *Homosexuality: An Annotated Bibliography* (New York: Harper & Row, 1972). Other works, in addition to those cited in subsequent notes, are Martin Hoffman, "The Male Prostitute," *Sexual Behavior,* 2:16–21 (August 1972); David J. Pittman, "The Male House of Prostitution," *Trans-Action,* March–April 1971, pp. 21–27; H. Laurence Ross, "The 'Hustler' in Chicago," *Journal of Student Research,* 1(1):13–19 (1959).
22. Donal E. J. MacNamara, "Male Prostitution in an American City: A Pathological or Socioeconomic Phenomenon?" (Paper presented to the American Orthopsychiatric Association, New York City, 1965). Abstracted in *Psychiatric Spectator* 2:5:6 (1965).
23. Simon Raven, "Boys Will Be Boys: The Male Prostitute in London," in *The Problem of Homosexuality in Modern Society,* ed. Hendrik M. Ruitenbeek (New York: Dutton, 1963).
24. Richard Burton, "Terminal Essay," in *The Arabian Nights,* originally published in 1886.
25. Donald J. West, *Homosexuality* (Chicago: Aldine, 1968).
26. Wainwright Churchill, *Homosexual Behavior among Males: A Cross-Cultural and Cross-Species Investigation* (Englewood Cliffs: Prentice-Hall, 1968), p. 57.

27. Ibid., p. 78.

28. Humphreys, op. cit., p. 116.

29. Albert J. Reiss, Jr., "The Social Integration of Queers and Peers," *Social Problems*, 9:102–120 (1961).

30. John Gerassi, *The Boys of Boise: Furor, Vice, and Folly in an American City* (New York: Macmillan, 1966).

31. Abraham Flexner, *Prostitution in Europe* (1914; reprint ed., Montclair: Patterson Smith, 1969), p. 31.

32. William W. Sanger, *History of Prostitution* (New York: Harper, 1858).

33. Robin Lloyd, *For Money or Love: Boy Prostitution in America* (New York: Vanguard, 1976).

34. Sivan E. Caukins and Neil R. Coombs, "The Psychodynamics of Male Prostitution," *American Journal of Psychotherapy*, 30:441–451 (1976); Reiss, op. cit.

35. Ibid.

36. Robert W. Deisher, Victor Eisner, and Stephen I. Sulzbacher, "The Young Male Prostitute," *Pediatrics*, 43:936 (1969).

37. Editorial, *Pediatrics*, 43:913–914 (1969).

38. Alan J. Davis, "Sexual Assaults in the Philadelphia Prison System," in *The Sexual Scene*, ed. John H. Gagnon and William Simon (Chicago: Aldine, 1970), p. 110.

39. Peter C. Buffum, *Homosexuality in Prison*, prepared for the Law Enforcement Assistance Administration (Washington, D.C.: Government Printing Office, 1971); John Irwin, cited in ibid., p. 13.

40. Buffum, op. cit., p. 13; John H. Gagnon, working paper presented to a 1971 conference on prison homosexuality, 1971), cited in ibid., p. 13.

41. Ronald L. Akers, Norman S. Hayner, and Werner Gruninger, "Homosexual and Drug Behavior in Different Types of Prisons," in *Corrections: Problems of Punishment and Rehabilitation*, ed. Edward Sagarin and Donal E. J. MacNamara (New York: Praeger, 1973), pp. 70–79.

42. George L. Kirkham, "Homosexuality in Prison," in *Studies in the Sociology of Sex*, ed. James M. Henslin (New York: Appleton-Century-Crofts, 1971), pp. 325–349.

43. Edward Sagarin, "Prison Homosexuality and Its Effect on Post-Prison Sexual Behavior," *Psychiatry*, 39:245–257 (1976).

44. Paul H. Gebhard, John H. Gagnon, Wardell B. Pomeroy, and Cornelia V. Christenson, *Sex Offenders: An Analysis of Types* (New York: Harper & Row, 1965).

45. Robert J. Kelly, commentary on "Sex in Prison" by Gene Kassebaum, *Sexual Behavior,* January 1972, p. 41.

46. David Ward and Gene Kassebaum, *Women's Prison: Sex and Social Structure* (Chicago: Aldine, 1965).

47. Kirkham, op. cit., p. 331.

48. Erving Goffman, *Stigma: Notes on the Management of Spoiled Identity* (Englewood Cliffs: Prentice-Hall, 1963).

49. Anthony M. Scacco, *Rape in Prison* (Springfield: Charles C. Thomas, 1975).

50. John H. Gagnon and William Simon, *Sexual Conduct: The Social Sources of Human Sexuality* (Chicago: Aldine, 1973).

51. Buffum, op. cit., p. 23.

52. Sagarin, "Prison Homosexuality."

53. Buffum, op. cit., p. 33.

54. Scacco, op. cit.

55. Don C. Gibbons, "Violence in American Society: The Challenge to Corrections," *American Journal of Corrections,* March–April 1969, p. 8.

56. Bruno Bettelheim, "Individual and Mass Behavior in Extreme Situations," *Journal of Abnormal and Social Psychology,* 38:417–452 (1943).

57. Gagnon and Simon, *Sexual Conduct,* pp. 246–247.

58. This theme, with the emphasis on the homosexual as victim, is described in detail in an earlier work by Sagarin and MacNamara. See Edward Sagarin and Donal E. J. MacNamara, "The Homosexual as a Crime Victim" (Paper presented at the First International Symposium on Victimology, Jerusalem, 1973), reprinted in part in *International Journal of Criminology and Penology,* 3:13–25 (1975), and in *Victimology: A New Focus,* ed. Israel Drapkin and Emilio Viano (Lexington: Heath, 1975), pp. 73–85.

59. Milton Helpern, in an answer to a question, *Medical Aspects of Human Sexuality,* May 1973, p. 225.

60. President's Commission on Law Enforcement and Administration of Justice, Task Force on Assessment, *Task Force Report: Crime and Its Impact—An Assessment* (Washington, D.C.: Government Printing Office), p. 12.

61. Ezzat A. Fattah, *La Victime: Est-elle coupable? Le Rôle de la victime dans le meurtre en vue de vol* (Montreal: Les Presses de l'Université de Montréal, 1971).

62. Gerald Walker, *Cruising* (New York: Stein & Day, 1970).

63. *Report of the Departmental Committee,* op. cit.

64. National Institute of Mental Health Task Force on Homosexuality,

Homosexuality: Final Report and Background Papers, ed. John M. Livingood (Washington: Government Printing Office, 1972). See particularly pp. 2–7.

Chapter 6.

1. Richard von Krafft-Ebing, *Psychopathia Sexualis* (1886; New York: Stein & Day, 1965; New York: Putnam, 1965).
2. Clifford Allen, *A Textbook of Psychosexual Disorders* (London: Oxford University Press, 1962).
3. John Money and Anke A. Ehrhardt, *Man & Woman, Boy & Girl: The Differentiation and Dimorphism of Gender Identity from Conception to Maturity* (Baltimore: Johns Hopkins Press, 1972).
4. Paul H. Gebhard, John H. Gagnon, Wardell B. Pomeroy, and Cornelia V. Christenson, *Sex Offenders: An Analysis of Types* (New York: Harper & Row, 1965), p. 380.
5. Ibid., p. 380.
6. Ibid., chap. 17.
7. Ibid., p. 399.
8. Albert Ellis and Ralph Brancale, *The Psychology of Sex Offenders* (Springfield: Charles C Thomas, 1956).
9. J. W. Mohr, R. E. Turner, and M. B. Jerry, *Pedophilia and Exhibitionism: A Handbook* (Toronto: University of Toronto Press, 1964), p. 115.
10. Gebhard et al., op. cit., chap. 16.
11. Arnold Birenbaum and Edward Sagarin, "The Deviant Actor Maintains His Right to Be Present: The Case of the Nondrinker," in *People in Places: The Sociology of the Familiar,* ed. Arnold Birenbaum and Edward Sagarin (New York: Praeger, 1973), pp. 68–82.
12. Clellan S. Ford and Frank A. Beach, *Patterns of Sexual Behavior* (New York: Harper, 1951, pp. 68–72.
13. Albert Ellis, *Reason and Emotion in Psychotherapy* (New York: Lyle Stuart, 1962).
14. Krafft-Ebing, op. cit.
15. The phrase is from John H. Gagnon and William Simon, eds., *Sexual Deviance* (New York: Harper & Row, 1967); it is used by Edward Sagarin, "Sex Deviance: A View from the Window of Middle America," in *Deviants: Voluntary Actors in a Hostile World,* ed. Edward Sagarin and Fred Montanino (Morristown: General Learning Press, 1977), pp. 429–462.

16. Havelock Ellis, *Studies in the Psychology of Sex* (New York: Random House, 1936), 2(pt. 1):72.

17. Robert Veit Sherwin, "Laws on Sex Crimes," in *The Encyclopedia of Sexual Behavior*, ed., Albert Ellis and Albert Abarbanel (New York: Hawthorn, 1961), pp. 627–628.

18. Benjamin Karpman, *The Sexual Offender and His Offenses: Etiology, Pathology, Psychodynamics, and Treatment* (New York: Julian, 1954), pp. 114–115.

19. Ibid., p. 356.

20. Irvin D. Yalom, "Aggression and Forbiddenness in Voyeurism," *Archives of General Psychiatry*, 3:305 (1960).

21. Ibid., p. 316.

22. Ibid., p. 318.

23. Gebhard et al., op. cit., p. 378.

24. Ibid.

25. William E. Hartman, Marilyn Fithian, and Donald Johnson, *Nudist Society: An Authoritative, Complete Study of Nudism in America* (New York: Crown, 1970).

26. Sherwin, op. cit., p. 627.

27. Barry Schwartz, "The Social Psychology of Privacy," *American Journal of Sociology*, 73:742 (1968).

28. Alan F. Westin, *Privacy and Freedom* (New York: Atheneum, 1967).

29. Edward Sagarin, "Power to the Peephole," *Sexual Behavior*, February 1973, pp. 2–7.

30. Westin, op. cit.

31. Quoted by Westin, op. cit., p. 361, from Hamberger v. Eastman, 206 A.2d 239 (N.H. 1964).

32. There is a considerable literature on cross-dressing. Havelock Ellis, op. cit., called it "eonism" and devoted a large part of *Studies in the Psychology of Sex* to the subject. There is a brief and interesting article by Hugo G. Beigel and Robert Feldman, "The Male Transvestite's Motivation in Fiction, Research, and Reality," in *Advances in Sex Research*, ed. Hugo G. Beigel (New York: Harper & Row/ Hoeber, 1963). A considerable amount of material is found in Robert J. Stoller, *Sex and Gender: On the Development of Masculinity and Femininity* (New York: Science House, 1968).

33. Sherwin, op. cit.

34. George L. Kirkham and Edward Sagarin, "Cross-Dressing," *Sexual Behavior*, April 1972, pp. 53–58.

35. Richard Green, "The Behaviorally Feminine Child: Pretranssexual? Pretransvestic? Prehomosexual? Preheterosexual?" in *Sex Differences*

in Behavior, ed. Richard C. Friedman, Ralph M. Richart, and Raymond L. Vande Wiele (New York: Wiley, 1974).

36. Daniel G. Brown, "Transvestism and Sex-Role Inversion," in Ellis and Abarbanel, op. cit., p. 1018.

37. The word was popularized by Harry Benjamin, *The Transsexual Phenomenon* (New York: Julian, 1966) but was used by Benjamin much earlier in "Transvestism and Transsexualism," *International Journal of Sexology,* 7:12–14 (1953).

38. Sherwin, op. cit.

39. Transsexualism is discussed in Robert J. Stoller, *Sex and Gender: On the Development of Masculinity and Femininity* (New York: Science House, 1968); also see Money and Ehrhardt, op. cit.; Richard Green and John Money, eds. *Transsexualism and Sex Reassignment* (Baltimore: Johns Hopkins Press, 1969); and Ethel S. Person and Lionel Ovesey, "The Psychodynamics of Male Transsexualism," in Friedman et al., op. cit., pp. 315–325.

40. On legal problems see "Medicolegal Aspects of Transsexualism," in Green and Money, op. cit., pp. 417–465; this section contains articles by Robert Veit Sherwin, John P. Holloway, Thomas E. James, Georg K. Stürup, and Jan Wålinder.

41. Gerhard O. W. Mueller, *Legal Regulation of Sexual Conduct* (New York: Oceana, 1961), p. 26.

42. Alfred C. Kinsey, Wardell B. Pomeroy, and Clyde E. Martin, *Sexual Behavior in the Human Male* (Philadelphia: Saunders, 1948).

43. Ellis and Brancale, op. cit.

44. S. Kirson Weinberg, *Incest Behavior* (New York: Citadel, 1955).

45. Herbert Maisch, *Incest* (New York: Stein & Day, 1972).

46. Edward Sagarin, "Incest: Problems of Definition and Frequency," *Journal of Sex Research,* in press.

47. Donald Hayes Russell, "Obscene Telephone Callers and Their Victims," *Sexual Behavior,* May 1971, p. 80.

48. *In re* Gault, 387 U.S. 1 (1967).

49. Gebhard et al., op. cit., p. 406.

50. *New York Post,* 3 Feburary 1976.

Chapter 7.

1. This term was suggested by Edward Sagarin, "Typologies of Sexual Behavior," *Journal of Sex Research,* 6:335–338 (1970).

2. Gerhard O. W. Mueller, *Legal Regulation of Sexual Conduct* (New York: Oceana, 1961), p. 46.

3. However, we were informed by faculty members that no effort is made to enforce the rule at the Utah university.

4. Gerhard O. W. Mueller, "Seduction and the Law," *Medical Aspects of Human Sexuality*, January 1972, p. 20.

5. Ibid.

6. Sagarin suggests that adultery is the most common form of sex deviance, and it fits very well into the concept "normal deviance," offered by John H. Gagnon and William Simon, eds., *Sexual Deviance* (New York: Harper & Row, 1967); Edward Sagarin, "Sex Deviance: A View from the Window of Middle America," in *Deviants: Voluntary Actors in a Hostile World*, ed. Edward Sagarin and Fred Montanino (Morristown: General Learning Press, 1977), pp. 429–462.

7. For a review of extramarital relations, particularly with knowledge and consent of spouse, see Roger Libby, "Extramarital and Co-Marital Sex: A Review of the Literature," in *Renovating Marriage*, ed. Roger Libby and Robert N. Whitehurst (Danville: Consensus, 1973), pp. 116–145; see also Jacquelyn J. Knapp, "An Exploratory Study of Seventeen Sexually Open Marriages," *Journal of Sex Research*, 12: 206–219 (1976); the best known book on the subject is probably Nena O'Neill and George O'Neill, *Open Marriage* (New York: Evans, 1972).

8. Among the works on group sex see Gilbert D. Bartell, *Group Sex* (New York: New American Library, 1974); Carolyn Symonds, "Sexual Mate-Swapping: Violation of Norms and Reconciliation of Guilt," in *Studies in the Sociology of Sex*, ed. James M. Henslin (New York: Appleton-Century-Crofts, 1971), pp. 81–109; and Charles A. Varni, "An Exploratory Study of Spouse Swapping," in *Beyond Monogamy*, ed. James R. Smith and Lynn G. Smith (Baltimore: Johns Hopkins Press, 1974), pp. 246–259. On the decline of group sex see Betty Fang, "Swinging: In Retrospect," *Journal of Sex Research*, 12:220–237 (1976).

9. Mueller, *Legal Regulation*.

10. This theme is discussed by Sagarin, "Sex Deviance," op. cit.

11. Ben B. Lindsey and Wainwright Evans, *The Companionate Marriage* (New York: Boni & Liveright, 1927).

12. Isabel Drummond, *The Sex Paradox* (New York: Putnam, 1953); Calvin C. Hernton, *Sex and Racism in America* (New York: Grove, 1966); and Alan Paton, *Too Late the Phalarope* (New York: Scribner's, 1953).

13. John Dollard, *Caste and Class in a Southern Town* (New York: Harper, 1937).

14. For an incisive sociological analysis of intermarriage see Robert K.

Merton, "Intermarriage and the Social Structure," in *Sociological Ambivalence and Other Essays,* ed. Robert K. Merton (New York: Free Press, 1976); this essay was originally published in 1941.

15. Irwin Deutscher, *What We Say/What We Do: Sentiments & Acts* (Glenview: Scott, Foresman, 1973).

16. H. Laurence Ross, "Traffic Law Violation: A Folk Crime," *Social Problems,* 8:231–241 (1960–1961).

Chapter 8.

1. Commission on Obscenity and Pornography, *Report* (New York: Random House; New York: Bantam, 1970); this commission, appointed in January 1968, was authorized by Congress under Public Law No. 90–100, enacted in October 1967. All references are to the Random House edition.

2. Ibid., p. 43.

3. Roth v. United States, 354 U.S. 476 (1957).

4. NY Penal Law §235.00 (McKinney).

5. Paul H. Gebhard, John H. Gagnon, Wardell B. Pomeroy, and Cornelia V. Christenson, *Sex Offenders: An Analysis of Types* (New York: Harper & Row, 1965).

6. Hamling v. United States, 94 S. Ct. 2887 (1974).

7. Marvin E. Wolfgang, "Violent Behavior," in *Current Perspectives on Criminal Behavior,* ed. Abraham S. Blumberg (New York: Knopf, 1974); Marvin E. Wolfgang and Franco Ferracuti, *The Subculture of Violence: Towards an Integrated Theory in Criminology* (New York: Barnes & Noble, 1967); see also Commission, op. cit., pp. 446–448.

8. John H. Gagnon and William Simon, "Pornography: Raging Menace or Paper Tiger" in *The Sexual Scene,* ed. John H. Gagnon and William Simon (Chicago: Aldine, 1970), p. 149.

9. Pamela Hansford Johnson, *On Iniquity: Some Personal Reflections Arising Out of the Moors Murder Trial* (New York: Scribner's, 1967).

10. Gebhard et al., op. cit., p. 669.

11. Ibid., p. 671.

12. Ned Polsky, *Hustlers, Beats, and Others* (Chicago: Aldine, 1967).

13. Gebhard et al., op. cit.

14. K. E. Davis and G. N. Braucht, "Exposure to Pornography, Character, and Sexual Deviance: A Retrospective Survey," in *Commission on Obscenity and Pornography Technical Reports* (Washington, D.C.: Government Printing Office, 1970), vol. 7.

15. Michael J. Goldstein, "Exposure to Pornography and Sexual Behavior in Deviant and Normal Groups," in *Commission Technical Reports*, vol. 7; and Michael H. Goldstein and Harold S. Kant, *Pornography and Sexual Deviance: A Report of the Legal and Behavioral Institute, Beverly Hills, Cal.* (Berkeley: University of California Press, 1973).

16. Bert Kutschinsky, "Sex Crimes and Pornography in Copenhagen: A Study of Attitudes," in *Commission Technical Reports*, vol. 7.

17. Commission, *Report*, p. 58.

18. Ibid., pp. 446–448.

19. Victor B. Cline, ed. *Where Do You Draw the Line? An Exploration into Media Violence, Pornography, and Censorship* (Provo: Brigham Young University Press, 1974).

20. Charles Winick, "A Study of Consumers of Explicitly Sexual Materials: Some Functions of Adult Movies," in *Commission on Obscenity and Pornography, Technical Reports* (Washington, D.C.: Government Printing Office, 1970), vol. 4.

21. M. Lipkin and D. E. Carns, "Poll of Mental Health Professionals," cited in Commission, *Report*, pp. 195–196.

22. Ginzburg v. United States, 383 U.S. 463 (1966); this case is briefly discussed in Commission, *Report*, pp. 431–432. See also Ralph Ginzburg, *Castrated: My Eight Months in Prison* (New York: Avant-Garde Books, 1973); and George D. Muedeking, "Pornography and Society," in *Deviants: Voluntary Actors in a Hostile World*, ed. Edward Sagarin and Fred Montanino (Morristown: General Learning Press, 1977), pp. 463–502.

23. Commission, *Report*, p. 54.

24. Ibid., p. 57.

25. Ibid., pp. 58–61.

Chapter 9.

1. Paul W. Tappan, "Sentences for Sex Criminals," *Journal of Criminal Law, Criminology, and Police Science*, 42:332–337 (1951).

2. Albert Ellis, "The Sex Offender and His Treatment," in *Legal and Criminal Psychology*, ed. Hans Toch (New York: Holt, Rinehart, 1961), p. 412.

3. Menachem Amir, *Patterns in Forcible Rape* (Chicago: University of Chicago Press, 1971).

4. Donal E. J. MacNamara, "Sex Offenses and Sex Offenders," *Annals of American Academy of Political and Social Science*, 376:153 (1968).

5. Alex. K. Gigeroff, J. W. Mohr, and R. E. Turner, "Sex Offenders on

Probation: Heterosexual Pedophiles," *Federal Probation,* 32(4):21 (1968).

6. Alex. K. Gigeroff, J. W. Mohr, and R. E. Turner, "Sex Offenders on Probation: Homosexuality," *Federal Probation,* 33(3):38 (1969).

7. Behavior modification as it is applied to homosexuality is described by M. P. Feldman and M. J. MacCulloch, *Homosexual Behavior: Therapy and Assessment* (Oxford and New York: Pergamon, 1971).

8. Georg K. Stürup, "Castration: The Total Treatment," in *Sexual Behaviors: Social, Clinical and Legal Aspects,* ed. H. L. P. Resnik and Marvin E. Wolfgang (Boston: Little, Brown, 1972), pp. 361–382.

9. E. Fuller Torrey, *The Mind Game: Witchdoctors and Psychiatrists* (New York: Emerson Hall, 1972; New York: Bantam, 1973).

10. Lawrence J. Hatterer, *Changing Homosexuality in the Male: Treatment for Men Troubled by Homosexuality* (New York: McGraw-Hill, 1970).

11. Samuel J. Brakel and Ronald S. Rock, eds., *The Mentally Disabled and the Law* (Chicago: University of Chicago Press, 1971), p. 341.

12. Ibid., pp. 362–364.

13. Ibid., p. 346.

14. *In re* Gault, 387 U.S. 1 (1967).

15. Edwin H. Sutherland, "The Diffusion of Sexual Psychopath Laws," *American Journal of Sociology,* 56:142–148 (1950).

16. Paul W. Tappan, "Some Myths about the Sex Offender," *Federal Probation,* 19(2):7–12 (1955).

17. Seymour L. Halleck, *Psychiatry and the Dilemmas of Crime: A Study of Causes, Punishment, and Treatment* (New York: Harper & Row/Hoeber, 1967), pp. 252–259.

18. Nicholas Kittrie, *The Right to Be Different: Deviance and Enforced Therapy* (Baltimore: Johns Hopkins Press, 1971).

Glossary

abnormal sex   generic term encompassing all criminalized or disvalued sexual behaviors, with the exceptions of adultery and fornication

abortifacient   oral medication taken with the intention of aborting the fetus; some abortifiacients are chemical compounds, even proprietary products; other are derived from folk medicine or the inventiveness of desperation; few actually work and many are dangerous or lethal

abortion   terminating pregnancy without giving birth; spontaneous abortion is without deliberate inducement, and is generally known as miscarriage; therapeutic abortion, to save the life or health of the mother, was once distinguished from illegal abortion, but most jurisdictions are now much more permissive with restrictions limited largely by the stage of fetal development

accost   term used by police and prosecutors to describe approaches in public, by males or females, for sexual solicitation

adultery   sexual intercourse between a man and woman at least one of whom is married but not to the other; compound or double adultery if both participants are married but not to each other

age of consent   statutory age, differing from jurisdiction to jurisdiction, which defines the legal capacity of a minor to give informed consent to sexual relations; to have sexual relations, even with consent, with a minor below the age of consent constitutes a crime (see statutory rape)

aggravated prostitution operating a brothel or call girl business

algolagnia sexual satisfaction derived from the anticipation of inflicting or suffering pain; a manifestation of sadomasochism

alienation of affections the basis in some jurisdictions for civil action for monetary damages brought by a husband or wife whose spouse has been wooed away by another; less frequently applied in the case of engaged couples

ambisexual bisexual; engaging in both heterosexual and homosexual activities

anal eroticism sexual behavior focusing on the anus; oral-anal contacts (rimming); insertion of the penis into the anus (sodomy); digital insertion into the anus; one of the paraphilias involves sexual stimulation by anal odors

anal-genital anal erotic behavior involving the penetration of the anus (male or female) by the penis

analism preoccupation with the anus as a focus of sexual satisfaction

anaphrodisiac a chemical preparation supposed to reduce or eliminate sexual erection in the male; saltpeter

androgen male sex hormone

androgynous possessing both male and female primary and/or secondary sex characteristics

androgyny inversion of the sexual identity; masculinization of the female

androsterone male sex hormone

anomaly, sexual an aberration or deviation either in the sex organs or in the sexual focus

antuitrin secretion of the anterior lobe of the pituitary gland important in the development of secondary sex characteristics in the male; injection or ingestion of antuitrin(s) is sometimes indicated in therapy for deficient sex drive and at one time was thought to be helpful in treatment of homosexuality

aphrodisiac a chemical substance supposed to stimulate sex interest and capability; cantharides; Spanish fly; any sex stimulant

artificial insemination technique of fertilizing the ovum with semen from the husband or a donor, inserted into the vagina by other than normal intercourse; sometimes used in cases of male impotence, sterility, impaired fertility, or injury to the genitalia

asexual uninterested in sex

asexualization castration

auntie older effeminate homosexual

autoeroticism (also **autoerotism**) masturbation and other forms of self-gratification

auto-monosexual perversion sexual actions performed on or with one's own body (e.g., self-fellation, self-abuse, self-mutilation)

autosexuality perversions performed on oneself, including self-fellation and sadomasochistic practices; also includes masturbation

badger game an act in which a prostitute solicits a client, takes him to her room, and while they are copulating her male partner enters, identifies himself as her husband or as a police officer, and shakes down the customer

basket term commonly used by homosexuals to describe the visible bulge at the crotch made by the penis and testicles; see size queen

bathroom (toilet) phobia fear of falling into toilet, or fear of monster coming from toilet to attack one's genitals; said to be present in male anal erotics

beat the dummy (meat) masturbate

bestialism, bestiality sexual contacts between human beings and infra-human animals; zoophilia

B-girl, B-boy employee of establishment serving alcoholic beverages, often attractive and scantily dressed, whose duty it is to hustle drinks; frequently available for prostitution

bisexual one who engages in or is interested in both heterosexual and homosexual behaviors

blow job fellatio

body language, sexual body gestures and/or postures that indicate to the knowledgeable observer a desire or readiness for sexual relations

bondage and discipline sadomasochism; generic term used to describe both actual relationships and pornographic materials (plays, pictures, stories) emphasizing dominance by Amazonic females, scantily clad in leather, inflicting whippings and punishment on submissive males; less frequently sex-role reversal with dominant males using harnessed females to pull dog sleds, for example; also found in homosexual sadomasochism

bowdlerize to excise (censor) unacceptable words from a manuscript, book, or other written material; usually but not always directed at words or phrases with sexual connotations

breach of promise a basis at one time in many jurisdictions for a civil action for monetary damages based on an alleged promise to marry, later reneged on; see also seduction

bubo visible symptom of serious venereal disease

buggery anal sodomy

bull dyke masculine lesbian

buns homosexual term for buttocks of other males

butch masculine lesbian

call boy male prostitute available for home or hotel visits through a central telephone answering service or registry

call girl female prostitute available for hotel or home visits through a telephone answering service or registry; usually higher priced and more attractive than street walkers or brothel prostitutes

cantharides an alleged aphrodisiac

carnal knowledge of a minor charge brought against an adult who has had copulative or sodomistic relations, no matter how slight the penetration, with a child under the age specified in a given jurisdiction

castrati male eunuchs castrated either for service in harems, to preserve the prepubertal voice range, for use as male prostitutes, or for religious reasons

castrating female aggressive, dominating female who deprives or attempts to deprive males of their masculine identity

castration asexualization; surgical excision of the male testes

castration, fear of phobia experienced by some males that sexual intercourse with a woman will result in injury to their testes and hence their potency

cat house house of prostitution

catamite homosexual prostitute or kept boy

celibacy state of sustained virginity; refraining from sexual relations and/or marriage, often for religious reasons (e.g., Catholic clergy)

chancroid visible symptom of venereal infection

chastity belt a device designed to prevent intercourse, at one time locked around a woman's genitals while her husband (father) was away

cherry the hymen; a virgin

chicken young male, usually in early adolescence, who makes himself available for sexual acts with older male partners, generally for money

chicken hawk older male who pursues chicken

child abuse usually physical abuse of young children, often by their parents, interpreted in some jurisdictions to include sexual assaults on child, carnal knowledge of child, etc.

child molester person, usually male, who seeks sexual satisfaction from very young children

circle jerk group masturbation; common in boys' boarding schools and in training schools of male delinquents; often prize is given to first boy to ejaculate

circumcision surgical removal of foreskin of penis for hygienic or religious reasons

clap gonorrhea

clitoridectomy surgical removal of all or part of clitoris

cock penis

cocksucking fellatio

cockteaser female who stimulates the male to a state of sexual excitation and then evades or refuses copulation

cod-piece protective covering for the male genitals, worn by some externally; worn sometimes to exaggerate or advertise size of penis

cohabit formerly used as euphemism for regular or at least repeated copulation between a male and female not married to each other; later tended to be restricted to such couples when domiciling together

cohabitation, lewd and lascivious charge brought in some jurisdictions against those living together openly without marriage to each other

cohabitation, nonmarital unmarried heterosexual couple domiciling together, usually without affront to community standards

coitus interruptus withdrawal of the penis from the vagina before emission to prevent unwanted pregnancy

common-law marriage relationship legally recognized in some jurisdictions in which certain legal rights inhere to the spouses and, in some cases, children after a statutorily defined period of living together openly, as if a marriage had taken place

community standards phrase used by the U.S. Supreme Court in Miller decision (1973) which would define material as pornographic and subject to criminal sanction if patently offensive in a given area

companionate marriage trial marriage; premarital cohabitation as man and wife to determine compatibility and suitability for a more permanent union

condom contraceptive device placed over penis to prevent entry of semen into woman's body; also used for prevention of veneral disease (hence known as prophylactic); rubber

conjugal visit sexual activity between a prison inmate and visiting spouse

consensual acts generic term covering acts between two or more persons that take place by mutual consent, with no threat or use of force; usually restricted to acts between adults

consolateur   a dildo; penis-shaped object utilized by females in auto-erotic practices or lesbian activities

consummate   the process of completing the marital union by having sexual intercourse

continence   refraining from sexual relations by act of will

contraceptive   a device, medication, or method of preventing pregnancy

contrary sexuality   term formerly used for homosexuality

contributing to the delinquency of a minor   charge brought against an adult who exposes a child to situations that might result in delinquent acts, e.g., introducing a child to narcotics, suggesting that a child commit a crime, encouraging homosexual activity or act with prostitute

coprolagnia   sexual pleasure derived from handling feces

coprolalia, coprophasia, coprophilia   sexual stimulation and/or satisfaction from use of or listening to obscene language or stories, particularly those focusing on excrement

coprophagia   sexual deviation focusing on excrement and/or urine; watching others evacuate the bowels or urinate; being urinated on; could include stimulation from writing graffiti on toilet walls

coprophobia   fear of excreting or excreta

copulatio analis   pederasty, anal sodomy

Cornelia complex   incestuous desire of mother for her son

cornhole   anal sodomy

crabs   pubic lice

cross-dressing   transvestism

cruising   seeking stranger for sexual encounter, usually restricted to homosexuality

cuckold   husband whose wife has committed adultery

cunnilinctus, cunnilingus   oral contact with the female labia

daisy chain   three or more males engaging in simultaneous anal-genital or oral-genital relations

defloration   intercourse with a virgin

degenerate   police-prosecutorial term for a person engaging in almost any form of disvalued or criminalized sexual activity

demi-vierge   literally a "half-virgin," used to denote a female who engages in many types of sexual activity except copulation; technical virgin

detumescence   the process of going from the erect to the flaccid state of the penis, normally occurring following ejaculation

deviate, sexual one whose sexual drive or focus is directed toward socially unaccepted channels; most often used for child molester

diaphragm a contraceptive device inserted into body of woman to prevent fertilization

dicky waver exhibitionist

dildo artificial penis

dimorphism having both male and female anatomical parts, sexual characteristics, or responses

dirt homosexual term for males who assault and/or rob homosexuals after having sexual relations with them

double standard value system that was more tolerant of male sexuality or promiscuity than female

drag queen effeminate homosexual who wears female clothing, jewelry, and may impersonate female

drag show entertainment featuring transvestite performers, principally males in female costume

droit du seigneur literally the right of the landholder, referring to the right to deflower female children of his serfs on their wedding night; see also jus primae noctis

dyke lesbian

eating pussy cunnilingus

effeminate being male and having pronounced feminine appearance and/or traits

ejaculation, premature emission of seminal fluid either prior to penetration or prior to readiness of female partner; ejaculatio praecox

Electra complex excessive, perhaps incestuous, interest of daughter in her father, including unconscious interest

emasculate asexualize, castrate; used literally and figuratively

endowment largely homosexual term for penis size, as heavily endowed, small endowment; see also size queen

entrapment vice squad technique in which either a plainclothesman or a decoy working with him inveigles homosexual or prostitute into soliciting, for the purpose of making arrest; widely used in criminal jurisprudence for nonsexual matters

eonism transvestism, cross-dressing, drag

erection the state of the sexually stimulated, tumescent penis; term is sometimes used when there is stimulation and hardening of clitoris or nipples

erogenous zones areas of body particularly sensitive to sexual stimulation

erotographomania conduct in which major sexual satisfaction is derived from viewing sexually explicit paintings, sculpture, or other objects

erotolalia deriving major sexual satisfaction from talking about or listening to talk about sex

erotomania compulsive interest in sexual matters

erotophilic strong interest in and concentration on erotic matters

erotophobic afraid of sex, hostile to evidences of sexuality

estrogen female sex hormone

estrus in heat, ready for sex

eunuch an emasculated male, asexualized, castrated

eunuchoid like a eunuch (usually not castrated)

exhibitionist one deriving sexual satisfaction from the showing of one's genitals to unwilling viewers; dicky waver, flasher

extracoital sexual connection between male and female not involving penetration of the vagina; may be oral, anal, intermammary, interfemoral, or other

extramarital sex outside of marriage by a married person, adultery

extravaginal extracoital

fag, faggot pejorative term used either for an effeminate homosexual or for a homosexual regardless of outward manifestations of effeminacy

fag-bar, fag-joint gathering place for homosexuals; gay bar

fairy pejorative term similar in use to fag, faggot

fellatio, fellation taking the penis into the mouth; the recipient can be male or female; cocksucking

fellator male insertee in fellatio

fellatrix female insertee in fellatio

fetishism the focus of the sex drive on a part of the body rather than on the person (usually not on the genitals), or on some bodily function, or on some inanimate object, often clothing, odorous object, etc.

fetishist one who has strong fetishistic compulsions

finger-fucking digital stimulation of one's own or another's genitalia or anus

fish queen male cunnilinguist

flagellation a form of sadomasochism in which sexual satisfaction is obtained from whipping or being whipped

flasher an exhibitionist

foreplay stimulation by touching, licking, tickling, pinching, kissing, or in some other form, prior to copulation, and not as end in itself

fornication copulation between a male and a female neither of whom is married

free love term used to denote high tolerance for sexual promiscuity, also sexuality and cohabitation without marriage

French envelope contraceptive, particularly a condom

French kiss entwining of tongues in kissing, also known as swapping spits; sometimes used as synonym for cunnilingus

French love fellatio and/or cunnilingus

French tickler a device attached to the tumescent penis to heighten sexual stimulation when inserted into vagina, often dangerous to female

feel fondling of another, particularly of buttocks of a female by a male

frigidity inability to respond to sexual stimulation

frottage derivation of sexual satisfaction by rubbing one's genitals, even when fully clothed, against body of another; also known as dry fucking; in female homosexuality, rubbing of genital areas of two females against each other

frotteur a person who frequents crowded places for the purpose of rubbing against the bodies of others

fruit male homosexual, often restricted to effeminate male

fuck to have sex, usually restricted to copulation and anal sex

full house having gonorrhea and syphilis concurrently, and perhaps pubic lice and other venereal manifestations.

gang bang multiple copulation with one subject, male or female, who may be willing participant or coerced

gay homosexual

gay bar bar that is reputed to be a gathering place for homosexuals

gay liberation movement to secure rights for homosexuals, to destigmatize behavior, decriminalize homosexuality, and end discrimination

gerontosexuality abnormal desire of a younger person for sexual relations with a much older male or female

gigolo a male kept or paid by a woman for sexual favors

glory hole homosexual term for an opening cut into the dividing wall between two public toilet cubicles, the male in one room inserting the tumescent penis into the hole so that it is fellated by the male in the adjoining cubicle

godemiche dildo, artificial penis

go down on to commit fellatio or cunnilingus

go-go girl (boy) attractive, scantily dressed or nude entertainer who performs sexually stimulating dances and gyrations

golden shower paraphilia in which the subject permits himself (on rare occasions herself) to be urinated on by one or more males and/or females for sexual stimulation

gonorrhea veneral disease characterized by an emission from the penis; clap

goose pinching of the anal region of another person, or putting finger along anal region, usually of clothed person

granuloma inquinale serious venereal disease

granuloma venereum serious venereal disease

Greek love anal sodomy usually with a young male as receptor

gymnopaedia Greek athletic festival featuring nude boy athletes; homosexual orgy with nude boys

gynandromorphy having both male and female anatomical parts

gynandry inversion of the female sexual identity; masculinization

gynecomastia development of female-type breasts on a male; condition fostered in transvestites and transsexuals by hormonal treatment

hand job masturbation, by oneself or on a person by another

hebephilia focusing of the sex drive on very youthful boys or girls; Lolita syndrome

hebephrenia mental disease at onset of menarche characterized by uncontrolled sexual promiscuity

hermaphroditism possession of some male and some female sex organs by one person; ambiguity as to whether the individual is male or female

heterosexual pertaining to individual or sex drive oriented toward gratification with other sex

homoerotophobia fear of being or being considered homosexual, also fear of homosexuality

homophile homosexual, and particularly associated with gay liberation movements; literally, love of same

homosexuality pertaining to individual or sex drive oriented toward gratification with same sex

homosexual marriage long-term monogamous homosexual relationships, not recognized as legal marriages, but consecrated as marital union by a few homosexually oriented churches

homosexual panic emotional crisis occasioned in some persons, particularly males, by fear of interest in homosexual gratification, by sight of male body that is stimulating, by solicitation for homosexual encounter, or by actual encounter, perhaps during state of intoxication

homosociality intimate but not necessarily sexual social relationship between persons of same gender

hooker a prostitute

horns, wearing descriptive term applied to a cuckold

horny sexually stimulated; if male, perhaps tumescent

hump to copulate with a female

hustler a male or female prostitute; also used for nonsexual connotations, as drug hustler

hymen the membrane which closes the opening to the vagina in virgins; cherry

hypersexuality oversexed; nymphomanic (female), satyriasis (male)

hypoplasia genitalia very small genitalia; micro-penis

impairing the morals of a minor charge brought against adults, lesser than carnal abuse, often but not always for sex-related offense, as fondling child's genitals, showing child pornographic material, or photographing a child engaging in sex play with other children

impersonator, female a male transvestite, a drag queen, one who cross-dresses; often an entertainer who cross-dresses

impotence a condition in which the male is physiologically or psychologically unable to get or maintain an erection at the time of intercourse; occasionally used to describe the female

incest sexual relations between persons of close blood kinship relationship; legally usually extended to relationships by adoption or through marriage, other than between spouses

indecent assault any uninvited touching of the genitals, buttocks, or breasts

indecent exposure exhibitionism; exposure of the genitals in public even if no sexual motivation is present, as in public urination, nude swimming, or sunbathing

infantosexuality focus of sexual desire on very young (prepubertal) children

insertor in fellatio and anal relations, the participant whose penis is inserted into the orifice of partner

instrumental masturbation use of a mechanical or electrical device, as a cow milking machine, for example, to effect ejaculation

intercourse term usually restricted to penile-vaginal copulation

interfemoral coitus placing the tumescent penis between the tightly closed thighs of partner and reaching emission through friction; thighing

interfered with police euphemism, particularly in England and Ireland, for rape

intermammary coitus placing the tumescent penis between the breasts of partner and effecting emission by friction

intermarriage marriage between persons of different races, religions, even nationalities; more restrictive term than miscegenation, which refers to sexual relations, with or without marriage, of such persons

intersexuality hermaphroditism; possessing some of the physical and/or psychological characteristics of both genders

intrauterine device contraceptive which prevents sperm from entering the womb; IUD

intromission the act of introducing semen into the vagina; often used as synonymous with heterosexual copulation

inversion term formerly used for homosexuality; later for having traits, characteristics, and manifestations of someone of the other sex (called sex-role inversion)

inversion, amphigenous bisexual psychosexually

invert term formerly used for a homosexual

irrumation fellatio

jerk off masturbate

jocker an aggressive male who plays insertor role in anal sodomy

john customer of a prostitute, usually used for heterosexual prostitution; trick is synonym used for homosexual and heterosexual customer

jus primae noctis literally "law of the first night"; feudal right of the landholder to deflower the virgin females of his serfs or tenants on their wedding night; see also droit du seigneur

Kama Kalpa Indian sex manual

Kama Sutra Indian sex manual

kept boy (girl) male (or female) supported, usually by older man, in return for sex favors

kept man gigolo, sweet man; male supported and/or paid in return for favors, usually to older woman

ki-ki sexual relations between two effeminate homosexuals

latent homosexuality capacity for homosexual satisfaction without overt experience, unconscious homosexual desires

lay to copulate; as noun, a female with whom one has (or wishes to have) intercourse; also get laid

leather bar gathering place, particularly bar, for homosexual sadomasochists, rough trade, motorcycle crowd, and apparently virile type of homosexuals

lecher one who is sensuous, lewd, grossly unchaste

lesbianism female homosexuality, sapphism, tribadism

lewd and lascivious police-prosecutorial term to describe criminalized, depraved, disvalued and perverse sexual behaviors

libido sexual drive

libido deficiens lacking in sexual drive

line up multiple copulation with one female, whether coerced or consensual; gang bang

living off the proceeds of prostitution charge brought against pimps, procurers, brothel keepers, and others who receive funds from prostitutes or their customers

locomotor ataxia tabés dorsalis, a venereal disease

loitering charge brought against male and female prostitutes who solicit in public places; also used against males who seek sex partners in public restrooms

love child child born out of wedlock, illegitimate child, bastard

lust murder homicide for sexual satisfaction; differs from homicide in course of attempted rape or sodomy, or to eliminate victim as witness-complainant, in that the violence and killing is basic to satisfaction of perpetrator's lust

lymphogranuloma inguinale venereal disease

lymphogranuloma venereum venereal disease

madam proprietor or manager of a house of prostitution; usually and traditionally woman heading female house; also used as male madam, for male heading homosexual house

masochism deriving sexual satisfaction from having pain inflicted on oneself

masturbation manual or instrumental stimulation of the genitalia, by oneself or another, to produce sexual satisfaction

Mattachine Society organization devoted to gay liberation

meat rack homosexual term for a place or area where homosexuals seeking partners display themselves, often in tight clothing emphasizing size of genitalia

ménage à trois two males and one female, or two females and one male, living in a sexual union, troilism

microphallus extremely small penis

miscegenation marriage or sexual relations between persons of different races, sometimes also applied to persons of different ethnic, religious and national groups

misogynist male who hates and/or fears women

mistress paid or supported female companion, concubine

mixoscopia deriving sexual satisfaction from watching other persons engage in sexual activity; some brothels have either viewing windows or two-way mirrors and charge fee to persons desiring this activity

mooning displaying the bare buttocks as gesture of contempt

moral leper degenerate, depraved, immoral, perverse (used for sexual and nonsexual descriptions)

morals squad vice squad

morphodite hermaphrodite

muff diving cunnilingus

multilateral sexuality play-dominated sexual interaction; together sex, party sex; swinging; orgy; multi-sex, group sex

mutual masturbation mutual stimulation of the genitals by two or more persons, of same or different genders

narcissism exaggerated self-love

narratophilia deriving principal sex satisfaction or stimulation from listening to sex stories

necrophagia see necrophilia

necrophilia sexual fantasies about or overt sexual contact with dead bodies

necrosadism deriving sexual satisfaction from defiling or mutilating dead bodies

nocturnal dreams (fantasies, ecstasies) sexually stimulating dreams, in male usually resulting in ejaculation

nocturnal emission (pollution) ejaculation during sleep as the result of dreams or fantasies, sometimes accompanied by friction of night clothing or bedding, or manual masturbation during sleep

noncoital extracoital

nuts testicles

nymphomania compulsive, excessive desire for sexual intercourse in female

obscene telephone calls use of forbidden sexual language over telephone by male to a female, usually stranger to caller, sometimes accompanied by verbal sexual advances; callers may be coprolaliacs or misogynistic sadists

obscenity material dealing with the genitalia, excremental functions, or with the sex process, dominated by prurient interests, and not acceptable by large numbers of people in society

Oedipus complex compulsive, excessive though usually unconscious sexual interest in mother by son

onanism   masturbation; term has also been used for coitus interruptus

one-night stand   term for one-time, nonaffectional, almost mechanical impersonal sex relationship, usually restricted to homosexual encounters

open cohabitation   unmarried couples living together without secrecy or circumspection

oral eroticism   fellatio, cunnilingus, rimming, any libidinal drive in which gratification is centered around mouth, tongue, oral cavity

oralism   oral eroticism

orgasm   physiological reaction that takes place in male or female upon achievement of maximum sexual satisfaction; climax; in male, usually accompanied by ejaculation

orgy   group sex, swinging

out of wedlock   illegitimate, bastard

PG   parental guidance; rating given a film with explicit sexual language or matter, but short of hard-core pornography

pandering   pimping, procuring

paraphilia   classification of sexual aberrations including fetishism, coprophilia, sadomasochism, scatology, and others

parathesia   perversion of the sexual instinct permitting sexual excitement from nonsexual and generally inadequate stimuli

parerosia, homosexual   sexual inversion

partialism   paraphilia in which sexual satisfaction is derived by rubbing one's genitals against a part of another's body other than the genitals

passing   term derived from race relations, when light-colored black pretended to be white, used for homosexual pretending to be heterosexual, and for impersonator pretending to be member of the other sex

passive homosexual   receptor in fellatio or anal sodomy

pasties   sequined patches pasted over the areola of the breasts of go-go girls, strip teasers, and others, to avoid arrest for indecent exposure

pederasty, pedication   love of boys (pedophilia), more commonly anal intercourse between males of any ages; sodomy

pederosis, pedophilia   love of very young (prepubertal or early pubertal) boys or girls

pedomania   compulsive sexual drive toward boys

pedophiliac   person addicted to pedophilia, almost invariably male

penilingus   fellatio

penis envy   Freudian concept in which young girls were said to have strong emotional problems because of their alleged feeling of deprivation at not having a penis

perversion, sexual   generic term for criminal, disvalued, socially unacceptable sex behaviors; sex aberrations, sex deviations; generally used pejoratively, but sometimes in a more neutral manner to describe any deflection of the sex drive from heterosexual intercourse

pervert   a person who attempts, practices, or harbors interest in the practice of sex perversions

petting   sex foreplay or substitute, as fondling, touching, kissing, licking, and other stimulating noncoital behavior

phallicism   phallic worship; excessive interest in the phallus of oneself or another; priapism

phallic symbol   a substitute that brings to mind the phallus, because of form, shape, or meaning imputed thereto

phallic worship   use of phallic symbols in religious rites, particularly fertility rites; worship of reproductive process

philanderer   promiscuous male, restricted to heterosexual usage, and usually to describe married or betrothed man

picacism, sexual   heterosexual aberrations, anomalies, deviances

pictophilia   deriving principal sexual satisfaction from erotic pictures of nude paintings, drawings, etc.

piece, piece of ass   a pejorative term about a woman, described solely as sex object

pimp   one who offers prostitutes to others; one who recruits, manages, and shares the earnings of prostitutes

pimpmobile   large, luxury-type automobile used by pimp to deliver prostitutes to assigned locations, supervise them, and collect their earnings

plainclothesman   vice squad cop or other policeman not wearing uniform and not readily identifiable as officer

platonic relationship   an affectional relationship without sexual involvement

play with oneself   masturbate

plural marriage   polygamy, polygyny, polyandry

pocket pool   manipulation of the genitals of a male by himself through side pants pockets; can also be conducted by another person

pollution   deriving sexual satisfaction by ejaculation of seminal fluid on a sex partner (rather than into an orifice), or by having fluid ejaculated on oneself by another

polyandry   one female with two or more husbands

polyerotism   deriving sexual satisfaction from a wide variety of sex objects and types of activity

polygamy multiple marriage, most commonly used as synonym for polygyny

polygyny one male with two or more wives

polymorphous perverse wide range of sexual interests in a variety of objects and activities; believed by Freudians to be normal developmental stage of persons, particularly males, previous to narrowing of interest in heterosexuality

ponce pimp, procurer

pornography written or pictorial material with overt sexual portrayal in a manner generally unacceptable in a society

potency, sexual virility, ability to have sexual (particularly heterosexual) intercourse

pouf derogatory term, widely used in England, for homosexual

premarital sex sex before marriage often used as synonymous with nonmarital sex

priapism condition in which there is an almost continuous and sometimes painful tumescence

profanation defiling and hence profaning inanimate objects for sexual stimulation or satisfaction; defiling a statue, particularly if it has religious meaning; defecating or urinating on the bedding of a sex partner; also called nihilisme de la chair

promiscuity indiscriminate or near indiscriminate sex behavior with wide variety of partners, usually but not necessarily all of one sex

prostitution sale of the body for sexual purposes to others for a fee, usually indiscriminately or nearly so

prudery extreme or exaggerated modesty; inhibition against being seen undressed, or against hearing discussion of sexuality

prurience lasciviousness, lewdness

pseudohermaphroditism condition in which there is partial anatomic development of both sexes

pseudohomosexuality sometimes used as synonymous with bisexuality; also having some interests associated with homosexuality and hence confusing oneself with homosexual

psychic masturbation ejaculation accomplished by deliberate fantasizing or daydreaming about sexually stimulating persons or situations

pubic hair hair growth on the lower abdomen around the penis base and the vulva

public indecency indecent exposure or lewd and lascivious conduct in public; may consist of public urination, fellatio, copulaton, or other act

public morals, crimes against generic classification for most sex crimes, as prostitution, sodomy, but usually not including forcible rape, which is classified as crime against the person

pull off masturbate

punk male passive receptor (insertee) in homosexual sodomy

puritanical exaggerated and rigid code of sex behavior

pussy female genitalia

put out to make oneself available for sexual intercourse, usually to describe female, but may be used homosexually as well

pyromania pathological fire setting, said to be frequently sexually motivated

queen effeminate male homosexual

queer homosexual (adj. or noun)

queer baiting badgering and assaulting homosexuals by males, usually adolescents or young adults; dirt

R restricted; rating for moving picture containing sexually oriented dialogue or situations, but not hard-core pornographic; children under 16 not admitted

rape, forcible sexual intercourse with an unwilling female by force or threat of force; also used in unusual case of impersonation of husband

rape, sodomistic anal intercourse accomplished on man or woman by force or threat of serious injury

rape, statutory consensual sexual intercourse between a male and a female, when the former is over and the latter under the age of consent; in some jurisdictions, term applies when there is a custodial-patient or custodial-inmate relationship

ravish rape

receptors insertees in fellatio or anal intercourse

redeeming social value standard set up by Supreme Court for judgment of pornography and obscenity cases; phrase used is "utterly without redeeming social value"

red light area (district) section of a city or town in which prostitution is permitted either by law or by police policy

rimming oral-anal contact, also called reaming; a major cause of hepatitis

rough trade virile, masculine-appearing, often delinquent adolescents and young male adults who prostitute themselves for homosexual clients, often beating and robbing the customer; also used for rough-looking males who seek females for one-night stands

rubber contraceptive, condom; also a frotteur

S & M (sadomasochism) behavior in which sexual satisfaction is obtained from inflicting pain or having pain inflicted; algolagnia, metatropism, submissionism, flagellation, bondage and discipline

sadism sexual satisfaction derived from inflicting pain on others

salacious lecherous, lustful, obscene

saliromania defilement or destruction of women's underclothing, or of nude statues or paintings of females

saltpeter an alleged anaphrodisiac, said to eliminate or reduce sexual appetite

sapphism lesbianism, tribadism

satyr an extremely highly sexed male

satyriasis compulsive male sexuality, almost always used for heterosexual; male counterpart of nymphomania; sometimes confused with priapism

scatological dirty, filthy, preoccupied with excrement or with excremental functions

scoptophilia deriving sexual pleasure and satisfaction from looking at the sexual organs of others; homosexual scoptophiliacs often loiter in public toilets, lockers and shower rooms; heterosexuals often become voyeurs; also scopophilia

score term used by male and female prostitutes (and occasionally by males, homosexual and heterosexual, in nonprostitutive pursuits) to indicate success in getting a sex partner

screw copulate, lay

scum male ejaculate; also come

scumbag condom; sometimes used as contemptuous term for prostitute or other promiscuous female

seafood homosexual term for a sailor

seduction act by which female permits intercourse only after a promise of male to marry her; her previous chastity was often considered sine qua non for act of seduction

self-abuse masturbation

sex aberration any of the sexual deviations or perversions; sexual anomaly, paraphilia

sex athlete one who is reputed to be extremely virile; male having a reputation for ability to have repeated ejaculations

sex change   a reassignment of gender, by surgical operation, hormonal treatment, and other measures; transsexualism

sex deviance   any criminalized, disvalued, or socially unacceptable sexual behaviors

sex education   program designed for use in elementary and junior high schools to acquaint children with human physiology and anatomy, reproductive process, birth control, and similar information

sexhibitionism   neologism indicating sexual satisfaction obtained from performing sex acts in front of audience

sex-induced guilt   feelings of remorse and often depression among some persons after indulging in or even fantasizing about sexual relations

sex murder   lust murder

sexo-esthetic inversion   sex role inversion, transvestism

sexology   science of sex, including reproduction, drives, relationships

sexopathy   sexual anomaly, aberration, abnormality

sex psychopath   legal term used in sex psychopath laws to classify those charged with certain sex-related offenses

sexual anomaly   a physical anomaly involving the genitalia, or an aberration of the sexual drive (paraphilia)

sexual assault   uninvited touching of the genitals, buttocks, or breasts of another; indecent assault

sexual equality   movement to end the double standard, giving equal freedom to women and men in sexual matters; also used by some to describe gay liberation

sexual freedom   movement to eliminate social prohibitions and inhibitions against previously disvalued sexual behaviors

sexualitis senilis   geriatric sexuality

short arm   penis

short arm inspection   examination of the penis in the military and merchant marine for evidence of unreported venereal disease

short eyes   prison jargon for someone incarcerated for carnal abuse of minor or child molestation; from shorties

situational homosexuality   engaging in homosexual relations in monosexual environment, although previously exclusively or principally heterosexual

sixty-nine, soixante-neuf   simultaneous oral-genital contact between two persons of the same or different genders

size queen   homosexual term for male with compulsive interest in partner with large penis, usually applied to effeminate homosexual; also basket queen

skinny dipping   nude swimming in public

sleep with   have sexual relations with

slut   prostitute or other promiscuous woman

snatch   female genital area, particularly pubic hair, muff, pussy

sodomy   anal intercourse, but often used to include all oral-genital relations, bestiality, and other acts

solicitation (for immoral purposes)   police-prosecutorial term for making an approach to potential sex customers by male or female prostitutes; also applied to approaches by males to other males for nonprostitutive sex

sotadic zone   purported geographic area circling the globe in the warmer climates, in which homosexuality and other sexual aberrations were said to have thrived

Spanish fly   an alleged aphrodisiac, cantharides

sponge, collagen   contraceptive device which prevents fertilization; said to be more comfortable and effective than IUD

statuophilia   love of statues and other inanimate replicas of human form; attempt to effect sexual relations with inanimate replica of human body

sterilization   surgical procedure which prevents passage of the reproductive cells into male seminal fluid without interfering with copulation and ejaculation

stigma   negative labeling; descriptive classification that causes persons to be disvalued or discriminated against

streaking   running nude in public places

streetwalking   solicitation for prostitution on a public street or thoroughfare

striptease   entertainment in which dancer removes her clothing in a highly suggestive manner

stud   virile male, sex athlete

submission   masochism

superfixation   inability to gain sex satisfaction except with an extremely specific sex object (as a slender blue-eyed blonde) or in a highly specific manner (as in the canine position)

superstud   extremely virile male, with large and thick penis and ability to ejaculate repeatedly

swapping spits   French kissing; insertion of tongue into mouth of sex partner

swing, swinging, swinger   lack of sex inhibition, and specifically participation in mate swapping, group sex, and/or orgies

syphilis   venereal disease

syphilomania   insanity resulting from exaggerated fear of contracting syphilis

syphilophobia   exaggerated fear of contracting venereal disease, particularly syphilis, sometimes leading to continence or satisfaction via masturbation

syphilopsychosis   tabes dorsalis, a venereal disease

tabes dorsalis (also known as tabes)   syphilitic disease attacking central nervous system, called locomotor ataxia and syphilopsychosis

taboo (tabu)   strongly held social mores, violation of which results in death, ostracism or severe criminal punishment; originally referred to prohibition against incestuous relations

tearoom   euphemism for public toilet, first used in England, later among homosexuals in America

tenesmus penile   priapism, chronic erection of penis

testosterone   male sex hormone

third sex   term formerly applied to homosexuals

top man   insertor in anal sodomy

toucher   frotteur

trade   male with exaggerated masculine demeanor, who makes himself available to passive homosexuals for fellatio, particularly for money; also used for heterosexual male of similar demeanor

tramp   sometimes used as pejorative synonym for prostitute

transsexual   person who has undergone a sex reassignment operation and who now adopts the opposite gender; also used for a person having desire and drive for such an operation

transvestism   cross-dressing, eonism

transvestite   one who cross-dresses, drag queen, female impersonator (when male)

tribadism   lesbianism, sapphism

trick, turn a trick   the customer of the prostitute; the john; to perform the sex act with the trick

troilism   sexual involvement among three persons, simultaneously or seriatim; similar to ménage à trois, but in troilism the sexuality is simultaneous or nearly so

undinism   urophilia; sexually responsive to the sight, smell, or taste of urine, or to sound of someone urinating

unisex   effacement of visible distinctions between the sexes other than anatomical

unnatural sexual aberrations and/or deviations; has particularly been applied to describe homosexuality and bestialism

uranism word formerly used for homosexuality

urethral masturbation digital or instrumental stimulation of the urethra in the female

urninde female homosexual, lesbian, tribade

urning male homosexual (obsolete)

urophilia deriving sexual satisfaction from urine, smell of urine, or being urinated on

VD venereal disease

vampirism, pseudovampirism sexual satisfaction from sight, smell or taste of partner's blood; act of biting until blood flows during sexual stimulation

vasectomy sterilization of male by surgery which prevents the passage of sperm into seminal fluid

venereal disease any of the diseases that are most commonly transmitted during sexual contact

vibrator artificial penis, often electrically or mechanically operated; dildo

vice squad police unit in charge of violations of laws relating to prostitution, homosexuality, pornography, and other sex matters

victimless crimes consensual acts, sexual and other, in which there is no complainant, no victim except a willing adult participant, and on which there is no agreement in society that they are harmful modes of behavior

virgo intacta virgin

virility masculinity, potency, ability to copulate with females; also used to describe ability to impregnate females

voyeur one deriving sexual satisfaction from viewing others in the nude, undressing, or in act of copulation, or by attending live sex shows or pornographic films; peeping Tom

watch queen one who stands on the lookout in public restroom while two males are having sex contact, and who gives signal when someone is approaching

wet dream nocturnal emission in response to sexually stimulating dream

white slavery compulsory prostitution, usually involving transportation of the victims to foreign countries or at least to other than their home areas

whore prostitute

whorehouse   house of prostitution, bordello, cathouse

wife-lending   custom in some societies to show hospitality to a guest by permitting him to enjoy sexual favors of wife; also of daughter

wife-swapping   early term for swinging, later changed to mate-swapping

wolf   male on the prowl for sexual satisfaction; used heterosexually for man seeking variety of partners and making frequent overtures; homosexually for one who seeks to subdue other, usually younger, male for sodomy

X rated, XX rated   rating applied to hard-core pornographic films depicting sexuality, and especially sex aberrations

XYY chromosome   biological anomaly in some males in which there is an extra Y chromosome, as distinct from normal chromosomal pattern in males of XY

zooerasty   zooeroticism

zooeroticism   deriving or seeking sexual satisfaction from relationships with animals

zoophilia   zooeroticism, bestiality

zoosadism   deriving sexual satisfaction from killing or inflicting pain on animals or birds

Selected Bibliography

ABRAHAMSEN, DAVID. *Report on a Study of 102 Sex Offenders at Sing Sing Prison.* Utica: State Hospital Press, 1950.

ACTON, WILLIAM. *Prostitution.* Edited with introduction and notes by Peter Fryer. New York: Praeger, 1968 (first published in 1857).

ALLEN, CLIFFORD. *A Textbook of Psychosexual Disorders.* London: Oxford University Press, 1962.

AMERICAN LAW INSTITUTE. *Model Penal Code.* Philadelphia: American Law Institute, 1962.

AMIR, MENACHEM. *Patterns in Forcible Rape.* Chicago: University of Chicago Press, 1971.

BARTELL, G. D. *Group Sex: A Scientist's Eyewitness Account of the American Way of Swinging.* New York: Wyden, 1971.

BEACH, FRANK A., ed. *Sex and Behavior.* New York: Wiley, 1965.

BEIGEL, HUGO G., ed. *Advances in Sex Research.* New York: Harper & Row, 1963.

BELL, ALAN P., and CALVIN S. HALL. *The Personality of a Child Molester: An Analysis of Dreams.* Chicago: Aldine-Atherton, 1971.

BENJAMIN, HARRY. *The Transsexual Phenomenon.* New York: Julian, 1966.

BENJAMIN, HARRY, and R. E. L. MASTERS. *Prostitution and Morality.* New York: Julian, 1964.

BERG, CHARLES, and CLIFFORD ALLEN. *The Problem of Homosexuality.* New York: Citadel, 1958.

BRAKEL, SAMUEL J., and RONALD S. ROCK, eds. *The Mentally Disabled and the Law.* Chicago: University of Chicago Press, 1971.

BREMER, JOHAN. *Asexualization: A Followup Study of 244 Cases.* New York: Macmillan, 1959.

BRINKLEY, ROLAND A., JR., JOHN C. WATKINS, DONALD J. WEISENHORN, and GEORGE G. KILLINGER. *The Laws Against Homosexuality.* Criminal Justice Monograph, vol. 2, no. 4. Huntsville: Institute of Contemporary Corrections and the Behavioral Sciences, Sam Houston State University, no date.

BROWNMILLER, SUSAN. *Against Our Will: Men, Women, and Rape.* New York: Simon & Schuster, 1975.

BUFFUM, PETER C. *Homosexuality in Prison.* Prepared for the Law Enforcement Assistance Administration. Washington, D.C.: Government Printing Office, 1971.

CAPRIO, FRANK S., and D. R. BRENNER. *Sexual Behavior: Psycholegal Aspects.* New York: Citadel, 1961.

CAULDWELL, DAVID O. *Transvestism: Men in Female Dress.* New York: Sexology Corp., 1956.

CHAPPELL, DUNCAN, ROBLEY GEIS, and GILBERT GEIS, eds. *Forcible Rape: The Crime, the Victim, and the Criminal.* New York: Columbia University Press, 1977.

CHOISY, MARYSE. *Psychoanalysis of the Prostitute.* New York: Philosophical Library, 1961.

CHURCHILL, WAINWRIGHT. *Homosexual Behavior among Males: A Cross-Cultural and Cross-Species Investigation.* New York: Hawthorn, 1967.

CLOR, H. M. *Obscenity and Public Morality: Censorship in a Liberal Society.* Chicago: University of Chicago Press, 1969.

COMMISSION ON OBSCENITY AND PORNOGRAPHY. *Report.* New York: Random House; New York: Bantam, 1970.

DAVIS, KINGSLEY. "The Sociology of Prostitution." *American Sociological Review,* 2:744–755 (1937).

DAVIS, KINGSLEY. "Illegitimacy and the Social Structure." *American Journal of Sociology,* 45:215–233 (1939).

DAVIS, KINGSLEY. "Sexual Behavior." In *Contemporary Social Problems,* edited by Robert K. Merton and Robert Nisbet, pp. 219–261. 4th ed. New York: Harcourt, Brace, 1976.

DE RIVER, J. PAUL. *The Sexual Criminal: A Psychoanalytic Study.* Springfield: Charles C Thomas, 1950.

DE RIVER, J. PAUL. *Crime and the Sexual Psychopath.* Springfield: Charles C Thomas, 1968.

DEVEREUX, GEORGE. *Abortion in Primitive Society.* New York: Julian, 1955.

DRUMMOND, ISABEL. *The Sex Paradox.* New York: Putnam, 1953.

EAST, NORWOOD. *Sexual Offenders.* London: Delisle, 1955.

EGEN, FREDERICK W. *Plainclothesman: A Handbook of Vice and Gambling Investigation.* New York: Greenberg, 1952.

ELLIS, ALBERT. *The Folklore of Sex.* New York: Charles Boni, 1951.

ELLIS, ALBERT. "The Sex Offender and His Treatment." In *Legal and Criminal Psychology,* edited by Hans Toch, pp. 400–416. New York: Holt, Rinehart, 1961.

ELLIS, ALBERT, and ALBERT ABARBANEL, eds. *The Encyclopedia of Sexual Behavior.* New York: Hawthorn, 1961.

ELLIS, ALBERT, and RALPH BRANCALE. *The Psychology of Sex Offenders.* Springfield: Charles C. Thomas, 1956.

ELLIS, HAVELOCK. *Studies in the Psychology of Sex.* 2 vols. New York: Random House, 1936.

FEDERAL BUREAU OF INVESTIGATION. *Uniform Crime Reports: Crime in the United States, 1975.* Washington, D.C.: Government Printing Office, 1976.

FORD, CLELLAN S., and FRANK A. BEACH. *Patterns of Sexual Behavior.* New York: Harper, 1951.

FREUD, SIGMUND. *Civilization and Its Discontents.* New York: Norton, 1965.

FREUD, SIGMUND. *The Sexual Enlightenment of Children.* New York: Collier, 1963.

FREUD, SIGMUND. *Three Contributions to the Theory of Sex.* New York: Dutton, 1962.

FURSTENBERG, FRANK F., JR. *Unplanned Parenthood: The Social Consequences of Teenage Childbearing.* New York: Free Press, 1976.

GAGNON, JOHN H., and WILLIAM SIMON. *Sexual Conduct: The Social Sources of Human Sexuality.* Chicago: Aldine, 1973.

GAGNON, JOHN H., and WILLIAM SIMON, eds. *Sexual Deviance.* New York: Harper & Row, 1967.

GAGNON, JOHN H., and WILLIAM SIMON, eds. *The Sexual Scene.* Chicago: Aldine, 1970.

GEBHARD, PAUL H., JOHN H. GAGNON, WARDELL B. POMEROY, and CORNELIA V. CHRISTENSON. *Sex Offenders: An Analysis of Types.* New York: Harper & Row, 1965.

GEBHARD, PAUL H., WARDELL B. POMEROY, CLYDE E. MARTIN, and CORNELIA V. CHRISTENSON. *Pregnancy, Birth, and Abortion.* New York: Harper, 1958.

GEIS, GILBERT. *Not the Law's Business: An Examination of Homosexuality, Abortion, Prostitution, Narcotics, and Gambling in the United States.* NIMH Pub. No. 72–9132. Rockville: National Institute of Mental Health, 1972.

GIBBENS, T. C. N., and J. PRINCE. *Child Victims of Sex Offences.* London: Institute for the Study and Treatment of Delinquency, 1963.

GIGEROFF, ALEX. K. *Sexual Deviations in the Criminal Law: Homosexual, Exhibitionistic, and Pedophilic Offences in Canada.* Toronto: University of Toronto Press, 1968.

GOLDSTEIN, MICHAEL J., and HAROLD S. KANT. *Pornography and Sexual Deviance: A Report of the Legal and Behavioral Institute, Beverly Hills, Cal.* Berkeley: University of California Press, 1973.

GREEN, RICHARD, and JOHN MONEY, eds. *Transsexualism and Sex Reassignment.* Baltimore: Johns Hopkins Press, 1969.

GREENWALD, HAROLD. *The Call Girl: A Social and Psychoanalytic Study.* New York: Ballantine, 1958.

GREENWALD, HAROLD, ed. *The Prostitute in Literature.* New York: Ballantine, 1960.

GUTTMACHER, MANFRED S. *Sex Offenses: The Problem, Causes and Prevention.* New York: Norton, 1951.

GUYON, RENÉ. *The Ethics of Sexual Acts.* New York: Knopf, 1934.

GUYON, RENÉ. *Sexual Freedom.* New York: Knopf, 1950.

HALLECK, SEYMOUR L. *Psychiatry and the Dilemmas of Crime: A Study of Causes, Punishment, and Treatment.* New York: Harper & Row/Hoeber, 1967.

HENSLIN, JAMES M., ed. *Studies in the Sociology of Sex.* New York: Appleton-Century-Crofts, 1971.

HERNTON, CALVIN C. *Sex and Racism in America.* New York: Grove, 1965.

HILL, PAUL. *Portrait of a Sadist.* New York: Avon, 1960.

HOFFMAN, MARTIN: *The Gay World: Male Homosexuality and the Social Creation of Evil.* New York: Basic, 1969.

HOLBROOK, D. *Sex and Dehumanization.* London: Pitman, 1972.

JERSILD, JENS. *Boy Prostitution.* Copenhagen: G. E. C. Gad, 1956.

KARPMAN, BENJAMIN. *The Sexual Offender and His Offenses: Etiology, Pathology, Psychodynamics, and Treatment.* New York: Julian, 1954.

KINSEY, ALFRED C., WARDELL B. POMEROY, and CLYDE E. MARTIN. *Sexual Behavior in the Human Male.* Philadelphia: Saunders, 1948.

KINSEY, ALFRED C., WARDELL B. POMEROY, CLYDE E. MARTIN, and PAUL H. GEBHARD. *Sexual Behavior in the Human Female.* Philadelphia: Saunders, 1953.

KIRKENDALL, LESTER A. *Premarital Intercourse and Interpersonal Relationships.* New York: Julian, 1961.

KITTRIE, NICHOLAS. *The Right to be Different: Deviance and Enforced Therapy.* Baltimore: Johns Hopkins Press, 1971.

KLING, SAMUEL G. *Sexual Behavior and the Law.* New York: Bernard Geis, 1965.

KRAFFT-EBING, RICHARD VON. *Psychopathia Sexualis*. Originally published in German in 1886. New York: Putnam, 1965; New York: Stein & Day, 1965.

KRONHAUSEN, EBERHARD, and PHYLLIS KRONHAUSEN. *Pornography and the Law: The Psychology of Erotic Realism and Pornography*. New York: Ballantine, 1959.

LINDNER, ROBERT. *Must You Conform?* New York: Grove, 1956.

LLOYD, ROBIN. *For Money or Love: Boy Prostitution in America*. New York: Vanguard, 1976.

LONDON, LOUIS S. *Sexual Deviations in the Male: Fourteen Detailed Case Studies*. 2 vols. New York: Julian, 1937, 1957.

LONGFORD, EARL OF. *Pornography: The Longford Report*. London: Hodder, 1972.

MADOW, LEO, et al. *The Dangerous Sex Offender: A Report of the Panel of Medical Advisors on Health and Welfare to the Joint State Government Commission*. Philadelphia: General Assembly of the Commonwealth of Pennsylvania, 1963.

MAISCH, HERBERT. *Incest*. New York: Stein & Day, 1972.

MARCUS, STEVEN. *The Other Victorians: A Study of Sexuality and Pornography in Mid-Nineteenth-Century England*. New York: Basic, 1966.

MARMOR, JUDD, ed. *Sexual Inversion: The Multiple Roots of Homosexuality*. New York: Basic, 1965.

MARSHALL, DONALD S., AND ROBERT C. SUGGS, ed. *Human Sexual Behavior: Variations in the Ethnographic Spectrum*. New York: Basic, 1971.

MASTERS, R. E. L., and E. LEA. *Sex Crimes in History*. New York: Julian, 1963.

McCAGHY, CHARLES H. "Child Molesters: A Study of Their Careers as Deviants." Ph.D. dissertation, University of Wisconsin, 1966. Excerpted in *Criminal Behavior Systems: A Typology*, edited by Marshall B. Clinard and Richard Quinney, pp. 75–88. New York: Holt, Rinehart & Winston, 1967.

McDONALD, JOHN M. *Rape: Offenders and Their Victims*. Springfield: Charles C. Thomas, 1971.

McDONALD, JOHN M. *Indecent Exposure*. Springfield: Charles C. Thomas, 1973.

MOHR, JOHAN W., R. EDWARD TURNER, and M. B. JERRY. *Pedophilia and Exhibitionism*. Toronto: University of Toronto Press, 1964.

MONEY, JOHN. *Sex Errors of the Body: Dilemmas, Education, Counseling*. Baltimore: Johns Hopkins Press, 1968.

Money, John, and Anke A. Ehrhardt. *Man & Woman, Boy & Girl: The Differentiation and Dimorphism of Gender Identity from Conception to Maturity*. Baltimore: Johns Hopkins Press, 1972.

Morland, Nigel. *An Outline of Sexual Criminology*. New York: Hart, 1967.

Morton, R. S. *Venereal Diseases*. Baltimore: Penguin, 1966.

Mueller, Gerhard O. W. *Legal Regulation of Sexual Conduct*. New York: Oceana, 1961.

Murtagh, John M., and Sara Harris. *Cast the First Stone*. New York: McGraw-Hill, 1957.

National Institute of Mental Health, Task Force on Homosexuality. *Homosexuality: Final Report and Background Papers*. John M. Livingood, ed. Rockville: The Institute.

North, M. *The Outer Fringe of Sex: A Study in Sexual Fetishism*. London: Odyssey, 1970.

O'Callaghan, Sean. *Damaged Baggage: The White Slave Trade and Narcotics Trafficking in the Americas*. New York: Roy, 1969.

Ovesey, Lionel. *Homosexuality and Pseudohomosexuality*. New York: Science House, 1969.

Platt, A. M. *The Child Savers: The Invention of Delinquency*. Chicago: University of Chicago Press, 1969.

Ploscowe, Morris. *Sex and the Law*. New York: Prentice-Hall, 1951.

Pomeroy, Wardell B. *Dr. Kinsey and the Institute for Sex Research*. New York: New American Library, 1973.

Radzinowicz, Leon, ed. *Sexual Offences*. London: Macmillan, 1957.

Reich, Wilhelm. *The Sexual Revolution: Toward a Self-Regulating Character Structure*. New York: Simon & Schuster, 1974.

Reinhardt, James M. *Sex Perversions and Sex Crimes: A Psychocultural Examination of the Causes, Nature and Criminal Manifestations of Sex Perversions*. Springfield: Charles C Thomas, 1957.

Reiss, Ira L. *The Social Context of Premarital Sexual Permissiveness*. New York: Holt, Rinehart & Winston, 1967.

Resnik, H. L. P., and Marvin E. Wolfgang, eds. *Sexual Behaviors: Social, Clinical, and Legal Aspects*. Boston: Little, Brown, 1972.

Rickles, N. K. *Exhibitionism*. Philadelphia: Lippincott, 1950.

Roberts, Robert W., ed. *The Unwed Mother*. New York: Harper & Row, 1966.

Sagarin, Edward, and Donal E. J. MacNamara, "The Problem of Entrapment." *Crime and Delinquency*, October 1970, pp. 363–378.

Sagarin, Edward, and Donal E. J. MacNamara. "The Homosexual as a Crime Victim": Paper presented at the First International Symposium on Victimology, Jerusalem, 1973. Reprinted in part in *International Journal of Criminology and Penology*, 3:13–25 (1975), and in *Victimology: A New Focus*, edited by Israel Drapkin and Emilio Viano, pp. 73–85. Lexington: Heath, 1975.

St. John-Stevas, Norman. *Life, Death and the Law: Law and Christian Morals in England and the United States*. Bloomington: Indiana University Press, 1961.

Sanger, William W. *The History of Prostitution: Its Extent, Causes and Effects Throughout the World*. New York: Eugenics Publishing, 1937.

Scacco, Anthony M. *Rape in Prison*. Springfield: Charles C. Thomas, 1975.

Schultz, Gladys D. *How Many More Victims? Society and the Sex Criminal*. Philadelphia: Lippincott, 1965.

Schur, Edwin M. *Crimes without Victims: Deviant Behavior and Public Policy: Abortion, Homosexuality, and Drug Addiction*. Englewood Cliffs: Prentice-Hall, 1965.

Sherwin, Robert Veit. *Sex and the Statutory Law*. New York: Oceana, 1949.

Slovenko, Ralph. *Sexual Behavior and the Law*. Springfield: Charles C. Thomas, 1965.

Socarides, Charles W. *The Overt Homosexual*. New York: Grune & Stratton, 1968.

Sorokin, Pitirim. *The American Sex Revolution*. Boston: Porter Sargent, 1956.

Stafford, Peter. *Sexual Behavior in the Communist World*. New York: Julian, 1967.

Stekel, Wilhelm. *Patterns of Psychosexual Infantilism*. New York: Liveright, 1952; New York: Grove, 1959.

Stekel, Wilhelm. *Sexual Aberrations: The Phenomena of Fetishism in Relation to Sex*. 2 vols. New York: Liveright, 1930, 1952.

Stoller, Robert J. *Sex and Gender: On the Development of Masculinity and Femininity*. New York: Science House, 1968.

Stoller, Robert J. *Perversion: The Erotic Form of Hatred*. New York: Delta, 1975.

Stürup, Georg K. *Treating the "Untreatable": Chronic Criminals at Herstedvester, Denmark*. Baltimore: Johns Hopkins Press, 1968.

Sutherland, Edwin H. "The Diffusion of Sexual Psychopath Laws." *American Journal of Sociology*, 56:142–148 (1950).

Tappan, Paul W. *The Habitual Sex Offender*. Report and Recommendations of the Commission on the Habitual Sex Offender. Trenton: State of New Jersey, 1950.

TERROT, CHARLES. *Traffic in Innocents: The Shocking Story of White Slavery in England*. New York: Dutton, 1960.

TRAINER, RUSSELL. *The Lolita Complex: A Clinical Analysis*. New York: Citadel, 1966.

TRAINI, ROBERT. *Murder for Sex*. London: William Kimber, 1960.

Uniform Crime Reports. See Federal Bureau of Investigation.

VEDDER, CLYDE, and PATRICIA KING. *Problems of Homosexuality in Corrections*. Springfield: Charles C. Thomas, 1967.

WALKER, MARCIA J., and STANLEY L. BRODSKY, eds. *Sexual Assault: The Victim and the Rapist*. Lexington: Heath, 1976.

WARD, DAVID, and GENE KASSEBAUM. *Women's Prison: Sex and Social Structure*. Chicago: Aldine, 1965.

WEINBERG, MARTIN, ed. *Sex Research: Studies from the Kinsey Institute*. New York: Oxford University Press, 1976.

WEINBERG, MARTIN S., and ALAN P. BELL, eds. *Homosexuality: An Annotated Bibliography*. New York: Harper & Row, 1972.

WEINBERG, S. KIRSON. *Incest Behavior*. New York: Citadel, 1955.

WEISS, CARL, and DAVID JAMES FRIAR. *Terror in the Prisons: Homosexual Rape and Why Society Condones It*. Indianapolis: Bobbs-Merrill, 1974.

WEST, DONALD J. *Homosexuality*. Chicago: Aldine, 1968.

WHITMAN, HOWARD. *Terror in the Streets*. New York: Dial, 1951.

WILDEBLOOD, PETER. *Against the Law*. New York: Messner, 1959.

WINICK, CHARLES, and PAUL KINSIE. *The Lively Commerce: Prostitution in the United States*. Chicago: Quadrangle, 1971.

WOLFENDEN, JOHN, et al. *Report of the Departmental Committee on Homosexual Offences and Prostitution*. London: Her Majesty's Stationery Office, 1956.

WOLFGANG, MARVIN E., and FRANCO FERRACUTI. *The Subculture of Violence: Towards an Integrated Theory in Criminology*. New York: Barnes & Noble, 1967.

YOUNG, WAYLAND. *Eros Denied: Sex in Western Society*. New York: Grove, 1964.

Index

Index